Globalization, Women, and Health in the Twenty-First Century

Edited by

Ilona Kickbusch, Kari A. Hartwig,
and
Justin M. List

GLOBALIZATION, WOMEN, AND HEALTH IN THE TWENTY-FIRST CENTURY

First published in 2005 by
PALGRAVE MACMILLAN™
175 Fifth Avenue, New York, N.Y. 10010 and
Houndmills, Basingstoke, Hampshire, England RG21 6XS
Companies and representatives throughout the world.

PALGRAVE MACMILLAN is the global academic imprint of the Palgrave Macmillan division of St. Martin's Press, LLC and of Palgrave Macmillan Ltd. Macmillan® is a registered trademark in the United States, United Kingdom and other countries. Palgrave is a registered trademark in the European Union and other countries.

ISBN 1–4039–7031–9

Library of Congress Cataloging-in-Publication Data

Globalization, women, and health in the 21st century / editors, Ilona Kickbusch, Kari A. Hartwig, and Justin M. List.
p. cm.
Includes bibliographical references and index.
ISBN 1–4039–7031–9
1. Women—Health and hygiene. 2. Women's health services.
3. Globalization—Health aspects. I. Kickbusch, Ilona, 1950– II. Hartwig, Kari A. III. List, Justin M.

RA778.G577 2005
362.1'082—dc22   2005049180

A catalogue record for this book is available from the British Library.

Design by Newgen Imaging Systems (P) Ltd., Chennai, India.

First edition: December 2005

10 9 8 7 6 5 4 3 2 1

Printed in the United States of America.

To our mothers

Contents

List of Tables and Figures

Tables

Figures

Foreword

Globalization exerts positive and negative impacts on health and has been linked to reduced government expenditures on health, education, and social programs, and restructured workplace and home life. Globalization is altering gender roles and relationships and influencing health determinants. Asymmetric rights and responsibilities, labor market segregation, consumption patterns, and discrimination are influenced differently by globalization and affect men and women's health in distinct ways. Gender dimensions of global public–private partnerships, trade agreements, economic, political, social, and health system reform, and labor trends were illuminated in international consultations conducted by the Canadian Institutes of Health Research Institute of Gender and Health in 2003 and 2004. Many of these critical issues are captured in this book.

This timely and transformative text portrays diverse perspectives, including ethical, economic, political, and social movement influences to illuminate the complex interrelationships at the intersection of gender, globalization, and health. This foreword draws attention to another crucial context in this debate: the United Nation's 2000 Millennium Declaration resolved to promote gender equality and empower women as strategies to combat poverty, hunger, and disease and stimulate sustainable development. Many millennium goals closely align with the issues raised in this book.

The initial Millennium goal "eradicate extreme *poverty*" has clear gender implications. Studies in the United States of America and Europe reveal differential mortality rates derived from social–economic disadvantage and gender roles. Moreover, female gender and low socioeconomic status were associated with limited access to health services and poor health status.

The Millennium Goal 3 "promote *gender equality* and empower women" refers to gender disparities in education, literacy, employment, and political involvement. The WHO (2002) defines gender equity in health as "the elimination of unnecessary, unjust, and avoidable differences between men and women" in their potential for good health, illness, disability, or death from preventable causes. Health disparities "or marked inequality between . . . population groups" is defined on the basis of gender, race, or ethnicity, educational level, literacy, or socioeconomic status.

Health conditions linked to *reproductive and sexual health* account for approximately 25 percent of the global disease burden faced by women. Reproductive health was identified as a major priority in our regional consultations. Relevant issues such as new reproductive technologies, access to contraception, and maternal mortality issues are articulated throughout this book. Although issues of men's health and the role of masculinity are not as prominent, unique voices and research studies focused on men are included here as well.

In addition, prominent attention is given to Millennium Declaration Goal 6 to "combat HIV/AIDS, malaria and other infectious diseases" as well as the spread of the tobacco epidemic around the globe.

The editors and authors of this book deserve commendation for this major contribution to the literature. Their insights highlight the importance of research to elucidate the conceptual and empirical underpinnings of the intersection of globalization, gender, and health and to design and test relevant interventions. These complex and critical investigations should engage scholars from the North and South working in partnership.

MIRIAM STEWART, PH.D.
Scientific Director
Institute of Gender & Health
Canadian Institutes of Health Research

Acknowledgments

From start to finish, the formation of this book has been a journey. A symposium at Yale University in June 2003—Globalization, Gender, and Health: The Gender Challenge—spurred the development of what follows. We thank the many participants of that symposium for their insightful comments on the relationships among what we called in short "GHG." Especially, for their financial support of that event, we thank Miriam Stewart, the Canadian Institutes for Health Research, Donald Green at the Yale Institute for Social and Policy Studies, the Yale University's Interdisciplinary Center for Bioethics, Stephanie Spangler—Yale University's Deputy Provost for Biomedical and Health Affairs, and Michael Merson, the director of the Center for Interdisciplinary Research on AIDS.

At the Yale University's Interdisciplinary Center for Bioethics, we especially thank Margaret Farley for her clarity, direction, and voice and Christiana Peppard and James Fleming for their meticulous organizing abilities.

We are very appreciative of the work our authors put into this book. These men and women lead truly international lives, and their perspectives, expertise, and experiences make this book the invaluable resource we believe it is. Despite language differences and the wide distances that separated the editors from the contributors, we were able to assemble a dynamic and truly global approach to the pressing issues at hand. We greatly appreciated their patience and ongoing involvement as the book took shape.

Many thanks go to Sharon Lu, Marina MacNamara and Corrie Paeglow who have both provided invaluable time editing and formatting these pieces. We also thank Anthony Wahl, Heather Van Dusen and Palgrave Macmillan press for their guidance and excitement to be a part of this endeavor. And, we also thank many of our friends and family members who have supported us along the way through their curiosity and encouragement.

Finally, we thank Carol Pollard at the Yale University's Interdisciplinary Center for Bioethics. From start to finish, she motivated us to move forward with this project offering us strategic advice, resources, a fresh eye to the content at hand, and her unceasing encouragement.

Introduction

Ilona Kickbusch, Justin M. List, and Kari A. Hartwig

The debate over the impact of globalization has widened from economic and political lenses to include both gender and health. There is an increasing body of work, which documents the extent to which the forces of global restructuring shape and determine community resources and economic opportunities for women and men.[1] Many important contributions examining the relationships between gender and health, gender and globalization, or health and globalization are available in the corpus of globalization literature.[2] This book contributes to that ongoing analysis; however, it is unique in its explicit attention to better understand both the dynamics of gender and health in the context of globalization. For the editors and contributors alike, analyzing these three domains together allows a more focused analysis of globalization forces and their impacts.

Many questions spurred the development of this book. Does globalization change gender relations and how? Does health or its absence impact global society in new ways? How does a global health challenge such as HIV/AIDS impact gender relationships? How do changing gender relations in turn impact health? In what way does health become an intermediary factor for a better life or a potential beacon for emancipation? Is health itself a major driving force for change? In different ways, the authors investigate and provide answers to these and other questions from their own research and experiences.

Surviving and Living in the Twenty-First Century

In the face of globalization, its impact and its discontents, Ulrich Beck states that the key political question we face today is "How do we want to live?"[3] This simple question focuses on the essence of life in a global society. How we live in New Haven, Manila, or Paris affects how our global neighbor lives in Jakarta, Toronto, and Accra. While answering this question may seem simple on one level, the ability of much of the world's people to live the way they would like hinges on development opportunities, capabilities, and resources. The question of "How do we survive?" becomes much more pertinent in the lives of many of the world's people. However, how some want to live in the world can critically impact how others survive in the world.

Health is created in the context of everyday life. The Ottawa Charter for Health Promotion articulates the dimensions of health:

> To reach a state of complete physical, mental and social well-being, an individual or group must be able to identify and to realize aspirations, to satisfy needs, and to change or cope with the environment. Health is, therefore, seen as a resource for everyday life, not the objective of living. Health is a positive concept emphasizing social and personal resources, as well as physical capacities.[4]

Therefore, health for all, a goal stated in the Declaration of Alma Ata,[5] ultimately understands health as a means to a better life rather than simply an end in and of itself. Furthermore, as they shape health, the gendered implication of globalization forces are felt at the individual, community, and household level in very tangible ways. Labor recruitment, work conditions, and the compensation practices of local and transnational corporations affect the health of men and women in different ways.

Health increasingly becomes a new global political space, global commodity, and key transboundary issue in both economic and social terms. This political space is increasingly complex and postnational in many aspects. Jan Scholte writes, "Even where contemporary states are legally entitled to do so, they have been quite unable singularly and fully to control the global spaces which affect their jurisdictions."[6] Shrinking national spaces have been replaced with increasing global ones. The Internet serves as an example of this global space, a space for organizing, learning, and sharing ideas. Similarly, disease and its spread have filled these global spaces and very few have been left insulated from its detriments. The method of achieving health—a global political space and commodity—free from disease in these spaces is contested.

To map the gendered impact of global processes in a new way will present a very different health landscape that takes us beyond nation-states into transborder flows of capital, people, goods, and services. Kickbusch and Buse point out that "transnational forces associated with globalization, particularly acceleration in mobility of people and goods, alter populations' susceptibility to ill health and disease and raise the risks for countries and the global community."[7] Although transborder flows have occurred for centuries, the current rapidity of these flows holds many consequences for health and its gendered impact on development. We reside in a new era of globalization, a globalization of the twenty-first century where new modes of communication, transportation, and political and cultural exchanges form a web of increasingly complex patterns of causation and impact.

The contributors in this volume find it easier to agree on the dimensions of health and gender than on a shared definition of globalization—and not all are agreed as to its exact impact on gender and health. The definition of globalization that one chooses largely defines the solution one proposes for addressing its ills and spreading its goods. For example, the contributors in this work frequently refer to two different definitions of globalization: (1) Kelley Lee has described globalization and its impact as a set of processes having three dimensions: spatial, temporal, and cognitive;[8] (2) Marianne Marchand and Anne Runyan prefer the term "global restructuring" and discuss it in terms of political change, regionalism, and resistance with impacts on gender as an integral part of viewing that change on symbolic, physical, and social levels.[9] Despite differences in defining globalization, all the authors agree that gender and health lie at the very core of mapping this understanding and they all show the interface between the constructs of globalization, gender, and health.

Globalization, Gender, and Health

This volume examines both the positive and negative influences of globalization on women and men's health and our changing gender roles. In critiquing the hegemony of economic and political global forces, it emphasizes the need for structural accountability, political representation of individuals and their communities, improved access to health care services, and gender equity as crucial components for development and economic security. New policy and research recommendations are a part of achieving these goals. Changing prevailing attitudes that run counter or prove ineffective to address gender and health inequities are a larger part toward achieving this end.

The structure of the book lets the reader participate in answering the introductory questions in a purposive progression from theory to experience. First, two frameworks are presented: Lesley Doyal examines conceptual dimensions of global restructuring pertinent to health and gender, and Lisa Cahill considers the impacts of and responses to globalization through the positive contributions of major religious and ethical traditions. In the following sections, lead chapters are accompanied by

"In Perspective" sections to complement the globalization and health theme from a different disciplinary and or regional perspective. As we develop a research agenda to deal with the interface of globalization, gender, and health, it becomes increasingly important *where* the discourse takes place.

Caren Grown begins with a global analysis of the direct and indirect pathways between trade liberalization and reproductive health. From Nepal, Mahesh Maskey provides an in-depth analysis on the impacts of trade agreements on the economic and social lives of Nepalese and unexpected consequences in both gender roles and health outcomes. From the perspective of an international agency working to facilitate positive changes in health, Wendy Harcourt from the Society for International Development documents how women and men outside academia and government structures are organizing to respond to the globalized impacts of trade agreements and trade-related aspects of intellectual property rights (TRIPS).

Resistance to various forms of globalization such as political ideologies, neoliberal economics, and perceived "Western values" perpetuated through the media can be seen side by side with peoples' and individuals adoption of new technologies, borrowing of cultural icons and rhythms, and challenging of local cultural definitions of appropriate gender roles. Exploring the interactions between sociocultural practices and global pressures, Jerry Spiegel and Cynthia Andruske take up some of these issues in their chapter on engendered resistance in daily living. Resistance to or acceptance of new technologies and established cultural norms come through in the following two "In Perspective" pieces. Marcia Inhorn looks at the impact of in vitro fertilization (IVF) and intracytoplasmic sperm injection (ICSI) technologies on gender relations and norms in Muslim societies. An applied medical anthropologist, Gillian Hundt relays her research experience of gendered resistance to violence in Israel, while also exploring gendered disease coping mechanisms as a combination of traditional healing systems and Western medicine in rural South Africa.

Manisha Desai focuses on the international women's health movement (IWHM) as one form of organized resistance to certain manifestations of globalization while also adopting the technologies of globalization that strengthen their networks. She argues that changing gender relations in the rise of this movement have raised women's health issues to a more prominent position in the global health arena and have contributed to community-level changes in gender roles and practices. In her "In Perspective" piece, Josephine Simbanegavi looks at historical aspects of globalization in the forms of precolonial, colonial, and postcolonial experiences in Africa and discordance among local and international policies and agendas, using Zimbabwe as a case study. Liliana Acero explains organized resistance against certain Norplant trials in Brazil as part of a larger discussion of the impact of globalization on sexual and reproductive issues in Latin America.

The last three book chapters and "In Perspective" sections begin with the issue of health and then draw out its global and gender implications. For this section, we specifically chose to focus on AIDS, the tobacco epidemic, and the emerging scientific attention to women's health research beyond reproductive health. The rapid spread of HIV/AIDS around the globe forced the public health community to recognize that it has a great deal to learn yet about infectious disease and that the sexual transmission of the virus forces us to examine our social, cultural, and legal policies—particularly in regard to gender—in new ways. Joanne Csete provides a global perspective of how international restructuring policies from trade agreements to legal protections for immigrants and domestic workers place individuals at risk for HIV and how their gender roles also are a determinant of risk. Theresa Kaijage and Michael Tan provide historical and gendered insights on the globalization of AIDS from their places in the world, Tanzania and the Philippines respectively. The tobacco epidemic—which has broad health implications for multiple chronic diseases such as heart disease, emphysema, and lung cancer—is being strategically marketed to populations who traditionally have not used tobacco: largely women in developing countries.

Jeff Collin traces how transnational tobacco companies—based on historical marketing efforts in the West—are now trying to make cigarettes and other tobaccos socially normative to women in non-Western countries. Stella Bialous narrates how she felt the pressures of tobacco advertising growing up in Brazil and how gender is manipulated to sell products. Further, Norbert Hirschhorn examines the medical and reproductive health implications of tobacco use on women—many of which have been underresearched and which we are still beginning to learn. This takes us to the last section of the book—moving women's health research onto the scientific agenda. Although much of this book focuses on gender roles in relation to the effects of globalization and health, the importance of better understanding how disease symptoms manifest themselves differently in men and women is indeed critical if we are to move into the twenty-first century with the tools and knowledge necessary to confront the next HIV virus or radiological symptom.

Carolyn Mazure documents the efforts of individual citizens and lobbyists in the United States to change federal law to require a broader base of female participation in clinical research trials. U.S. dominance in the global marketplace and media markets is often perceived as a negative consequence of globalization; but that very strength of presence is having consequences in areas such as women's clinical research in other parts of the world as Ulrike Maschewsky-Schneider's case study from Germany tells us. Throughout the book, each author highlights where we need to go next in terms of research and policy. The systemic gaps in our knowledge due to a lack of consistent gender analysis often is highlighted alongside the undertow of cultural changes as societies respond to the rapid alterations surrounding them.

There are ideological and disciplinary differences reflected in the chapters of this book. Each of the chapters in this volume describes in a different way why gender is a necessary consideration when understanding the status of health in all societies. As one will see in the course of reading this work, some of our authors took issue with a tendency to equate "gender" with "women." This remains a challenge, if we are to adequately understand the pathways to change and to develop policy proposals with long-term impact. The position taken by most authors however is that local and global forces disproportionately and negatively impact women.

While each chapter stands alone in terms of its content, the union of these diverse approaches provides an important interdisciplinary perspective necessary for constructively confronting the sheer complexity of globalization and proposing ethical alternatives toward a more just distribution of opportunity and knowledge for development. Globalization brings with it new identities and social relations, and each and every one of the elements we analyze can imply freedom for some and oppression for others. Only after collaborative solutions to the question of "how do we survive?" are achieved can many of the world's people begin answering the question of how we want to live.

Notes

1. M. H. Marchand and A. S. Runyan (2000), *Gender and Global Restructuring: Sightings, Sites and Resistances*, London: Routledge; S. Sassen (1998), *Globalization and Its Discontents*, New York: The New Press; A. Giddens (2003), *Runaway World: How Globalisation is Reshaping Our Lives*, New York: Routledge; A. Giddens (2000), *The Third Way and Its Critics*, Oxford: Blackwell Publishers, Inc.; N. A. Naples and M. Desai, eds. (2002), *Women's Activism and Globalization: Linking Local Struggles and Transnational Politics*, New York and London: Routledge.
2. K. Lee (2003), *Globalization and Health: An Introduction*, London: Palgrave Macmillan; R. L. Harris and M. Seid, eds. (2004), *Globalization and Health*, International Studies in Sociology and Social Anthropology Series, Volume 95,

Leiden: Brill; C. McMurray and R. Smith (2001), *Diseases of Globalization: Socioeconomic Transitions and Health*, London: Earthscan Publications Ltd.; G. Sen, A. George, and P. Ostlin, eds. (2002), *Engendering International Health: The Challenge of Equity*, Cambridge, MA: The MIT Press; K. Lee, K. Buse, and S. Fustukian, eds. (2002), *Health Policy in a Globalising World*, Cambridge: Cambridge University Press.

3. U. Beck (2000), *What is Globalization?* Translated by Patrick Camiller, Cambridge, UK: Polity Press, p. 215.

4. http://www.who.int/hpr/NPH/docs/ottawa_charter_hp.pdf, accessed February 18, 2005.

5. http://www.euro.who.int/AboutWHO/Policy/20010827_1, accessed February 18, 2005.

6. J. Scholte (2000), *Globalization: A Critical Introduction*, New York: Palgrave Macmillan, p. 136.

7. I. Kickbusch and K. Buse (2001), Global influences and global responses: International health at the turn of the twenty-first century, in M. Merson, R. Black, and A. Mills, eds., *International Public Health* (pp. 701–733), Gaithersbrug: Aspen Publishers, p. 707.

8. K. Lee (2003), Introduction, in K. Lee, ed., *Health Impacts of Globalization: Towards Global Governance* (pp. 1–12), London: Palgrave Macmillan, p. 5.

9. M. Marchand and A. Runyan (2000), Introduction, in M. Marchand and A. Runyan, eds., *Gender and Global Restructuring: Sightings, Sites, and Resistance*, London: Routledge; M. H. Marchand (2003), Challenging globalization: Toward a feminist understanding of resistance, *Review of International Studies*, Special Issue (29): 145–160.

1

Understanding Gender, Health, and Globalization: Opportunities and Challenges*

Lesley Doyal

Introduction

This chapter offers a framework for understanding the links between globalization, health, and gender relations. These very complex connections are explored from two different perspectives: how existing gender relations affect the globalization of health and (more briefly) how the globalization of health may affect future patterns of gender relations. The chapter begins with some preliminary comments on the three different concepts under review: globalization, health, and gender relations.

Defining Globalization

Over the past three decades, there has been a dramatic increase in the volume and speed of economic, financial, technical, and cultural interchanges between different countries.[1] For some individuals and communities these developments have been positive, giving them greater access to a range of valued resources. But the daily lives of others have been transformed in more negative ways. At the same time there has been a significant reduction in the capacity of many nation-states to respond effectively to the changing patterns of need within their populations.

The concept of "globalization" is often used as a major variable in explaining these changes. But because the term itself is so broadly defined and so widely contested, it can be of little value in making sense of specific instances of social reality. If we are to tease out the links between gender, health, and global change we will need to be very clear about which developments we are talking about, when they are taking place, and where. For this reason, the analysis presented here will refer to processes of "global restructuring" rather than the singular and often deterministic concept of "globalization."[2] This will provide the canvas upon which to paint a more accurate picture of the fragmented and often contradictory dimensions of global change that are affecting the health of individuals and local communities.

Too often, the term globalization is often used in a way that presumes a unified process leading toward greater homogeneity. Moreover the focus is mainly on the economic sphere with other aspects of society receiving much less attention. The concept of global restructuring offers a more flexible framework for understanding what has been described as "a set of multi-dimensional, multispeed and disjuncted processes."[3] It incorporates a range of social, cultural, and other dimensions of change and also allows for the impact of human agency. Hence it can be used as the broad canvas upon which to paint a more accurate picture of the complex and contradictory global trends that are affecting the well-being of individual women and men.

Putting Health on the Agenda

There is now a large literature exploring the relationships between global restructuring and human health. Balance sheets have been drawn up and the resulting profit/loss accounts have been widely debated.[4] The failure to come to any overall consensus reflects in part the very variable effects of these different processes. But it also reflects the very high level of generality at which most of the debate has so far been conducted.[5]

Links have been made between indicators such as economic growth and mortality rates or life expectancy. However relatively few attempts have been made to move beyond these macro-level statistical relationships. If our understanding of these processes is to be enhanced, there will need to be much more detailed case studies of the messy reality that lies behind any observed correlations. In particular we will need to disaggregate trends in the different diseases, disabilities, and illness that are consolidated into the broader indicators of mortality and life expectancy.

Recent work on the global burden of disease is a valuable resource in this context since it provides evidence on the contribution of specific diseases to the number of healthy years of life lost to death and disability in different parts of the world.[6] These numbers will need to be treated with care since they are likely to underestimate the health problems facing women as many women's ailments remain invisible.[7] Used with gender sensitivity, however, this approach can provide one element in the conceptual tool kit necessary for mapping the links between social and economic change and trends in male and female patterns of morbidity and mortality.

The drawing of this map will pose significant methodological challenges. Changes in the realms of politics, economics, culture, and technology are reshaping physical and social environments in different parts of the world. The task for us here is to understand the causal relationships between these changed conditions of life and the health of individuals and communities. This will not be achieved without more cooperation between researchers trained in very different disciplinary traditions. Most importantly, it will need creative collaboration across the boundaries of the natural and social sciences.

The last decades of the twentieth century were marked by a growing recognition of the limitations of the biomedical paradigm in explaining patterns of morbidity and mortality. This has led to a growing use of insights and methods from other disciplines in exploring the wider determinants of health. At the same time, many social scientists have moved beyond their fears of biological determinism to bring different notions of the body back into discourses on health.[8] These converging trends offer the opportunity to develop genuinely interdisciplinary methodologies which in turn will help us to make sense of the combination of factors that combine to create characteristically gendered patterns of health and illness.[9]

Bringing Gender Relations into the Picture

Most work in the broad area of globalization or global restructuring has been gender blind.[10] With a few exceptions, commentators have paid little or no attention to the ways in which women and men may experience these changes differently. In recent years this gap has begun to be filled with the emergence of a new literature focused on gender and development issues.[11] But many more studies are needed of the differential impact of global change on women and men in specific social settings. And a central focus of this research should be the ways in which biological sex and social gender mediate the impact of restructuring on individual well-being.

The most obvious differences between women and men are to be found in the realm of biology. Women's capacity for reproduction makes them vulnerable to a wide range of health problems if they are not able to control their fertility and go safely through pregnancy and childbirth. Similarly, both women and men are susceptible to sex specific diseases such as cancers of the uterus or prostate. However recent research has also identified differences in the vulnerability of women and men to diseases that affect both sexes.[12]

It is widely recognized for example, that men are inherently more likely than women to die prematurely from heart disease. It is less well known that they are more susceptible to many infectious diseases including tuberculosis and pneumonia. Women on the other hand are more likely than men to contract HIV from a single encounter with an infected partner and are also more likely to develop autoimmune diseases such as diabetes and rheumatoid arthritis. Though they rarely act alone, these biological differences between women and men will need to be part of our conceptual framework for exploring the links between global restructuring and health.

In combination with these biological determinants, male and female patterns of morbidity and mortality are also shaped by social relationships including those associated with gender.[13] All societies assign specific characteristics to individuals depending on whether they are defined as male or female. There are also differences in the duties they are expected to perform and in their entitlement to a wide range of social and economic resources. This gendered division of responsibilities and rewards means that women and men may face different threats to their well-being while also having differential access to health-promoting resources.

The nature of these gender differences, however, will vary between societies and communities. Stratification by gender operates within the context of a range of other variables including age, race, caste, class, and ethnicity. Thus the implications of "maleness" or "femaleness" for health will show some similarities between a middle-class London suburb and a rural village in Bangladesh but there will also be very marked differences. And it is here at the busy intersection between a range of social, economic, and biological variables that we can begin to seek out some of the most immediate effects of global restructuring on health.

How do Gender Relations Shape the Impact of Globalization on Human Health?

There are many different ways of talking about gender relations. Indeed the complex debates found in contemporary gender studies offer a bewildering variety of definitions and interpretations. For the purposes of this discussion we adopt a framework, which can be operationalized in relatively simple ways across a range of settings. The approach proposed here is an examination of the links between globalization, health, and gender relations in two separate but interconnected domains: the division of labor and the distribution of resources. Illustrative examples are used to suggest possible causal links and to indicate future areas of research. Though the main focus is on the health of poor women, the gendered implications of restructuring for men will also be highlighted where appropriate.

Gendered Divisions of Labor and Global Restructuring

One of the most obvious characteristics of most societies is the gendered nature of the division of labor.[14] Historically, women have been given responsibility for what takes place in the home while men have been seen as the main actors in the public arena. Of course, this was never an accurate reflection of reality and one of the effects of restructuring has been to move the global division of work even further from this mythical complementarity of male and female roles.

The last decades have seen major changes in the way goods and services are produced. These changes have not been universal and their impact has differed markedly between regions, communities, and countries. However, it is clear that in most parts of the world they have been gendered in their effects.[15] Most importantly, many more women have taken on paid work in both the formal and the informal sectors.[16] In some countries, this increased employment among females has been accompanied by a decline in paid work among males. Yet there is little evidence of concomitant changes in the gender division of household labor.

These developments have had implications for the health of both sexes. In the transition economies of Eastern and Central Europe, for example, it is clear that the health of many men has been profoundly damaged by loss of paid work and by other changes in the nature of daily life.[17] However on a global scale, it is probably (poor) women who have been most affected as they come under increasing pressure to manage their families' survival strategies both at work and at home.

Gender, Health, and Waged Work

It is clear that increased access to waged work can potentially be good for women's health.[18] If they are able to earn (and keep) an independent income, this will make it easier for them to buy what they need to promote their own health whether that is a better diet or a safe space to live, away from abuse. Evidence from a number of studies suggests that the workplace may also be an important source of social support. However for many women (and especially for the poorest) the conditions of work and the way it is organized will place severe constraints on the realization of these potential health benefits.

The global restructuring of production is based on the demand by employers for flexible labor that will meet their needs at the lowest possible cost. This has led to increased pressure on many men to risk their lives in order to support their families. It is also the context in which many of the world's poorest women have entered the labor force for the first time. Most live in countries where regulatory regimes are weak and wages are low and as a result they often face both new and old hazards to health.[19]

Exposure to new hazards is especially common in the Export Processing Zones in Asia and Latin America where women usually make up the majority of the workforce.[20] In the case of the electronics industry for example, a number of studies have shown that the reality of life on the production line is far from its clean and pollution-free image.[21] Here, young women are often exposed to a multiplicity of toxic substances with chronic effects on both their physical and their mental health.

It is important that these new risks associated with "modern" technologies are given appropriate attention. However, the greatest impact has probably been on the many women in developing countries now exposed to the traditional hazards of old industries such as textiles. Millions are also being pulled or pushed into the informal sector to eke out a precarious living.[22] The work in these settings is usually strenuous, monotonous, and poor ergonomically; yet, such damaging effects on well-being go largely unacknowledged.[23]

In rural areas, there have also been alarming increases in the numbers of agricultural workers whose health is damaged by exposure to certain pesticides and other environmental chemicals.[24] This reflects changes in patterns of agricultural production especially the increased use of agrichemicals. Women are often in the greatest danger both because of their preponderance in the agricultural labor force and because chemicals are frequently stored in or near their homes.[25] Their biological susceptibility to some of these toxins is greater than that of men and some will be passed on to babies in breast milk. Yet the social invisibility of their labor means that they are less likely than men to have access to protective clothing.

Gender, Health, and Domestic Work

There is growing evidence that global restructuring has also had an impact on the nature of unpaid labor. Some women now have the resources to ease their own burden of housework through hiring the services of other (usually migrant) women.[26] Meanwhile, most of these women continue to have the primary responsibility for domestic work and this often has to be done alongside paid employment and sometimes subsistence agriculture. This leaves them carrying what has been called the double or even triple burden.

For many of the world's poorest women these daily labors have become significantly more hazardous as a result of environmental changes associated with global restructuring.[27] In parts of India for example, women now have to walk many extra hours each day for a head-load of firewood while in many African communities water may be several hours away. Women may be at risk of musculoskeletal injures as they scramble to acquire the necessities of life in increasingly inhospitable terrains.[28] And in some parts of the world, there has been an increase in the huge burden of lung disease suffered by women as deforestation increases the levels of pollution from cooking stoves.[29]

Because of the insecurity and the destabilization that often accompanies restructuring, both the volume and the intensity of domestic work have increased for many women.[30] Some women have been forced to migrate in order to find work or to avoid situations of conflict. For many, the pressures are exacerbated as public sector services are withdrawn and traditional sources of support disappear. Frequent childbearing will be an additional hazard especially if food is in short supply. This can lead to iron-deficiency anemia and greater vulnerability to pregnancy related disorders and to a range of infectious diseases.[31] It also renders women more vulnerable to depression and other mental health problems.[32]

This section has identified some examples of the complex links between gender, work, and health in the context of global restructuring. But much more research is needed into aspects of illness and disability that are extremely difficult to measure. We need to know more about the changing circumstances under which waged work is both good and bad for women's and men's health. More studies are also needed of the complex hazards facing women in the course of their combined labors both inside and outside the home. We need a fuller class analysis of labor conditions that pose health hazards to men and the relationships between health, labor, and migration. Additionally, we need to have a much clearer understanding of the fatigue and the "time famine" that characterizes the lives of so many poor women.[33]

Gender and the Distribution of Resources

Gendered criteria for the allocation of work are mirrored by gender inequalities in the allocation of resources. Women and men are expected to do different kinds of work and they are rewarded differentially for the labors they carry out. In most societies, the pattern is one where women have less entitlement than men to the most valued resources and this may limit their capacity to promote and protect their own health. In many parts of the world, global restructuring has exacerbated these inequalities.

Gender, Poverty, and Health

The links between poverty and ill health are long established and it is clear that the numbers of people in poverty have increased in recent decades.[34] While this cannot be attributed in any simplistic way to global restructuring, it does appear that deprivation is now appearing in new guises and different settings.

It is frequently claimed for example, that recent developments have led to a "feminization of poverty" and that women now make up around 70 percent of the poor. The scarcity of gender disaggregated poverty data makes it impossible to judge the accuracy of such global estimates.[35] However, recent studies from the United Nations do suggest that more women than men are in poverty in 12 out of the 15 developing countries for which there is appropriate data.[36] More importantly perhaps, the evidence also indicates that women and men fall into poverty by different routes and that it differently influences their well-being.[37]

In many (but by no means all) settings, women who are single heads of households are at greater risk than their male counterparts of being in poverty.[38] Excess poverty among women can also result from gender bias in household resource allocation. In many (but again not all) societies, cultural norms state that women and girls are entitled to less than their male counterparts.[39] This applies not only to money but to a wide range of other resources including food, land, credit, time, status, and physical security. As a result, women in poor households may end up being the most deprived of all, while even in more affluent families gender bias may push women into invisible poverty.

These gender differences in the causes of poverty are also reflected in its effects. It has long been recognized that being poor can damage the health of both males and females. But biological sex and social gender are important factors mediating this relationship. Both women and men will have to work very hard in conditions of poverty and will also be short of material resources. The nature and the meaning of their work will vary markedly as will their physical capacity to carry it out. Men and women will also have differential access to the economic and social support that can be used to limit the harmful effects of their labors.[40]

The impacts of these differences on well-being are hard to decipher. Poverty does appear to be more damaging to women's health than to men's. This is reflected in a recent study comparing the causes of the burden of disease in rich and poor countries.[41]Communicable diseases are much more common among the poorest 20 percent of the world's population than among the rich. It is women who carry the heaviest burden of death and disability from these causes, suffering 7.5 percent more deaths and losing 11.4 percent more disability adjusted life years (DALYs) than men. This excess is due in part to the inclusion of maternal deaths in the calculation. But even when this is excluded, the greater female burden persists (5.4 percent more deaths and 7.8 percent more DALYs lost).[42]

The gendered impact of poverty on health can also be illustrated by examining the changing nature of the HIV/AIDS epidemic.[43] The last decade has seen a huge increase in the numbers of women infected so that they now constitute the majority of HIV positive people.[44] In situations where they have few options for supporting themselves and their families, many women may feel compelled to stay with a male partner even when this is putting their life at risk. For some, paid sex work may be the only source of income and adolescent girls are particularly at risk in such circumstances. This reflects their greater biological vulnerability but also their lack of alternative means of subsistence where the rapidity of global restructuring has cut away the support networks that previously existed even in impoverished communities.

Similar links can be made between the gendered nature of poverty and the health burden of intimate violence. Of course, violence against women is found in all communities and not just among the poor. A growing number of studies have indicated that violence is often exacerbated under the conditions of insecurity and social conflict that so often accompany restructuring.[45] Men may feel emasculated as they lose their sense of identity and social status while women's lack of access to financial and other resources forces them to remain in a situation that may threaten their health.[46]

Gender Inequalities in Access to Health Care

Gendered inequalities in access to resources in general are also reflected in the context of health care. As we have seen, women's reproductive capacities mean that they have sex-specific needs, which must be met if they are to realize their potential for health. But there is growing evidence that changes accompanying global restructuring have placed new constraints on the ability of some women to meet both their sex-specific and also their more general health care needs.

Global restructuring has included policies designed to reshape the economies of many developing countries and these initiatives have had a particular impact on the delivery of health care. During the 1980s and early 1990s the combination of economic crisis and structural adjustment policies led to a dramatic decline in both the quality and quantity of public services especially in the poorest countries.[47] Partly as a response to these problems, the World Bank, WHO, and a number of other agencies championed what came to be known as health sector reform.[48]

During the period of fiscal crisis and structural adjustment, the cost of health care rose dramatically with the introduction of user fees. This led to a major flight to the private sector and an increase in out-of-pocket expenditure as well as a rise in self-treatment.[49] Studies to evaluate the impact of these trends have been rare and few have been gender-sensitive. The evidence now becoming available does suggest that in many parts of the world women have been disproportionately affected.[50] Where gender inequalities shape the allocation of household resources, this is often reflected in decisions about health care expenditure and women are most likely to miss out.[51]

At the same time, it has become clear that despite the global impact of the 1994 Cairo International Conference on Population and Development, sexual and reproductive health has not been high on the agenda of health sector reformers.[52] The main emphasis in this process has been on the reshaping of financing mechanisms and human resources with relatively little attention being paid to the form or content of the care being offered. In more recent years, attention has shifted toward priority setting between different types of services but the main tool has been the burden of disease model, which tends to underestimate the impact of reproductive health problems.[53]

Under these circumstances health sector reformers have too often neglected sexual and reproductive health services, sidelining them as "special interest" programs.[54] They have not recognized their centrality to women's health and this has contributed to continuing high levels of maternal morbidity and mortality.[55] Over the past five years, the global total of maternal deaths has increased significantly and now stands at around 600,000 per year. Women in Sierra Leone and in Afghanistan for instance, still have a one in seven chance of dying from maternal causes.[56] While the causes of these deaths are complex it is clear that both poverty and lack of access to appropriate medical care play crucial roles.

These examples have highlighted the need for more research on the gendered nature of the poverty associated with global restructuring. This will provide the basis for a better understanding of the complex effects of material and social deprivation on the health status of both women and men. In particular, there is an urgent need for more rigorous analysis of the gendered impact of health sector reform especially in the area of sexual and reproductive health.

How will the Globalization of Health Affect Patterns of Gender Relations?

Thus far, we have examined the role of sex and gender in shaping the impact of global restructuring on health. In this final section, we look at a different formulation of the same equation: how might the globalization of health affect gender relations themselves? Since this topic remains largely unexplored in the wider literature, the account presented here serves only as a very brief introduction to possible topics for future work.

The last few years have seen a growing interest in the policy implications of the links between gender and global restructuring. The United Nations broke new ground with its compilation of data *The World's Women 2000: Trends and statistics*[57] and two volumes on *Progress of the World's Women*.[58] At the same time, the work of UNDP has increasingly taken on a gender focus with the introduction of the Gender Empowerment Measure and the Gender Development Index.[59]

These are valuable resources that form part of a much wider range of materials now emerging from other international organizations, from NGOs, and from academia. All of them explore the impact of global restructuring on women's lives and many focus on health effects in particular. Few have turned the question around to see how health might affect gender relations but a perusal of the literature does suggest two areas where this process might be taking place. These are the changing relations of caring in households and the increasing involvement of women in health politics.

The Globalization of Health and Changes in Relations of Caring in Households

There is now a growing literature on the changing nature of gender relations in households. It is suggested that as women replace men in some parts of the labor force, the traditional "patriarchal bargain" is being undermined.[60] During this period of what a recent World Bank report called "gender anxiety" both women and men are becoming increasingly unclear about their rights and responsibilities within the family setting.[61] Some respond by attempting to reinforce old values based on outmoded economic patterns. But in other settings, the space has opened up for the renegotiation of gender relations.

Thus far, changing patterns of health have received little attention as causal factors in these processes but recent studies suggest that they may have a part to play. There has been widespread recognition of the growing burden taken up by women as the HIV/AIDS epidemic generates a huge increase in the need for care. However, there are signs that in some settings, these traditionally gendered divisions in caring are beginning to break down. As more women become ill and die, and traditional support systems are destroyed, young men in particular are beginning to take on responsibilities that they would previously have rejected as inappropriate.

These developments may be reinforced by the process of ageing now taking place in most countries in the world. This global trend is having a particular impact in developing countries where the number of people over the age of 60 will double over the next 25 years and the majority of these will be women. This will clearly have a major impact on the demand for health services and it seems likely that again there will be pressures for change in the balance of caring between women and men. In some communities, global demographic changes and the impact of epidemic diseases may therefore combine with changing patterns of employment to reshape gender relations within households.

The Increasing Involvement of Women in the Politics of Health

Alongside changes within households, there is also evidence that in many parts of the world more women are becoming more active in the public arena. As the effects of global restructuring have become more visible, many women have responded by becoming involved in politics.[62] These activities have been very diverse and have varied by time and place but health has often been a central focus.[63] Campaigns led by women have clearly had a major impact on both global and local health politics.[64] It can be argued that their impact is likely to be even greater as new forms of organizing contribute to more fundamental changes in gender relations.

The decades of globalization have witnessed the greatest ever mobilization of women into politics. Not surprisingly, their campaigns have been firmly rooted in everyday life as they have tackled the challenges of survival in the context of uncertainty. The most intensive campaigning has involved sexual and reproductive health and gender violence.[65] But women have also been involved in a variety of needs-based campaigns relating to poverty and subsistence.[66] Occupational and environmental health have also been high on women's political agendas as global restructuring has exposed both them and their families to new hazards.[67]

As many states have withdrawn from the care of their citizens, the organizations making up "civil society" have taken on greater responsibilities. Women have been especially active in this context with many moving from the role of volunteer service provider to community activist.[68] At the same time, some of those entering the labor force have become involved for the first time in collective action to defend themselves against threats to their well-being.[69] This transition of increasing numbers of women from the private world of the household to the public world of activism and politics is likely to have implications for gender relations at both individual and institutional levels.

For a few women, the expansion of their sphere of activity has been especially dramatic. Using new information technologies and deploying the universalizing framework of human rights they have highlighted the political potential of partnerships and "virtual communities" in a globalized world.[70] They have moved beyond the confines of their own communities and are now working to promote global health in both national and international contexts. Despite major differences in material circumstances and sociocultural identities, they are working together to promote more equitable gender relations as part of the wider campaign for a healthier world.

Conclusion

This chapter offered a brief outline of some of the major conceptual challenges we face in analyzing the links between gender, health, and global restructuring. It presented a preliminary framework for understanding these complex processes and offered some suggestions for future research. We have seen that the success of this project is dependent on two things: a capacity to draw on the widest possible range of intellectual resources and a willingness to engage in empirical (but theoretically informed) investigations in a wide variety of settings. Only if these conditions are met will we be able to produce a coherent account of the complex and ever-changing realities currently (re)shaping the health of both women and men in different parts of the world.

Notes

* This is an amended version of a paper first published in *Third World Quarterly* 23(3): 233–249, Copyright: Taylor & Francis.

1. F. Lechner and J. Boli, eds., (2000), *The Globalization Reader*, Oxford: Blackwell; D. Held, A. McGrew, D. Goldblatt, and J. Perraton (1999), *Global Transformations: Politics, Economics and Culture*, Cambridge: Polity Press; A. Giddens (1990), *The Consequences of Modernity*, Cambridge: Polity Press.

2. M. Marchand and A. Runyan (2000), Introduction, in M. Marchand and A. Runyan, eds., *Gender and Global Restructuring: Sightings, Sites and Resistance*, London: Routledge; S. Sassen (1998), *Globalization and Its Discontents*, New York: New Press.

3. M. Marchand and A. Runyan, Introduction, p. 7.

4. G. Cornia (2001), Globalization and health: Results and options, *Bulletin of the World Health Organization* 79(9): 834–841; D. Dollar (2001), Is globalization good for your health? *Bulletin of the World Health Organization* 79(9): 827–833; N. Drager and R. Beaglehole (2001), Globalization: Changing the public health landscape, *Bulletin of the World Health Organization* 79(9): 803; R. Feachem (2001), Globalization is good for your health, mostly, *British Medical Journal* 323: 504–506; M. Weisbrot, D. Baker, E. Kraev, and J. Chen (2001), The scorecard on globalization 1980–2000: Twenty years of diminished progress, *CEPR Briefing Paper*, Washington DC: Center for Economic and Policy Research; D. Yach, and D. Bettcher (1998), The globalization of public health threats and opportunities, *American Journal of Public Health* 88: 735–8.

5. K. Lee (1998), Globalization and health, *LSHTM Policy Discussion paper*, London: London School of Hygiene and Tropical Medicine, p. 1.

6. C. Murray and D. Lopez, eds. (1996), *The Global Burden of Disease*, v.1, Cambridge, MA: Harvard School of Public Health on behalf of the World Health Organization and the World Bank.

7. K. Hanson (1999), Measuring up: Gender, burden of disease and priority setting techniques in the health sector, *Working Paper no 12*, Cambridge: Harvard Center for Population and Development.

8. L. Birke (2002), Anchoring the head: The disappearing (biological) body, in G. Bendelow et al., eds., *Gender, Health and Healing: The Public/Private Divide*, London: Routledge; K. Davis (1997), *Embodied Practices*, London: Sage; C. Shilling (1993), *The Body and Social Theory*, London: Sage.

9. G. Sen, A. George, and P. Ostlin, Engendering health equity: A review of research and policy, in G. Sen, A. George, and P. Ostlin, eds., *Engendering International Health: The Challenge of Equity* (pp. 1–33), Cambridge: MIT Press.

10. M. Marchand and A. Runyan, Introduction; Sassen, *Globalization and Its Discontents*.

11. R. Pearson (2000), Moving the goalposts: Gender and globalization in the twenty first century, in C. Sweetman, ed., *Gender in the Twenty First Century*, Oxford: Oxfam; C. Jackson and R. Pearson (1998), *Feminist Visions of Development*, London: Routledge; N. Kabeer (1994), *Reversed Realities: Gender Hierarchies in Development Thought*, London: Verso.

12. T. Wizeman and M. Pardue (2001), *Exploring the Biological Contribution to Human Health*, Washington DC: National Academy Press.

13. L. Doyal (1995), *What Makes Women Sick: Gender and the Political Economy of Health*, Basingstoke: Macmillan; Sen, George and Ostlin, Engendering health equity: A review of research and policy.

14. N. Kabeer, *Reversed Realities: Gender Hierarchies in Development Thought*.

15. Panos (1999), Globalization and employment: New opportunities, real threats, *Briefing 33*, London: Panos. http://www.panos.org.uk/global/reportdetails.asp?id=1000&reportid=1015.

16. United Nations (1999), *World Survey on the Role of Women in Development: Globalization, Gender and Work*, New York: United Nations; United Nations (2000), The world's women 2000: Trends and statistics, *Social Statistics and Indicators Series K*, 16, New York: United Nations; UNIFEM (2000), *Progress of the World's Women 2000*, New York: UNIFEM; UNIFEM (2003), *Progress of the World's Women 2002*, New York: UNIFEM.

17. V. Sholnikov (1997), The Russian health crisis of the 1990's in mortality dimensions, *Working Paper no 97.01*, Cambridge: Harvard Center for Population and Development Studies; L. Chenet (2000), Gender and socio-economic inequalities in mortality in Central and Eastern Europe, *Social Science and Medicine* 40(10): 1355–1366; P. Watson (1995), Explaining rising mortality among men in Eastern Europe, *Social Science and Medicine* 41(7): 923–924.

18. L. Doyal, *What Makes Women Sick: Gender and the Political Economy of Health*.

19. A. Chhachhi and R. Pittin (1996), Introduction, in A. Chhachhi and R. Pittin, eds., *Confronting State, Capital and Patriarchy*, Basingstoke: Macmillan; M. Fontana, S. Joekes, and R. Masika (1998), Global trade expansion and liberalization: Gender issues and impacts, *BRIDGE Report 42*, Brighton: IDS; P. Ostlin (2002), Examining work and its effects on health, in G. Sen, A. George, and P. Ostlin, eds., *Engendering International Health: The Challenge of Equity*.

20. Coalition for Justice in the Maquiladoras (1993), *The Issue is Health: Toxic Samplings, Environmental Conditions and Health Concerns along the US/Mexico Border*, San Antonio: CJM; R. Loewenson (2000), Occupational hazards in the informal sector: A global perspective, in K. Isaksson et al., eds., *Health Effects of the New Labour Market*, New York: Kluwer Academic/Plenum; R. Loewenson (2001), Globalization and occupational health: A perspective from Southern Africa, *Bulletin of the World Health Organization* 79(9): 863–868.

21. S. Theobald (1999), Community responses to the electronics industry in Thailand, *Development* 42(4): 126–129.

22. J. Delahanty and M. Shefali (1999), Improving women's health and labour conditions in the garment sector, *Development* 42(4): 98–102; Loewenson, Occupational hazards in the informal sector: A global perspective. United Nations, *The World's Women 2000: Trends and Statistics*.

23. L. Doyal, *What Makes Women Sick: Gender and the Political Economy of Health*.

24. J. Sims and M. Butter (2000), Gender equity and environmental health, *Working Paper Series* 10(6), Cambridge: Harvard Center for Population and Development.

25. M. Jacobs and B. Dinham (2003), *Silent Invaders: Pesticides, Livelihood and Women's Health*, London: Zed Books; P. Ransom (2001), *Women, Pesticides and Sustainable Agriculture*, available: https://www.earthsummit2002.org/wcaucus (accessed September 12, 2001).

26. B. Anderson (2000), *Doing the Dirty Work? The Global Politics of Domestic Labour*, London: Zed Books; B. Ehrenreich and A. Hochschild (2004), *Global Woman: Nannies, Maids and Sex Workers in the New Era*, London: Granta.

27. M. Awumbila and J. Momsen (1995), Gender and the environment: Women's time use as a measure of environmental change, *Global and Environmental Change* 5(4): 337–346; D. Davidson and W. Freudenburg (1996), Gender and environmental risk concerns—a review of available research, *Environment and Behavior* 28(3): 302–339; J. Sims and M. Butter (2000), Gender equity and environmental health, *Working Paper* 10(6), Cambridge: Harvard Center for Population and Development.

28. B. Kettel (1995), Women, health and environment, *Social Science and Medicine* 42(10): 1367–1379; G. Martine and M. Villarreal (1997), Gender and sustainability: Re-assessing linkages and issues, *Working Paper no 97.11*, Cambridge: Harvard Center for Population and Development.

29. J. Sims and M. Butter, Gender equity and environmental health; V. Mishra, R. Retherford, and K. Smith (1999), Biomass fuels and prevention of TB in India, *International Journal of Infectious Diseases* 3(2): 119–129.

30. J. Avorti and V. Walters (1999), You just look at our work and see if we have any freedom on earth: Ghanaian women's accounts of their work and their health, *Social Science and Medicine* 48: 1123–1133.

31. B. Brabin and M. Hakimi et al. (2000), An analysis of anemia and pregnancy—related mortality, *Journal of Nutrition* 131(supplement): 6045–6155.

32. J. Astbury (1999), Gender and mental health, *Working Paper 99.8*, Cambridge: Harvard Center for Population and Development Studies.

33. C. Jackson and R. Palmer-Jones (1998), *Work Intensity, Gender and Well-Being*, Geneva: UNRISD.

34. V. Navarro (1998), Neoliberalism, globalization, unemployment, inequalities and the welfare state, *International Journal of Health Services* 28(4): 607–682.

35. C. Jackson (1998), Rescuing gender from the poverty trap, in C. Jackson and R. Pearson, eds., *Feminist Visions of Development*, London: Routledge; Z. Oxaal and S. Cook (1998), *Health and Poverty Gender Analysis: A briefing prepared for SIDA by BRIDGE*, Brighton: IDS.

36. UNIFEM (2001), *Gender and HIV /AIDS: Facts and Statistics*, available: https://www.unifem.undp.org/hiv_aids/hiv_facts.html.

37. N. Cagatay (1998), Gender and poverty. *Working Paper 5*, New York: UNDP Social Development and Poverty Elimination Division; C. Jackson, Rescuing gender from the poverty trap.

38. A. Varley (1996) Women heading households: Some more equal than others? *World Development* 24(3): 505–520.

39. E. Messer (1997), Intra-household allocation of food and health care: Current findings and understandings-introduction, *Social Science and Medicine* 44(11): 1675–1784.

40. C. Jackson and R. Palmer-Jones (1998), *Work Intensity, Gender and Well-Being*.

41. D. Gwatkin and M. Guillot (2000), *The Burden of Disease among the Global Poor: Current Situation, Future Trends and Implications for Strategy*, Washington DC: World Bank and Global Forum for Health Research.

42. L. Reichenbach (2001), Priority setting in International Health: Beyond DALY's and cost effectiveness analysis, *Working Paper Series no 99.06*, Cambridge MA: Harvard Center for Population and Development Studies.

43. P. Gordon and K. Crehan (1997), *Dying of Sadness: Gender, Sexual Violence and the HIV Epidemic*, New York: UNDP Gender and Development Program; P. Farmer, M. Connors, and J. Simmons, eds. (1996), *Women, Poverty and AIDS: Sex, Drugs and Structural Violence*, Monroe: Common Courage Press.

44. UNAIDS (2004), *2004 Report on the Global AIDS Epidemic*, Geneva: UNAIDS.

45. C. Garcia Moreno (1999), Violence against women, gender and health equity, *Working Paper Series no 99.15*, Cambridge: Harvard Center for Population and Development Studies; D. Narayan, et al. (2000), *Voices of the Poor: Can Anyone Hear Us?* Washington DC: World Bank.

46. Panos (1998), *Intimate Enemy: Gender Violence and Reproductive Health*, London: Panos.

47. C. Simms, M. Rowson, and S. Peattie (2001), *The Bitterest Pill of All: The Collapse of Africa's Health System*, London: Save the Children Fund, UK.

48. P. Berman (1995), *Health Sector Reform in Developing Countries*, Boston: Harvard University Press; A. Cassells (1995), Health sector reform: Key issues in less developed countries, *Journal of International Development* 7(3): 329–347; J. Kutzin (1995), Experience with organizational and financing reform of the health sector, *Current Concerns SHS Paper no. 8 (SHS/CC/94.3)*, Geneva: WHO; World Bank (1993); *World Development Report: Investing in Health*, New York: Oxford University Press.

49. A. Cassells, Health sector reform: Key issues in less developed countries.

50. H. Standing (1999), Frameworks for understanding gender inequalities and health sector reform, *Working Paper Series no 99.06*, Cambridge: Harvard Center for Population and Development Studies.

51. I. Evans (1995), SAPping maternal health, *Lancet* 346(8982): 1046; F. Nyonator and J. Kutzin (1999), Health for some? The effects of user fees in the Volta Region of Ghana, *Health Policy and Planning* 14(4): 329–341; P. Sparr (1994), *Mortgaging Women's Lives: Feminist Critiques of Structural Adjustment*, London: Zed Books.

52. P. Nanda (1999), Global agendas, health sector reforms and reproductive health and rights: Opportunities and challenges in Zambia, *Development* 42(4): 59–63; H. Standing (2002), An overview of changing agendas in health sector reforms, *Reproductive Health Matters* 10(20): 19–28; V. Subramanian (1999), The impact of globalization on women's reproductive health and rights: A regional perspective, *Development* 42(4): 145–149; Women's Environment and Development Organization (1999), *Risks, Rights and Reforms; A 50 Country Survey Assessing Government Actions Five Years after the International Conference on Population and Development*, New York: WEDO.

53. K. Hanson (1999), Measuring up: Gender, burden of disease and priority setting techniques in the health sector, *Working Paper no 12*, Cambridge: Harvard Center for Population and Development; E. Nygaard (2000), Is it feasible or desirable to measure burdens of disease as single number? *Reproductive Health Matters* 8(15): 117–127.

54. H. Standing, Frameworks for understanding gender inequalities and health sector reform.

55. Panos (2001), *Birth Rights: New Approaches to Safe Motherhood*, London: Panos, available: http://www.panos.org.uk/briefing/birth_rights_files/ birth_ rights.htm.
56. K. Hill, C. AbouZahr, and T. Wardlaw (2001), *Estimates of Maternal Mortality for 1995*, Geneva: Bulletin of the World Health organization.
57. United Nations, *The World's Women 2000: Trends and Statistics*.
58. UNIFEM (2000), *Progress of the World's Women 2000*, New York: UNIFEM; UNIFEM (2003), *Progress of the World's Women 2002*, New York: UNIFEM.
59. UNDP (1995), *Human Development Report 1995*, New York: UNDP.
60. D. Kandiyoti (1998), Gender, power and contestation: Rethinking bargaining with patriarchy, in C. Jackson and R. Pearson, eds., *Feminist Visions of Development*, London: Routledge.
61. D. Narayan, *Voices of the Poor: Can Anyone Hear Us?*
62. A. Basu (1995), *The Challenge of Local Feminisms: Women's Movements in Global Perspective*, Boulder: Westview Press; A. Chhachhi and R. Pittin, Introduction; S. Rowbotham and S. Mitter (1994), *Dignity and Daily Bread: New Forms of Organizing Among Poor Women in the Third World and the First*, London: Routledge; S. Rowbotham and S. Linkogle (2001), Introduction, in S. Rowbotham and S. Linkogle, eds., *Women Resist Globalization: Mobilizing for Livelihood and Rights*, London: Zed Books.
63. L. Doyal, *What Makes Women Sick: Gender and the Political Economy of Health*.
64. Ibid.
65. R. Petchesky and K. Judd (1998), *Negotiating Reproductive Rights: Women's Perspectives across Countries and Cultures*, London: Zed Books; N. Purewal (2001), New roots for rights: Women's responses to population and development policies, in S. Rowbotham and S. Linkogle, eds., *Women Resist Globalization: Mobilizing for livelihood and rights*; L. Bennett and L. Manderson (2000), *Eliminating Sexual Violence against Women: Towards a global initiative*, Geneva: Global Forum for Health Research; Panos, *Intimate Enemy: Gender Violence and Reproductive Health*.
66. S. Rowbotham and S. Linkogle, Introduction.
67. Women's Environment and Development Organization (1998), *Women Transform the Mainstream: 18 Case Studies of Women and Sustainable Development*, New York: WEDO.
68. A. Lind (1997), Gender, development and urban social change: Women's community action in global cities, *World Development* 25(8): 1205–1223; A. Basu, *The Challenge of Local Feminisms: Women's Movements in Global Perspective*.
69. A. Chhachhi and R. Pittin, Introduction; S. Theobald (1999), Community responses to the electronics industry in Thailand, *Development* 42(4): 126–129; F. Parveen and K. Ali (1996), Research in action: Organizing women factory workers in Pakistan, in A. Chaachhi and R. Pittin, eds., *Confronting State, Capital and Patriarchy*, Basingstoke: Macmillan.
70. Amnesty International (1995), *Human Rights are Women's Rights*, London: Amnesty International; M. Keck and K. Sikkink (1998), *Activists Beyond Borders*, London: Cornell University Press; I. Kickbusch (2000), The development of international health policies-accountability intact? *Social Science and*

Medicine 51: 979–989; I. Kickbusch & J. Quick (1998), Partnerships for health in the 21st century, *World Health Statistics Quarterly* 51(1): 68–74; D. Stienstra (2000), Dancing resistance from Rio to Beijing: Transnational organizing and women's conferences, in M. Marchand and A. Runyan, eds., *Gender and Global Restructuring: Sightings, Sites and Resistances*, London: Routledge; A. Cassells (1996), Aid instruments and health systems development: An analysis of current practice, *Health Policy and Planning* 11(4): 193–198.

2

Philosophy and Religion: Do Activists for Women's Health Need Them?

Lisa Sowle Cahill

Introduction

As virtually all of the contributors to this volume illustrate eloquently, women suffer from egregious health inequities worldwide. As Lesley Doyal points out in her opening chapter women make up about 70 percent of the poor globally, the aggregate number of maternal deaths has increased to around 600,000 annually, and women now constitute the majority of those infected by HIV. A recent overview of the intersections of gender, health, and equity confirms that the "most powerful determinants" of health are social, cultural, and economic conditions, including "income distribution, sanitation, housing, nutrition, consumption, work environment, employment, social and family structures, education, community influences, and individual behaviors."[1] Health is, then, embedded in a web of multiple social factors that are interdependent with power relations in society. According to this same review, gender "is a key form of social stratification, which also determines unequal access to resources, biased public representation, and discriminatory institutional policies."[2] Therefore, addressing health equity for women involves exposing, analyzing, and challenging cultural norms that assign women to places of inferior social influence and privilege. These cultural norms are pervasive and well entrenched, rationalized with theories of women's nature, sacralized by religious ideologies, and reinforced by daily practices that both express and vindicate the ideas behind them.

The most immediate and self-evident response to discrimination against women in access to health care is practical resistance. Activists on behalf of women's welfare form practical organizations and coalitions to fight inequitable conditions. They adopt local, national, regional, and global strategies to promote more equitable policies, promote concrete access to essential services, and to reduce gender bias in communities and cultures, as well as to empower women specifically to change their own situations.[3] Usually such activism relies on tacit ethical judgments that are not explicitly examined or defended. Such judgments may be expressed by using value-laden terms to describe women's situation or to advocate change, or simply by proclaiming or enumerating women's "rights." For example, the aforementioned overview describes strategies in favor of women's health in the following way:

> The most effective interventions have been those with an *empowerment* focus. They aim to help disadvantaged women to gain their rights, improve their access to essential facilities and services, address perceived deficiencies in their knowledge, acquire personal or social skills, and thereby improve their health. . . .[4]

More than a simple description, this statement is premised on several ethical evaluations. Women have a right to health equal to that of men; women's disadvantage in this regard is a moral evil, or unjust; ethics and justice demand intervention; and the empowerment of disenfranchised women themselves is not only an effective but a morally praiseworthy way to remedy gender-based health inequities. Similarly, Lesley Doyal's chapter in this book (chapter 1) concludes by noting that women are moving increasingly into the world of activism and politics, and "are working to promote global health in both national and international contexts," as well as "more equitable gender relations as part of the wider campaign for a healthier world."

Feminist philosophers and theologians, along with activists, concur in such aims, applaud such developments, and are heartened by evidence of effectiveness in changing the low health status of women. But what is the specific role or importance of feminist ethical theory, as well as of religious theory ("theology") and religious practice, in validating and creating changes? To engaged activists, explanatory theories may seem like an irrelevant academic pastime, while religion and theology may even appear dangerous, given the record of the historic faith traditions on the subordination of women. To philosophers and theologians, ethical theory is an indispensable complement of ethical practice.

My thesis is that ethical theory, both philosophical and religious, has several important functions that can assist social change on behalf of women's welfare. I briefly enumerate and discuss four relevant purposes of philosophical ethics, and four different philosophical approaches to ethics (each of which can fulfill these purposes). I then outline four purposes and four types of religious or theological ethics that point toward a philosophically and socially informed feminist theological ethics that can play a transformative role vis-à-vis women's global health concerns.

Purposes of Philosophical Ethics

The first and most fundamental role of philosophical ethics is to mount more strong and coherent challenges to situations of "injustice" by aiding the formulation of reasonable, consistent, and persuasive analyses of the meanings of justice and injustice. In classical terms, the essential definition of justice is to give to each person what is due. The debate over what this means, however, has always been contentious, from Plato's *Republic* down to our own day. In fact, it is not disagreement about whether women are owed justice that is at the root of debates about women's rights to health care, but disagreement over what is in fact just for women. Are women owed treatment that is equal to that of men, differentiated according to different characteristics (and what are the relevant characteristics?), or differentiated according to social status? Philosophical ethics probes the meaning and conditions of justice, examining in particular whether persons should be treated identically, or according to merit or desert, or to need. Most feminists would argue that women should be treated according to the basic needs they share in common with all human beings, as well as consideration of the needs they have as women (e.g., reproductive needs).

What is viewed as "discriminatory" by feminists is viewed as "just" by those who regard women as having a different and lower status than men. This is why it is not sufficient simply to state that one's aim is gender "justice," or even "equity." For some, justice and equity mean that women are less entitled than men to have basic needs met. In fact, in such a view, sex differences exist in order to enable women to fulfill roles in male-oriented institutions of marriage and family. Women are seen as secondary, subordinate, and less deserving, rather than as entitled to equal or special consideration. The success of activists for women's health will be compromised to the extent that they employ a vocabulary of "justice" and "rights" for women without carefully examining the reality of different assumptions about what constitutes the meaning or content of such terms, and how such assumptions have been validated and can be challenged within different cultural matrices.

A second role of philosophical ethics is to clarify the means and goals of action based on agreed-upon values or definitions of justice. This is especially important in conflict cases, or in cases of uncertainty and ambiguity. For example, granting that women have a right to basic health care and to special care for special needs, advocates for women might still disagree over what is appropriate and ethical in reproductive, prenatal, perinatal, and maternal care. Are certain types of family planning measures ethically preferable to others, at least in certain situations or cultures? What if the most "effective" means of preventing pregnancy is more "intrusive" than alternatives? To what degree should parents or families be involved in decision making about the reproductive health of teenage girls? Is prenatal sex selection an appropriate and ethical form of pregnancy services? How about the administration of nevirapine to pregnant women to avoid giving birth to infants with HIV/AIDS? What if the only availability of nevirapine is in an experimental research program?

Philosophical ethics tries to weigh values like autonomy, distributive justice, beneficence, and nonmaleficence in a context of practical wisdom or prudence, sensitive both to social needs and values, and to respect for the individual. Though there are many conflicts philosophical analysis cannot resolve definitively, it can at least sponsor more careful, reflective, self-critical, and nuanced types of action, carried out with greater appreciation of concerns on multiple sides of an issue.

Third, philosophy can provide a vocabulary and set of "moral lenses" that continue to function within social action, reinforcing commitments and practices. This is the function most commonly or obviously seen in activism for women's health, where a position or agenda is put forward in value terms that enhance the attractiveness of the goal, and serve to unite advocates around the same goals. Terms like equality, equity, empowerment, justice, rights, and fairness help confirm and advance moral convictions among those who are trying to put them into practice in the face of strong social resistance. Advocates rely on philosophical premises such as the basic equality of women and men, and the importance of social and political participation for all persons.

For instance, introducing a collection of papers representing the efforts of a worldwide health advocacy network, the prime minister of Bangladesh announced that

> The question of inequity in different aspects of life is a global problem. Inequality or, more importantly, inequity, is a matter of great concern for us all. We are stunned to see the perpetuation of inequities between men and women, between urban and rural areas, and between rich and poor. . . . It is essential to ensure equal rights between women and men in all spheres of life.[5]

In this statement, the prime minister does not lay out the reasons behind his view that men and women, rich and poor, should have equal rights or equal access to health care. In fact, he does not spell out why health care could be considered a right, much less whether all social classes and economic groups have a right to the same level of care, nor whether health care should be purchased with public or private funds. He does not differentiate treatments and options that should or should not be covered in universal health care. The rhetoric of justice and equality functions rather as an effective tool to exhort and encourage those who together, despite obvious cultural differences, share the fundamental practical goal of improving health care for women.

A fourth and complementary role of philosophical ethics is to provide a basis of intentional collaboration among activists from different political, cultural, and/or religious traditions, who share (or can come to share) similar reactions to situations of injustice. The ability to articulate intellectual understandings similarly will interface with and enhance similar moral commitments or a shared plan of action. The self-understanding, aims, and language of many activists actually move close to and indicate this extended role for philosophy.

According to one analysis, "awareness of health equity as an international issue has reached the point where sufficient momentum has built up to stimulate the types of collaborative action that are necessary to monitor and advocate for health equity worldwide."[6] Further, "more collaborative work should be encouraged to focus minds on refining methods and tools for monitoring and analysis, particularly for use in low-income settings," as well as "research," "innovative thinking," and "strong efforts" to introduce "equity" into "current policy debates."[7] Though focused on concrete and practical initiatives, these proposals obviously entail the need for incisive, higher-level analysis of values, principles, and interpretations of a just society or a just global health picture. This is even more true of these authors' concluding call for a "world conscience" (embodied in World Health Organization policy) to "play a leadership role."[8]

Although philosophies and philosophical theories are as diverse as the cultures of the world, common problems and commitments urge the importance of finding ways to identify at least some common ethical values, principles, and explanations of justice. The next section reviews four prominent types of ethical theory before offering the "capabilities approach" of Martha Nussbaum as one rather eclectic theory that is based on commitment to the practical needs of women, and that might interface helpfully both with different cultural contexts and with religious ethics.

Approaches to Philosophical Ethics

The most common type of ethical theory employed in North American feminism is a liberal rights–based theory.

> Common to all variants of the liberal tradition is a definite conception, distinctively modern in character, of [humanity] and society. What are the several elements of this conception? It is *individualist*, in that it asserts the moral primacy of the person against the claims of any social collectivity; *egalitarian*, inasmuch as it confers on all [people] the same moral status and denies the relevance to legal or political order of differences in moral worth among human beings; *universalist*, affirming the moral unity of the human species and according a secondary importance to specific historic associations and cultural forms; and *meliorist* in its affirmation of the corrigibility and improvability of all social institutions and political arrangements.[9]

In accord with this definition, liberal feminism asserts the autonomy and right to self-determination of individual women, claims equal rights for men and women in all societies, views all societies as having the same basic mandate to protect women's human rights, and is activist and positive in its approach to social change.

Liberalism is not without its critics, however. For one thing, the emphasis on individual freedom and "rights" that lies at the heart of this approach does not cohere well with cultural traditions in which membership in community and social roles define individual identity. For another, liberalism is the guiding ideology behind market capitalism as well as modern feminism.[10] Although liberalism has been a powerful force for the recognition of human rights worldwide, critics accuse liberals of claiming a universality for their moral ideals that is not borne out in fact, and of defining so-called human rights in ways that are biased toward Western political traditions and agendas.

"Postmodern" moral theory—as well as deconstructive and poststructuralist critiques—is a response to liberalism. Notoriously hard to define, postmodernism essentially rejects the modern liberal premise of universal reason as a foundation for a worldwide morality and politics of human rights. Instead, postmodern thinkers call attention to the plurality of global cultures and the dependency of all philosophical, religious, and political ideas on the cultures within which they are generated. The moral edge of postmodernism is the undermining of all dominating, "totalizing," or "hegemonic" views of human nature, morality, or the good society. The goal of postmodern ethics is to lift up and empower persons and peoples who have been marginalized by the overriding racist, sexist, and capitalist theories and practices that serve the interests of elites in North Atlantic cultures. In this sort of perspective, women's health equity is not best served by letting liberal economics and politics define the feminist cause, but by empowering oppressed women from a diversity of cultures to define their own needs and solutions.

In the words of Judith Butler, "to establish a set of norms that are beyond power or force is itself a powerful and forceful conceptual practice that sublimates, disguises, and extends its own power play through recourse to tropes of normative universality."[11] She asks, "to what extent is cultural conflict understandable as the clashing of a set of presumed and intransigent 'universalities,' a conflict which cannot be negotiated through recourse to a cultural imperialistic notion of the 'universal' or, rather, which will only be solved through such recourse at the cost of violence?"[12]

Since transforming the situation of women globally requires communication and cooperation across communal boundaries, implying the permeability and fluidity of identities, as well as shared goals, many feminist theorists have nuanced the postmodern idea that worldviews are incommensurable. For example, Uma Narayan thinks that some ability to generalize about human rights is necessary in order to have "effective political agendas."[13] However, generalizations about "salient similarities" must always be critically examined in terms of "empirical accuracy" and "political utility or risk."[14] Moreover, "universal visions of social justice (for example, that women's rights are human rights)" should be grounded in participatory local practices and implemented according to local priorities.[15]

A third philosophical theory that recognizes communication among stakeholders to be an essential component of justice is "discourse theory" or "communicative action" theory, deriving from Kantian "respect for persons," as interpreted by Jurgen Habermas and others. The basic insight represented by this approach is that all who are affected by a decision, practice, or policy have a right to participate in the discussion or discourse on the basis of which it is formulated or continued. Without submerging the cultural differences stressed by postmodernism, discourse theory strives to maintain "universality" in the form of respect and inclusion, so that cross-cultural critiques of injustice are still possible. Seyla Benhabib remarks, " 'universality' is a regulative ideal that does not deny our embodied and embedded identity, but aims at developing moral attitudes and encouraging political transformations that can yield a point of view acceptable to all." It is "a concrete process in politics and morals of concrete, embodied selves, striving for autonomy."[16] This third type of approach is procedural rather than substantive, and as such has a good deal in common with the liberal approach endorsing respect for equality and freedom. With the postmodern approach, it recognizes that the content of individual well-being or of "rights" is highly context-dependent, and opens a space for equal representation of feminist aims from a variety of contexts.

Though they affirm the basic value of autonomy, all three of the above approaches otherwise avoid construals of the concrete goods necessary to constitute justice or, specifically, the well-being of women. There is a good reason for this: such construals often or even usually represent particular historical and cultural constructions that are universalized at the cost of genuine sensitivity to the diverse experiences, needs, and standpoints of women around the globe. Nevertheless, activism for women's rights, perhaps most especially in the area of health, reveals that there are certain basic human needs and goods that are in fact universal, however different the ways in which they are culturally mediated and institutionalized may be.

At the very least the human body establishes parameters of goods and harms that can be commonly recognized. Recognition of common ground often begins with experiences of deprivation or suffering, such as rape, domestic abuse, HIV infection, or maternal and infant deaths. The flip side of these evils are the social goods of bodily integrity and freedom from violence, sexual self-determination, the need for essential medications to relieve life-threatening conditions, and competent care during pregnancy and childbirth, as well as adequate nutrition and clean water. These goods are not culturally relative.

A fourth type of philosophical theory moves beyond the shared view of liberal, postmodern, and discourse theory that justice is best understood in procedural terms, and attempts to offer substantive definitions of human goods and the good society. A prominent feminist version of this sort of approach is the "capabilities theory" of Martha Nussbaum.[17] Originally a "liberal," Nussbaum has incorporated elements of both postmodernism and discourse theory, and has a strong investment in advocating for specific essential goods, on the basis of her work in women's "human development,"[18] especially in India and Bangladesh. Unlike classic liberals, Nussbaum uses an explicitly inductive method, and places material goods as well as civil liberties on her list; but, like liberals and unlike postmodernists, she does not shy away from talking about "universal obligations."[19]

According to Nussbaum, the minimum conditions of a life with dignity are certain "human capabilities," on which societies ought to agree, no matter what their overarching conceptions of the good, or specific social institutions are.[20] These conditions include life; bodily health; bodily integrity; senses, imagination, thought; emotions; practical reason; affiliation (relationship to others); relationship to other species; play; and political and material control over one's environment.[21] One tension in Nussbaum's thought is that, while lifting up a social theory of human well-being that implies social interdependence and the importance of social institutions to the common good, she continually falls back on the key value of liberal autonomy and individual rights as her basic premise.[22] Yet the autonomy focus tends to neglect social and institutional responsibility to provide positive material conditions of social belonging, such as access to health care, which Nussbaum wants to secure for women.

In her analysis of Nussbaum's internationalist theory of human goods, Hilary Charlesworth notes that the capabilities approach transcends "the standard Western obsession with civil and political liberties at the expense of economic and social equity."[23] Still, Nussbaum's language "may indicate that greater weight is accorded to civil and political rights" than to the material necessities that are also necessary to women's ability to function. Moreover, the rights of groups are not considered at all in the capabilities approach. Rather than "universalism," Charlesworth proposes the term "transversalism" to indicate a method of inquiry that does not derive from preexisting premises, but is built up by empathetic and mutually critical dialogue.[24] Such dialogue would reveal and include other sociocultural perspectives in which communal belonging, social roles, and material rights have more import than in traditional liberal political theory. A "transversal" method also aims at moral agreement or consensus on basic aspects of women's value and rights, while hoping to overcome the disproportionate influence of one perspective in the formation of the consensus.

This review of four theories has certainly not been comprehensive in relation to philosophical positions, but it is adequate to show some shared concerns and contributions of feminist philosophy today. In sum, there has been a major trend since the middle of the twentieth century to recognize the diversity of cultures, and hence to advocate for women's well-being primarily by seeking greater guarantees of procedural justice. However, the increasing visibility and effectiveness of activism for women has been an important factor in driving renewed efforts to seek substantive consensus, through dialogue across cultural standpoints, about the goods essential to a secure and fulfilling human life.

An important final point is that feminist philosophy is almost by definition activist, politically engaged, and at least relatively confident that change in favor of women is not only possible but already occurring.[25] It may even be that the most dangerous adversary of activism for women's rights is not patriarchy, but "political realism," the stance that self-interest has always governed social relationships and always will.[26] Whether in the realm of foreign policy, military conflict, economic globalization, or gender hierarchy, a politically "realist" outlook contradicts the very possibility of social transformation toward greater justice for all, and discourages efforts in that direction as naive and bound to fail. Philosophically cogent defenses of justice and rights are an important tool in proving "realism" wrong.

Approaches to Religious or Theological Ethics

Philosophical and theological ethics can be allies in meeting the challenges of sexism and political realism; women's rights movements often include women with strong commitments to their religious traditions. In fact, in many cultures, purely "secular" political movements are in the minority or nonexistent. For that matter, even in North America and Europe, political action and social ethics are always indebted to communities and traditions of identity and meaning, even if they are identified pluralistically or without specific attribution to religious roots. Moreover, although religious institutions and authorities can be dogmatic, hidebound, reactionary, or fundamentalist—and so underwrite traditional norms oppressing women—religions can also be sources of countercultural and liberating analysis and action. Religions are, after all, as internally pluralistic as other types of community, and are constantly being renegotiated in contact with cultural developments and historical trends. For example, Christian feminists, inspired by changing cultural roles of women and modern commitments to equality, often go back to the Bible to rediscover and reappropriate models of women's behavior, or female leaders, such as Mary Magdalene, an important disciple in all four gospels.[27]

The special contribution of religious feminists to activism for women's health stems from the fact that religious narratives, symbols, and practices are profoundly formative for most of the world's peoples. Often such formation involves attitudes toward gender that need to be changed. However, religious traditions and formation also provide powerful sources of moral conversion and motivation. Religious traditions place human practices and projects against the horizon of transcendent meaning and value. At the heart of religious traditions, though expressed in a variety of forms and sometimes hidden, lies a prophetic call to repentance, compassion, and reform. For example, "Jesus' passion as an act of solidarity with his people is relived among the militant, protesting Filipino women who have taken up the struggle on behalf of their sisters and of the rest of the suffering poor."[28] The Abrahamic religions (Judaism, Christianity, and Islam) share the belief that all humans are made "in the image of God," and that all are called to love God and their fellow human beings. Such values can become the basis of social practices of solidarity and inclusion that empower women and allow entrenched assumptions about women's roles and rights to be questioned.

Though hardly complete as an overview of feminist theology, four types of feminist theological ethics can be identified as having special importance for activism on women's health issues. The first is a trajectory focused on women's autonomy and rights, deriving from liberal Protestant social ethics, and gathering energy from the pro-choice abortion rights movement of the 1970s. Genuine liberation for women entails respect for the "body-selves" through which we are connected to the world: "our bodies *are* ourselves, and they *should be* ours, unmediated by others' power to determine, control, manipulate, or seduce."[29] Linking women's welfare with religious ethics, Harrison claims that "we encounter God through relationship with all that nurtures and sustains life."[30]

For many of the same reasons that postmodernism appeared as a challenge to liberal philosophy, so postmodern feminist theologians have challenged their liberal sisters. Mary McClintock Fulkerson takes issue with any appeal to women's experience that assumes "there is a natural referent, 'women,' the 'we' who share oppression and common humanity."[31] Experience, reality, discourse, and power can never be separated, so "the standard for 'full humanity' is precisely what we do not have."

Feminists working out of the Catholic common good tradition and feminist liberation theologians provide two further streams of theological ethics that aim to bridge cultural divides and name specific conditions of women's well-being, while empowering women locally and respecting cultural differences. The Catholic common good tradition has been embodied in modern times in the line of papal social encyclicals beginning in 1891 with Leo XIII's *Rerum Novarum (On the Condition of Labor)*.[32] These encyclical letters define justice in terms of the participation of all members of society in the common good, and define participation in terms of mutual rights and duties, having to do with both material and social goods. The social nature of the person is essential to this tradition. Since the 1960s, the common good (and civil government) have been defined in more democratic and inclusive ways, and the assumption of stable social hierarchies has been reduced. Women's rights to equal pay for equal work, freedom from violence, and the right of all to a decent standard of living, including health care, have been affirmed. The common good has been understood increasingly as a "universal common good" that requires the reduction of disparities between rich and poor and stipulates the obligation of the privileged nations to aid international development and to take steps toward world peace. Anything but politically "realist," this tradition has often been criticized for being too naive and idealistic.

Feminist reinterpreters find this tradition helpful because of the ways in which it grounds obligations in shared aspects of human nature, employs the premise of the inherently social nature of the individual to advance the participation of all in social processes and benefits, and places advancement of the most marginal members of society at the forefront of its moral agenda. According to one recent work, the principle of the common good makes the situation of the most disenfranchised its standard.[33] Specifically identifying access to health care as an issue, Suzanne DeCrane calls for "fidelity to the task of laboring to bring into existence more just relationships," while appreciating that "no social system can or will reflect . . . the ideal of justice and equity that the transcendent horizon of God as the ultimate common good establishes."[34]

One shortcoming of Catholic social teaching, from a feminist perspective, is that, in its "official" expressions, it has always tended to assume that change will emanate from responsible authorities at the top of the social pyramid, and that the role of religious and moral voices is to call them to account and encourage a greater sense of fairness. Feminist theology, to the contrary, stresses the responsibility and empowerment of women, and it is exactly "empowerment from below" that is the rallying cry of liberation theology. Beginning in the 1960s in Latin America with Catholic (often Marxist-influenced) activists, liberation theology came into its own with Gustavo Gutierrez's groundbreaking *A Theology of Liberation*.[35]

Liberation theology shapes the work of feminist theologians and ethicists from Latin America, Asia, and Africa, as well as by Latina, Asian American, and African American women theological ethicists. In 1986, a Women's Commission was created within the Ecumenical Association of Third World Theologians (EATWOT), to combat the sexism present even within the liberation movement.[36] Third World women's theology expresses their distinctive struggles and seeks empowerment through faith for social action. "The context of poverty, multiple oppression, and tokenism shows up as a common experience" of Asian, African, and Latin American women. "The Third World is a cross-ridden universe of economic, political, and religio-cultural oppressions within which women are doubly or triply burdened."[37] Many feminist theologians in this world find in the spirituality and suffering of Christ a divine identification with women's suffering, and an inspiration to take an active role in changing human conditions so that they more accurately reflect the in-breaking "reign of God."[38]

An important current development, with clear implications for women's health equity, is the emergence of collaborative interreligious liberation movements, focused on practical problems, and deriving power from analogous prophetic elements that exist across traditions. Robert Schreiter writes of "global theological flows" that are uniting different traditions and worldviews around similar justice concerns.[39] He sees religion as a powerful source of the renewal of civil society in the face of globalization, and believes that theological discourse can help create communities of resistance against some of globalization's pernicious effects. Though distinct in their cultural settings and practices, religious critiques are intelligible to one another, and join together voices of protest against the "failure of global systems." This has already occurred in theologies of liberation, and in religious and other movements inspired by feminism, ecology, and human rights.[40]

Examples of Local, Interreligious, and Transnational Religious Advocacy for Women's Health

In *Gathering Power*, Paul Osterman writes of the role of the churches in the southwest United States in forming labor unions and demanding rights.[41] He offers a case study of two Mexican women—one with a college degree and one with little formal education—who started a health clinic in Texas. They came together with others through an interfaith organization that, in concert with the Industrial Areas Foundation, had resolved to address the lack of primary health care for the uninsured in their community. They met with county commissioners, won a renegotiation of the budget to accommodate more health care funds, and worked to diminish the opposition of the local health care establishment to the free clinics, which it feared would undermine plans for a research facility. After negotiating with local medical leaders, the business community, and city officials, the women obtained the donation of a facility by a city government, and identified a nonprofit corporation to manage the center. The Milagro ("miracle") Clinic opened in McAllen Texas on the feast of Our Lady of Guadalupe in 1996.[42]

Muslim women in Afghanistan have also organized to provide better care for women in their society. Afghanistan has among the world's highest rates of infant and maternal mortality.[43] Women and children suffer from a combination of poor nutrition, stunted growth, lack of skilled medical care, life in remote villages, lack of education, teenage marriages, pressure to have large families, and cultural traditions that prohibit examination of women by male doctors. Most women go through a constant cycle of pregnancy and birth with little or no medical care. With the help of Aide Medicale Internationale (A.M.I.), a French agency, some Muslim midwives are being trained to serve village women, and share knowledge in the local communities about how to assist at births, in some cases even thwarting taboos against male physicians.[44]

A transnational and interreligious instance of religious women's cooperation toward health care access for women was described by Marianne Farina, C.S.C.[45] Farina spent 12 years working in Bangladesh, and recounted a project sponsored with Muslim women in the 1970s and 1980s. The project cut across continents, religious traditions, and social classes, though it began with the very concrete experience of Catholic religious sisters working with Muslims who had been taught that women receive less food, clothing, health care, and education than men, without complaining. One of the Holy Cross women, Sister Bruno, received funds from Caritas International, a Catholic relief agency, to enable Muslim village women make macramé plant hangers and coasters in their homes. Because the women were not allowed to leave their households, Sister Bruno collected the products for sale and then returned to redistribute the money. This enabled the families to purchase new seed for the rice fields, giving the women's work prestige and economic power.

When the handicrafts became too numerous for Sr. Bruno to transport, she established a collection center in the mission, but husbands still objected to women's travel. In a creative reinterpretation of Catholic patriarchy, the mission was defined as "father's household" (referring to the mission priest), so that the Muslim women would be seen as remaining under male protection. At the mission, the sisters took the opportunity to instruct local Christian and Muslim women together in health care classes. They had a program in natural family planning, a "low-tech" and culturally acceptable method that elicited cooperation from the men, and began to change the nature of their marriage relationships. In the process, Muslim women saw the daughters of the Christians being educated, and succeeded in gaining the same benefit for their own, under the rationale that educated girls would be easier to marry off. Eventually, the Muslim women were allowed to travel to Dhaka to participate in a nationwide women's macramé export business, which, of course, greatly enhanced their status and access to other resources. Sister Marianne concluded her paper by saying, "The women pursued not only their own political, social, and religious rights and freedoms, but are willing unselfishly to become dynamic agents for the justice of others. They dare to ask the question, 'Who are the poor, oppressed, and marginalized in our society now?'"

In sum, feminist religion and theology (and feminist currents within the historic faith traditions) are prophetic, activist, and hopeful of significant social changes. They increasingly build interreligious and hence intercultural alliances, and take advantage of transnational networks and institutions (including religious institutions) to seek change. These networks are important for feminist work toward health care justice because they maximize the potential of religious identity, a defining reality for most women in the world, to underwrite "the preferential option for the poor" (a phrase of liberation theology and Catholic social teaching). They are also important because they connect "grassroots" women to other local communities and broader social movements that incorporate religious identity and motivation, empowering social transformation.

This suggests that it is important for theorists and policy makers to take into account the positive roles of religious communities and feminist theologians in addressing women's health needs. At a basic level, the infrastructure of virtually every culture worldwide includes religious institutions and practices, and these are an indispensable means of influencing identities, beliefs, and behaviors as they affect women. Religion is frequently oppressive of women, but it can also serve as a locus of empowerment and conversion. Health care policy should engage religious institutions and representatives both in order to formulate programs of action that are responsive to and coherent with local values and needs, and to take advantage of a potentially powerful agent of implementation. Working as much as possible through women's religious participation, advocates for women's health can challenge and begin to change aspects of religious traditions that discriminate against women.

Theoretical or conceptual research on the meanings of respect and justice as they bear on women's access to health resources will also find a valuable resource in religion. Theology engages in theoretical, systematic, and critical reflection on religious traditions and practices. Feminist theology undertakes a critical examination of religion in light of the situation and needs of women. Theology also examines the relation of faith traditions to society and politics. Feminist theology evaluates present injustices in the light of a higher realm of value and a spiritual reality that calls human beings to compassion and accountability; invoking the divine claim and command provides a vital source of judgment and commitment. Feminist philosophy and theology can complement and reinforce the practical aims of activists and policy makers committed to health equity for women. Therefore future research on global health equity for women should take these theoretical disciplines and their practical counterparts into account as serious conversation partners in the project to analyze and to realize women's greater access to health and well-being.

Notes

1. P. Ostlin, A. George, and G. Sen (2000), Gender, health, and equity: The intersections, in T. Evans, M. Whitehead, F. Diderichsen, A. Bhiuya, and M. Wirth, eds., *Challenging Inequities in Health: From Ethics to Action* (p. 182), Oxford: Oxford University Press.
2. Ibid., p. 175.
3. Ibid., p. 183.
4. Ibid., p. 186.
5. S. Hasina (2000), Foreword, in T. Evans, M. Whitehead, F. Diderichsen, A. Bhiuya, and M. Wirth, eds., *Challenging Inequities in Health: From Ethics to Action* (p. vii).
6. M. Whitehead, G. Dahlgren, and L. Gilson (2000), Developing the Policy Response to Inequities in Health: A Global Perspective, in T. Evans, M. Whitehead, F. Diderichsen, A. Bhiuya, and M. Wirth, eds., *Challenging Inequities in Health: From Ethics to Action* (pp. 309–323).

7. Ibid., p. 321.
8. Ibid., p. 322.
9. J. Gray (1986), *Liberalism* (p. 8), Minneapolis: University of Minnesota Press.
10. John Gray, the author of the above definition, was an economic advisor to Margaret Thatcher.
11. J. Butler (1995), Contingent foundations: Feminism and the question of "postmodernism," in S. Behabib, J. Butler, D. Cornell, and N. Fraser, eds., *Feminist Contentions: A Philosophical Exchange* (p. 39), New York and London: Routledge.
12. Ibid., p. 40.
13. U. Narayan (2000), Essence of culture and a sense of history: A feminist critique of cultural essentialism, in U. Narayan and S. Harding, eds., *Decentering the Center: Philosophy for a Multicultural, Postcolonial, and Feminist World* (p. 89), Bloomington and Indianapolis: Indiana University Press.
14. Ibid., p. 97.
15. A. Ferguson (2000), Resisting the veil of privilege: Building bridge identities as an ethico-politics of global feminisms, in *Decentering the Center* (pp. 189–207, 197).
16. S. Benhabib (1992), *Situating the Self: Gender, Community and Postmodernism in Contemporary Ethics*, New York: Routledge, p. 153.
17. M. Nussbaum (1999), *Women and Human Development: The Capabilities Approach*, New York and Cambridge: Cambridge University Press.
18. M. Nussbaum (2000), *Sex and Social Justice*, New York and Oxford: Oxford University Press.
19. Ibid., p. 30.
20. M. Nussbaum, *Women and Human Development*, p. 5.
21. Ibid., pp. 78–80.
22. M. Nussbaum, *Sex and Social Justice*, p. 102.
23. H. Charlesworth (2000), Martha Nussbaum's feminist internationalism, *Ethics*: 111 (accessed at www.jstor.org).
24. Ibid., pp. 76–77.
25. M. E. Keck and K. Sikkink (1998), *Activists Beyond Borders: Advocacy Networks in International Politics*, Ithaca and London: Cornell University Press.
26. J. J. Mearsheimer (2001), *The Tragedy of Great Power Politics*, New York and London: W.W. Norton & Company.
27. E. Schussler Fiorenza (1983), *In Memory of Her: A Feminist Reconstruction of Christian Origins*, New York: Crossroad.
28. V. Fabella (1989), A Common Methodology for Diverse Christologies? in V. Fabella and M. A. Oduyoye, eds., *With Passion and Compassion: Third World Women Doing Theology* (pp. 108–117, 110), Maryknoll, NY: Orbis Books.
29. B. Harrison (1983), *Our Right to Choose: Toward a New Ethic of Abortion* (p. 106), Boston: Beacon Press.
30. Ibid., p. 108.
31. M. M. Fulkerson (1994), *Changing the Subject: Women' Discourses and Feminist Theology* (p. 107), Minneapolis: Fortress Press.

32. The social encyclical are available in David J. O'Brien and Thomas A. Shannon, eds. (1992), *Catholic Social Thought: The Documentary Heritage*, Maryknoll, NY: Orbis.

33. Suzanne Decrane (2004), *Aquinas, Feminism, and the Common Good*, Washington, DC: Georgetown University Press.

34. Ibid., p. 150.

35. G. Gutierrez (1973), *A Theology of Liberation: History, Politics and Salvation*, Maryknoll, NY: Orbis Books.

36. V. Fabella and M. A. Oduyoye, *With Passion and Compassion*.

37. V. Fabella (1989), Introduction, in V. Fabella and M. A. Oduyoye, eds., *With Passion and Compassion: Third World Women Doing Theology* (pp. i-xv).

38. Ibid., p. xiv.

39. Robert J. Schreiter (1998), *The New Catholicity: Theology between the Global and the Local*, Maryknoll, NY: Orbis Books.

40. Ibid., p. 16.

41. P. Osterman (2002), *Gathering Power: The Future of Progressive Politics in America*, Boston: Beacon Press.

42. Ibid., pp. 84–87.

43. C. Gall (2003), Afghan motherhood in a fight for survival: Women struggle against staggering infant and maternal mortality rates, *New York Times International*, May 25: 3.

44. Ibid.

45. M. Farina (1997), *Ethics of Sex and Gender*, final paper, unpublished: Boston College.

3

The Pathways between Trade Liberalization and Reproductive Health: A Review of the Literature and Some Propositions for Research and Action*

Caren Grown

Introduction

There is, by now, a fairly large literature on the relationship between globalization and health.[1] Within this literature, however, there is relatively little attention given to the implications of the liberalization of international trade, one aspect of globalization, for reproductive health, which is a subset of overall health.[2] This chapter considers the linkages between trade liberalization and provision of and access to sexual and reproductive health services.

This linkage is important for several reasons. First, as many have argued, international and macroeconomic policies create an "indispensable enabling environment for reproductive and sexual rights to become practical realities."[3] Second, many countries are progressively liberalizing their economies, including the health sector, unilaterally or by entering into multilateral, regional, or bilateral trade agreements, which require them to reduce barriers to imports and exports. Such liberalization is likely to affect provision of and access to quality reproductive health services and commodities. At a theoretical level, trade liberalization can create new opportunities for improving reproductive health, but it can also make it more difficult to advance reproductive/sexual health and rights objectives in policies, programs, and services. For instance, a more liberalized health trading system can improve a country's competitive capacity, attract foreign investment, allow for a greater mobility of personnel, which enables knowledge exchange between medical personnel coming from diverse backgrounds and from different levels of expertise, create employment for women, increase income levels, improve access to reproductive health technologies, and ultimately raise the quality of health care delivery.[4] On the other hand, there is concern about higher costs of services and supplies, concentration of services that may restrict access of lower-income or remote populations, lower quality of services, and shortages of critical medical personnel (e.g., doctors, nurses, and midwives) that result from migration both from the public to the private sector and from developing to developed countries as health professionals opt for higher salaries and better opportunities for professional development. Ample skepticism also exists about governments' willingness to institute public policies that redistribute gains from export revenue to improve the public health care system and mitigate the effects of rising health care costs for the poor due to privatization of health services and the emergence of joint ventures between public and foreign health providers.

Unfortunately, there is more heat than light about each of these effects, and the net impacts are not yet well documented. What is needed are clearer analytical frameworks and reliable empirical evidence. This is a long-term task, but a first step is to identify the relevant variables and suggest some pathways by which trade liberalization affects reproductive health problems and services. Ultimately, it is important for those interested in the guarantee of economic justice and women's rights to understand exactly how these pathways and linkages work in order to find effective entry points for advocacy and action.

The outline of this chapter is as follows. The first section defines the concepts of trade liberalization and reproductive health and reviews trends in each area. The second section presents a conceptual framework for understanding the linkages between trade liberalization and reproductive health, and discusses the challenges in tracing the linkages at the national or subnational level. Given that the linkages between health and trade are both direct and indirect and operate at multiple levels (household, country, international), distinguishing empirically the effects of trade policies and changes in reproductive outcomes from other policies and forces (e.g., health sector reform) may be difficult. This section discusses possible approaches to address this challenge. The final section concludes with recommendations for future research and policy to advance women's reproductive health and rights in a more globalized world.

The analysis in this chapter focuses largely on developing countries, although occasional reference is made to industrialized countries. It is based largely on a review of literature from economics, sociology, and anthropology as well as literature published by activist organizations in industrialized and developing countries.

Trends and Definitions

Trade Liberalization

The flows of goods and services that are exported across national borders increased substantially following World War II. Since 1948, the volume of global trade grew by an average of 6 percent every year.[5] From the early 1980s, exports of developing countries grew faster than the world average, and now account for about one-third of world trade.[6] Moreover, between 1990 and 2000, the share of imports and exports in Gross Domestic Product (GDP) of developing countries increased by 30 percent. The increase was most significant in Europe and Central Asia and in East Asia and the Pacific where the increase was by more than 50 percent (see table 3.1).[7]

Much of that growth has been in manufactures, which today account for 70 percent of developing country exports. East Asia and Latin America have experienced the most rapid growth in manufacturing exports.[8] At the same time, trade in services, including health services, has also increased rapidly (estimated as 20 percent of all exports in 2003).[9] Although comprehensive

Table 3.1   Ratio of exports and imports to Gross Domestic Product (GDP)

Ratio of Exports and Imports to GDP; 1980, 1990, and 2000
(In 1995 constant US$)

	1980	1990	2000	% change 1980–1990	% change 1990–2000
Developed Countries	0.52	0.62	0.89	23.43	46.21
East Asia and the Pacific	0.74	0.92	1.29	19.56	52.34
Europe and Central Asia	2.87	0.96	1.11	−31.46	53.37
Latin America and the Caribbean	0.76	0.76	0.84	7.10	25.95
Middle East and North Africa (MENA)	0.88	0.76	0.76	−5.47	13.13
South and West Asia	0.42	0.40	0.65	−3.54	25.07
Sub-Saharan Africa	0.92	0.74	0.80	−11.46	11.82

Notes: N = 106 for 1980, N = 128 for 1990, N = 144 for 2000;
    N = 105 for % change 1980–1990—105 countries have data for both 1980 and 1990;
    N = 124 for % change 1990–2000—124 countries have data for both 1990 and 2000;
    MENA does not include data on major oil exporting countries in the region.

Source: World Development Indicators, World Bank 2004.

and internationally comparable data are not available, it appears that cross-border delivery of health services has increased through movement of personnel and consumers and through cross-border trade in data process-ing and other activities.[10] There has also been significant growth in foreign direct investment in the health sector. While trade in health services is modest at present, the continuing removal of some of the regulatory barriers to trade at the regional, multilateral, and national levels means that trade in health services is likely to take on greater importance in the future.[11]

Reproductive Health and Rights

Over the past decade, the concept of reproductive health and rights has broadened considerably, from a narrow focus on the control of fertility to a multidimensional framework encompassing demographic, medical, and sociopolitical components.[12] In its demographic aspects, reproductive health covers control over fertility, access to contraception, and safe abor-tion. In its medical aspects, reproductive health comprises safe pregnan-cies, lactation, better nutrition and child survival, and freedom from diseases of the reproductive tract and HIV/AIDS. Finally, reproductive health in its sociopolitical manifestation encompasses access to informa-tion and freedom to exercise reproductive choice, freedom from violence and threat, and the right to enjoy a healthy sexual life. Thus, reproductive health is a broad framework to analyze the needs of women and men in their sexual relationships and reproductive behavior.[13]

Reproductive and sexual health cannot be accessed by women without the guarantee of a concomitant body of rights.[14] Reproductive rights include: the right of all couples and individuals to decide freely and responsibly the number, spacing, and timing of their children and to have the information and means to do so; the right to attain the highest standard of sexual and reproductive health and the right to services and information that make this possible; and the right to make decisions con-cerning reproduction free of discrimination, coercion, and violence.[15] Sexual rights include freedom from violence, mutilation, and sexual assault, the right to the highest standard of sexual well-being, the right to the necessary information and services to attain sexual well-being without discrimination on the basis of age, gender, sexual orientation, marital status, race, class, caste, and soon. The rights agenda moves from a negative preven-tive stance focused on reproductive health problems to an affirmative one emphasizing overall well-being.

Table 3.2 summarizes recent trends in some of the salient components of women's reproductive heath status.[16] As shown in the first three columns in the table, fertility decline has already occurred in most parts of

Table 3.2 Key reproductive health indicators for selected countries: 1990–2003

	Total fertility rate			Maternal deaths per 100,000 live births			Percent of women among pop.15–49 living with HIV/AIDS	
	1990	1995	2002	1990	1995	2000	1997	2003
Afghanistan	6.90	6.90	6.80	1700	820	1900		
Albania	3.03	2.64	2.23	65	31	55		
Algeria	4.49	3.68	2.75	160	150	140		15.56
Angola	7.20	7.08	7.00	1500	1300	1700	52.00	59.09
Antigua and Barbuda	1.78	1.70	1.70					
Argentina	2.90	2.70	2.44	100	85	82	18.33	20.00
Armenia	2.62	1.63	1.15	50	29	55		36.00
Australia	1.91	1.82	1.75	9	6	8	5.00	7.14
Austria	1.45	1.40	1.31	10	11	4	18.67	22.00
Azerbaijan	2.74	2.29	2.07	22	37	94		
Bahamas	2.12	2.18	2.12	100	10	60	33.87	48.08
Bahrain	3.76	3.46	2.30	60	38	28		<83.33
Bangladesh	4.12	3.35	2.95	850	600	380	14.76	
Barbados	1.74	1.74	1.75	43	33	95	33.33	32.00
Belarus	1.91	1.39	1.25	37	33	35		
Belgium	1.62	1.57	1.62	·10	8	10	36.11	35.00
Belize	4.39	3.72	2.95		140	140	24.76	37.14
Benin	6.62	6.15	5.30	990	880	850	50.00	56.45
Bhutan		5.79	5.10	1600	500	420		
Bolivia	4.85	4.36	3.75	650	550	420	14.23	27.08

Continued

52

Table 3.2 Continued

	Total fertility rate			Maternal deaths per 100,000 live births			Percent of women among pop.15–49 living with HIV/AIDS	
	1990	1995	2002	1990	1995	2000	1997	2003
Bosnia and Herzegovina	1.70	1.60	1.30		15	31		
Botswana	5.07	4.55	3.82	250	480	100	48.95	57.58
Brazil	2.74	2.45	2.14	220	260	260	22.81	36.92
Brunei Darussalam	3.20	2.92	2.47	60	22	37		<100
Bulgaria	1.81	1.23	1.25	27	23	32		
Burkina Faso	7.02	6.84	6.30	930	1400	1000	48.57	55.56
Burundi	6.80	6.49	5.77	1300	1900	1000	50.00	59.09
Cambodia	5.56	4.74	3.80	900	590	450	50.00	30.00
Cameroon	6.00	5.20	4.60	550	720	730	48.39	55.77
Canada	1.83	1.64	1.52	6	6	6	13.02	23.64
Cape Verde	5.50	4.12	3.46		190	150		
Central African Republic	5.46	5.06	4.60	700	1200	1100	50.00	54.17
Chad	7.06	6.75	6.20	1500	1500	1100	50.60	55.56
Channel Islands	1.71	1.75	1.75					
Chile	2.58	2.37	2.15	65	33	31	18.00	33.46
China	2.10	1.92	1.88	95	60	56	12.00	22.89
Colombia	3.07	2.82	2.48	100	120	130	15.28	34.44
Comoros	5.80	4.85	4.05	950	570	480		
Congo, Dem. Rep.	6.70	6.70	6.70	870	940	990	50.00	57.00
Congo, Rep.	6.29	6.29	6.29	890	1100	510	49.47	56.25
Costa Rica	3.20	2.78	2.30	55	35	43	26.00	33.33
Cote d'Ivoire	6.18	5.40	4.55	810	1200	690	49.25	56.60

Croatia	1.63	1.58	1.45	95	18	8	32.14	33.33
Cuba	1.69	1.48	1.58	5	24	33		
Cyprus	2.42	2.13	1.90	15	0	47		32.00
Czech Republic	1.89	1.28	1.20		14	9		18.00
Denmark	1.67	1.81	1.73	9	15	5	24.84	55.95
Djibouti	5.98	5.62	5.20	570	520	730	50.00	
Dominica	2.70	2.14	1.90					
Dominican Republic	3.38	3.24	2.60	110	110	150	33.33	27.06
Ecuador	3.71	3.27	2.76	150	210	130	13.89	34.00
Egypt, Arab Rep.	3.97	3.63	3.05	170	170	84	10.49	13.33
El Salvador	3.85	3.58	2.90	300	180	150	24.44	34.29
Equatorial Guinea	5.89	5.89	5.51	820	1400	880	47.83	
Eritrea	6.50	5.97	4.80	1400	1100	630		56.36
Estonia	2.04	1.32	1.25	41	80	63		33.77
Ethiopia	6.91	6.23	5.60	1400	1800	850	48.00	55.00
Fiji	3.09	3.30	2.60	90	20	75	<38.46	33.33
Finland	1.78	1.81	1.73	11	6	6	20.00	<33.33
France	1.78	1.71	1.88	15	20	17		26.67
French Polynesia	3.25	2.93	2.50		20	20		
Gabon	5.09	4.64	4.05	500	620	420	50.00	57.78
Gambia, The	5.90	5.52	4.80	1100	1100	540	48.46	57.14
Georgia	2.21	1.41	1.10	33	22	32		33.33
Germany	1.45	1.25	1.35	22	12	8	19.43	22.09
Ghana	5.50	4.55	4.11	740	590	540	50.00	56.25
Greece	1.40	1.32	1.32	10	2	9		20.00
Guam	3.34	3.81	3.75		12	12		
Guatemala	5.33	5.10	4.30	200	270	240	24.81	41.89
Guinea	5.90	5.60	5.02	1600	1200	740	50.00	55.38
Guinea-Bissau	7.10	7.10	6.60	910	910	1100	51.82	

Continued

Table 3.2 Continued

	Total fertility rate			Maternal deaths per 100,000 live births			Percent of women among pop.15–49 living with HIV/AIDS	
	1990	1995	2002	1990	1995	2000	1997	2003
Guyana	2.61	2.49	2.31		150	170	33.00	55.45
Haiti	5.42	4.93	4.20	1000	1100	680	33.89	57.69
Honduras	5.16	4.79	4.00	220	220	110	24.39	55.93
Hong Kong, China	1.27	1.30	0.96	7			38.71	34.62
Hungary	1.84	1.57	1.30	30	23	16		
Iceland	2.31	2.08	1.95	0	16	0		<100
India	3.80	3.40	2.92	570	440	540	24.39	38.00
Indonesia	3.04	2.80	2.32	650	470	230	25.49	13.64
Iran, Islamic Rep.	4.68	3.28	2.00	120	130	76		12.26
Iraq	5.88	5.10	4.05	310	370	250		
Ireland	2.12	1.87	1.90	10	9	5		30.77
Israel	2.82	2.90	2.70	7	8	17		
Italy	1.26	1.18	1.25	12	11	5	30.00	32.14
Jamaica	2.94	2.78	2.30	120	120	87	31.43	47.62
Japan	1.54	1.42	1.33	18	12	10	5.59	24.17
Jordan	5.40	4.35	3.50	150	41	41		
Kazakhstan	2.72	2.26	1.80	80	80	210		33.54
Kenya	5.64	4.90	4.23	650	1300	1000	48.75	65.45
Korea, Dem. Rep.	2.39	2.15	2.07	70	35	67		
Korea, Rep.	1.77	1.75	1.45	130	20	20	12.90	10.84
Kuwait	3.44	2.97	2.52	29	25	5.		
Kyrgyz Republic	3.69	3.31	2.40	110	80	110		<20.51

Lao PDR	6.00	5.50	4.80	650	650	650	52.00	<29.41
Latvia	2.02	1.25	1.16	40	70	42		33.33
Lebanon	3.22	2.74	2.22	300	130	150		<17.85
Lesotho	5.08	4.85	4.30	610	530	550	50.00	56.67
Liberia	6.80	6.50	5.80	560	1000	760	50.00	56.25
Libya	4.72	3.92	3.32	220	120	97		
Lithuania	2.03	1.49	1.27	36	27	13		<38.46
Luxembourg	1.62	1.68	1.78	0	0	28	<33.33	
Macedonia, FYR	2.06	1.97	1.75		17	23		
Madagascar	6.22	5.88	5.20	490	580	550	50.00	58.46
Malawi	7.00	6.55	6.05	560	580	1800	49.25	56.79
Malaysia	3.77	3.40	2.85	80	39	41	19.70	16.67
Maldives	5.70	4.82	4.00		390	110		
Mali	6.86	6.68	6.40	1200	630	1200	50.00	59.17
Malta	2.05	1.83	1.81	0	0	21		
Mauritania	6.02	5.30	4.60	930	870	1000	49.15	57.30
Mauritius	2.25	2.14	2.00	120	45	24		
Mexico	3.31	2.90	2.40	110	65	83	11.67	33.13
Mongolia	4.03	3.13	2.43	65	65	110		<40
Morocco	4.01	3.42	2.75	610	390	220		
Mozambique	6.34	5.61	5.00	1500	980	1000	48.33	55.83
Myanmar	3.76	3.42	2.80	580	170	360	20.91	30.31
Namibia	5.39	5.28	4.80	370	370	300	50.00	55.00
Nepal	5.26	4.55	4.15	1500	830	740	40.00	26.67
Netherlands	1.62	1.53	1.70	12	10	16		20.00
New Zealand	2.18	2.01	1.90	25	15	7	14.62	<14.28
Nicaragua	4.80	3.87	3.44	160	250	230	24.39	33.87
Niger	7.64	7.47	7.10	1200	920	1600	50.82	56.25
Nigeria	6.04	5.72	5.07	1000	1100	800	50.00	57.58

Continued

Table 3.2 Continued

	Total fertility rate			Maternal deaths per 100,000 live births			Percent of women among pop.15–49 living with HIV/AIDS	
	1990	1995	2002	1990	1995	2000	1997	2003
Norway	1.93	1.87	1.75	6	9	16		<25
Occupied Palestinian Territory		58.2			120	100		
Oman	7.38	5.56	3.97	190	120	87		<38.46
Pakistan	5.84	5.20	4.50	340	200	500	19.35	12.19
Panama	3.01	2.73	2.42	55	100	160	25.00	41.33
Papua New Guinea	5.55	4.76	4.30	930	390	300	50.00	30.00
Paraguay	4.60	4.33	3.84	160	170	170	17.74	26.00
Peru	3.68	3.39	2.64	280	240	410	15.49	33.75
Philippines	4.12	3.78	3.24	280	240	200	30.43	22.47
Poland	2.04	1.61	1.30	19	12	13		
Portugal	1.43	1.38	1.54	15	12	5		
Puerto Rico	2.20	2.00	1.90		30	25	19.43	19.55
Qatar	4.34	3.32	2.48		41	7		
Republic of Moldova	1.84	1.34	1.32	60	65	36		
Romania	1.89	1.34	1.28	130	60	49		
Russian Federation				75	75	67		33.72
Rwanda	7.15	6.51	5.70	1300	2300	1400	48.57	56.52
Samoa	4.76	4.54	4.00	35	15	130		
Saudi Arabia	6.56	5.98	5.30	130	23	23		
Senegal	6.20	5.67	4.90	1200	1200	690	50.00	56.10
Serbia and Montenegro	2.08	1.88	1.74		15	11		20.00

Seychelles	2.82	2.34	2.09	1800	2100	2000	50.00	
Sierra Leone	6.50	6.24	5.59	10	9	30	19.68	24.39
Singapore	1.87	1.71	1.37		14	3		
Slovak Republic	2.09	1.52	1.30	13	17	17		
Slovenia	1.46	1.29	1.15		60	130		
Solomon Islands	5.87	5.68	5.26		1600	1100		
Somalia	7.25	7.25	6.95	1600	340	230		
South Africa	3.32	3.08	2.80	230	8	4	50.00	56.86
Spain	1.33	1.18	1.28	7	60	92	20.83	20.77
Sri Lanka	2.53	2.28	2.10	140	1500	590	29.85	17.14
Sudan	5.42	5.06	4.40	660	230	110		57.89
Suriname	2.64	2.54	2.40		370	370	32.96	34.00
Swaziland	5.30	4.86	4.20	560	8	2	50.62	55.00
Sweden	2.13	1.73	1.64	7	8	7	24.33	25.71
Switzerland	1.59	1.47	1.50	6	200	160	34.17	30.00
Syrian Arab Republic	5.34	4.20	3.40	180	120	100		<40
Tajikistan	5.05	3.70	2.87	130	1100	1500		
Tanzania	6.25	5.75	5.03	770	44	44	48.57	56.00
Thailand	2.27	2.02	1.80	200	850	660	37.66	35.71
Timor-Leste			6.50		980	570		
Togo	6.60	5.40	4.90	640			51.25	56.25
Tonga	4.16	4.18	3.40					
Trinidad and Tobago	2.36	1.89	1.75	90	65	160	32.84	50.00
Tunisia	3.50	2.67	2.08	170	70	120		<50
Turkey	3.00	2.65	2.23	180	55	70		
Turkmenistan	4.17	3.75	2.70	55	65	31		
Uganda	6.98	6.72	6.00	1200	1100	880	49.43	60.00
Ukraine	1.85	1.40	1.20	50	45	35		33.33
United Arab Emirates	4.12	3.62	3.00	26	30	54		

Continued

Table 3.2 Continued

	Total fertility rate			Maternal deaths per 100,000 live births			Percent of women among pop.15–49 living with HIV/AIDS	
	1990	1995	2002	1990	1995	2000	1997	2003
United Kingdom	1.83	1.71	1.66	9	10	13		29.79
United States	2.08	2.02	2.10	12	12	17	19.75	25.53
Uruguay	2.51	2.60	2.19	85	50	27	17.31	32.76
Uzbekistan	4.07	3.60	2.35	55	60	24		33.64
Vanuatu	5.54	4.94	4.26280	32	130			
Venezuela, RB	3.43	3.10	2.72	120	43	96	14.81	32.00
Vietnam	3.62	2.67	1.87	160	95	130	19.77	32.50
Yemen, Rep.	7.53	6.48	6.00	1400	850	570		
Zambia	6.32	5.92	5.05	940	870	750	50.68	56.63
Zimbabwe	4.78	4.10	3.65	570	610	1100	51.43	58.13

Source: UN Statistical Database, World Development Indicators 2004, and UNAIDS Report on the Global Epidemic 1998, 2004.

the world, except for very slight increases in a handful of countries in Western Europe and North America. Maternal mortality rates remain a cause of concern in many developing countries: maternal deaths per 100,000 live births are well over 1,000 in almost all sub-Saharan African countries.[17]

Globally, in 2003, about half of the 37.8 million adults ages 15–49 with HIV/AIDS were women. According to UNAIDS,[18] the overall proportion of HIV-positive women has increased steadily since 1997, with heterosexual sex being the dominant mode of transmission. The epidemic is most "feminized" in sub-Saharan Africa, where 57 percent of infected adults are women and 75 percent of infected 15–24 year olds are women and girls.[19] The prevalence of HIV-infected women also increased slightly in South and Southeast Asia, and somewhat more so in North America, Latin America and the Caribbean, Eastern Europe, and Central Asia. Although there are distinct country trends and modes of transmission, many analysts attribute gender inequality—especially the rules governing sexual relationships and sexual violence—as a major factor driving the increase of the epidemic.[20]

Direct and Indirect Pathways between Trade Liberalization and Reproductive Health

Trade liberalization is multidimensional. Trade liberalization can occur through an autonomous decision of a government to remove or reduce barriers to exports, eliminate subsidies to domestic industries and firms, and privatize goods and services, all of which are intended to result in the freer movement of capital, goods, and labor across borders. But, trade liberalization more commonly occurs as a result of multilateral trade negotiations of the World Trade Organization (WTO), through regional or bilateral trade agreements, or via conditions attached to IMF or World Bank loans.[21]

Sexual and reproductive health is also multidimensional, involving the prevalence, nature, and distribution of both reproductive health problems and needs within a given population, the quantity, quality, type, cost, and distribution of reproductive health services, and finally, the "fit" between problems and services, for example, the extent to which women and men can access the services they need.[22] In both theoretical and empirical work, it is important to distinguish these different aspects of both trade liberalization and reproductive health.

Figure 3.1 summarizes some of the salient dimensions to be included in considering the impacts of trade liberalization on reproductive health. It distinguishes between trade agreements, trade policies, and trade flows on

Trade agreements relevant for reproductive health	**Reproductive health services likely to be affected**

• World Trade Organization
  GATS
  TRIPS
• Regional (e.g., NAFTA)
• Bilateral (e.g., U.S.-Thailand)
	• Changes in quantity and geographic distribution of reproductive health services (e.g., family planning, STD diagnosis/ treatment, prenatal care, and assisted delivery).
	
	• Changes in availability and cost of drugs such as antibiotics, diagnostic kits, contraceptive supplies, HIV vaccines, vacuum aspiration kits, etc.
	
	• Changes in availability and cost of services by trained health professions at different levels (midwives, nurses, doctors) in different regions (rural, urban, etc).
	
	• Distribution of health services between public and private sectors.
	
	• Changes in quality of services across different sectors and regions.

Domestic trade policies relevant for reproductive health	
• Reduction of tariff and non-tariff barriers to imports of medicines and equipment • Removal of domestic subsidies in the health sector (e.g. for local pharmaceutical firms and health insurance companies). • Elimination of restrictions on entry and terms of practice by foreign health service providers • Changing of enterprise ownership through privatization • Regulatory changes in areas such as accreditation and licensing requirements.	**Reproductive health problems/needs** • Nature • Prevalence • Distribution
Trade flows	
Volume and monetary value of trade in • Goods • Services	

Figure 3.1   Dimensions of trade and reproductive health.

the right side, and reproductive health supplies and services, and reproductive health needs and problems on the left side. Figure 3.2 illustrates
two different pathways through which these different dimensions of trade
liberalization affect different aspects of reproductive health problems and
services: the *direct pathway* through which trade policies affect the supply
of reproductive health services, and the *indirect pathway* through which
trade policies and movements in goods and services affect women's
demand for services indirectly through changes in their labor force
participation.

These figures are very simplified illustrations of complex forces. The
effects of trade flows and trade rules on reproductive health services and
needs are likely to be multiple, separated in time, and country-specific
depending on the policies, market conditions, and other factors that
prevail at any given time in a country. Furthermore, the framework in
figure 3.2 indicates that assigning causality may be complicated as the arrows
go in multiple directions, for example, from trade policies to reproductive

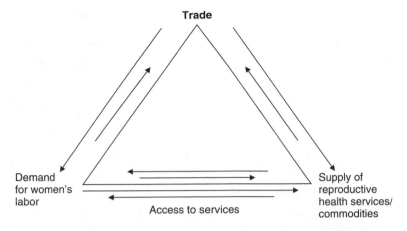

Figure 3.2   Direct and indirect pathways of trade liberalization on health.

health, but also from health outcomes and health services to trade flows. For example, improved access to prenatal and delivery services can help to lower infant mortality rates and contribute to a subsequent reduction in the birthrate as families choose to have fewer children. Parents can then invest more per child, raising children's education and health levels and their subsequent labor productivity in a trade-oriented economy.[23] Well-designed prospective longitudinal research that tracks the direction and order of magnitude of effects within countries and over time is therefore an important future task for understanding the causal linkages.

Direct Pathways

The most salient WTO agreements for reproductive health are the General Agreement on Trade in Services (GATS) and the Agreement on Trade-Related Aspects of Intellectual Property (TRIPS). The GATS, established in 1994, is the first multilateral agreement to provide a framework for countries to determine which service sectors of the economy they wish to open up to foreign suppliers and to competition, and what restrictions countries wish to implement to limit trade.[24] Under the GATS services can be traded through four modes: (1) *cross-border supply*, the provision of services from a practitioner in one country to a patient or practitioner in another predominantly through the Internet, satellite transmission of medical images, teleconference, and international telephone calls; (2) *consumption abroad*, which occurs when consumers travel across borders to obtain health services in another country; (3) *commercial presence*, which is when a foreign company invests in or opens up a subsidiary office in another country to provide health services; and (4) *the presence of natural persons*, which refers to health professionals (doctors, nurses, specialists, paramedics, midwives, etc.) travelling across borders to deliver services on a temporary basis.[25]

Lipson[26] argues that Mode 2 (consumption abroad) and Mode 3 (commercial presence) appear to have the greatest relevance to the cross-border delivery of reproductive health services, while Grown and Duron[27] posit that, in spite of limited commitments to date, Mode 4 (presence of natural persons) will also impact reproductive health infrastructure and delivery systems, with implications for the quality of care, access, and informed choice. As of 2005, however, the impacts of this agreement are seen to be relatively modest:

> There is scant evidence showing that GATS rules and individual country commitments have had a direct or significant impact on national policies concerning reproductive health, at least so far because such services are delivered largely by the public sector, or by non-profit organizations, and because government options under GATS, both with respect to liberalizing flexibility in specific sectors and the ability to make exceptions for public morals or health reasons, have to date allowed governments to implement reproductive health policies of their choosing. However, as for-profit actors gain ground in the delivery and financing of reproductive health services, GATS and public regulation of providers could have greater impact. Private, commercial activity in a service sector brings into play some basic GATS rules concerning foreign supplier participation. In those situations where reproductive health services are profitable, such as infertility services for the elite, abortion and other surgical procedures, or sales of certain contraceptive supplies, foreign providers may well show greater interest in the rules governing their entry and operations in other countries' markets.[28]

The TRIPS agreement, formally adopted by the World Trade Organization in January 1995, requires signatory countries of the WTO to recognize and protect both process and product innovations in all technological fields, including pharmaceuticals.[29] This agreement is likely to affect research, production, and distribution of pharmaceuticals, reproductive technologies, supplies, and vaccines, with implications for access, quality of care, and informed choice. Although it is commonly asserted that the TRIPS will increase costs of reproductive drugs, supplies, and vaccines, thereby limiting women's access, there is little systematic evidence to bear out these claims.[30]

Similar to the GATS, there are few studies of the impacts of the TRIPS agreement on reproductive health supplies and technologies, with the exception of products to treat HIV/AIDS. It has been argued that average price increases for essential medicines could be in the range of 200–300 percent for many low-income countries.[31] However, some studies conducted on the impact of patents on drug prices in a set of developing countries showed that patents increase drug prices between a far smaller range of 12–68 percent.[32] Even those increases, however, may be prohibitive for poor households. In some countries, as a result of lawsuits and pressure from activists, drug companies have dramatically reduced prices of patented anti-retrovirals and other essential medicines.[33]

It is important to point out that TRIPS permit countries to override a patent, for example, if prices are too high or if supplies are limited or if it faces a public health emergency. The TRIPS "safeguards" allow access to more affordable generic drugs, which has important implications for price competition through compulsory licensing that allows countries to grant compulsory licensing for the production and importation of cheaper generic drugs, parallel imports, and the Bolar provision.[34] While these safeguards are potentially important, many governments lack the legal and administrative capacity to implement them while others have not availed themselves of the opportunities.[35] As a result, many activists argue for modifying the patent rules and strengthening the safeguards.

Indirect Pathways: Trade Liberalization, Women's Employment, and Reproductive Health

One indirect pathway through which trade liberalization affects reproductive health is through gendered changes in labor markets.[36] Trade liberalization has effects on both the demand and supply side, but this chapter focuses on changes in the demand side brought about by freer movements of capital as a result of foreign direct investment, reduction of tariffs, or other means.

As noted earlier, different components of trade will affect labor demand differentially. For instance, foreign direct investment may give rise to considerable labor mobility that is gender-differentiated, that is, to job shifts across and within sectors, to geographical mobility, and to transitions in and out of the labor force.[37] The elimination of tariffs, quotas, subsidies, and other instruments of trade policy can also affect labor demand differentially according to a number of factors, including: geographic location; worker characteristics, for example, age, sex, marital status, education, skill level, and so on; economic sector, for example, agriculture, manufacturing, services; type and size of economic enterprise, for example, public, private, or parastatal, formal and informal, family-based enterprises; type of employment, for example, wage and salary, own-account, unpaid family labor; and conditions of work, including nature or employment contract, job security, seasonality, benefits, working hours, and so on. The next section reviews the empirical evidence on the impact of trade liberalization on different dimensions of women's employment.

The Effect of Trade Liberalization on Women's Employment

A large literature shows that trade liberalization has increased the demand for female labor and provided women access to manufacturing, services, and some types of agricultural employment in many countries. Notably, semi-industrialized economies that emphasize export manufacturing have experienced a rise in the female share of employment, especially in the early phases of industrialization, although as these economies mature, the process of feminization of export employment may decline or even reverse.[38] In Taiwan, Hong Kong, South Korea, and Singapore, as well as in Mexico's *maquiladoras*, women's share of manufacturing employment first increased and then fell in later stages of industrialization.[39]

In agriculturally oriented developing economies that have emphasized exports of cash crops as part of their liberalization strategy, women have increased job opportunities as seasonal or contract workers or as laborers on husbands' or relatives' land in the production of export cash crops.[40] In some countries, such as in Latin America, economic restructuring and globalization have led to the feminization of agriculture as women seek remunerative employment to supplement declining family income.[41] Some women have also become producers of nontraditional agricultural exports (NTAEs). In Latin America and South Africa, NTAEs are often produced on large-scale enterprises, with women forming up to 80 percent of the workforce.[42]

In developing economies that rely heavily on service exports to propel growth (such as informatics and tourism), women also constitute a large share of export workers.[43] An additional benefit of service sector export labor is the remittances of workers who emigrate to work as nurses and domestics, which generate foreign exchange for the home economy.[44] The large majority of these workers are female.[45]

Direct Effects of Trade-Induced Changes in Female Employment on Reproductive Health and Rights

The importance of women's employment on the indirect path from trade to reproductive health and rights can be summarized primarily in its influence (positive or negative) on girls' and women's sexual and reproductive health problems and on their access to services through their health coverage and their ability to pay.[46] Work-related health problems include occupational health and safety issues (such as birth defects or infertility caused by chemicals), exhaustion, stress, sexual harassment on the job, forced pregnancy tests, or a myriad of other problems and needs. Positive relocation may also lead to better reproductive health conditions, such as improved self-image or self-esteem. Work-related health insurance coverage or ability to pay for services can include the gain or loss of a variety of health benefits, private or public, such as eligibility for national health insurance paid by employer and employee contributions, or cash incomes to pay for services. Refusal to permit time off of work for health-related reasons, or a woman's concern about loss of income if she does take time off can interfere with her access to services for herself and her family. The next section reviews the evidence that exists on the positive and negative effects of different types of trade-induced employment impacts on women's reproductive health problems and access to services.[47]

Factory Employment

Export-oriented employment work can be both positive and negative for women's reproductive health and rights. This mixed nature of the effects is evident, for instance, in Bangladesh, where the recruitment of adolescent girls into the burgeoning garment industry has had the positive effect of delaying marriage and childbirth.[48] Some studies find that as women's access to outside income rises, they are better able to renegotiate the distribution of resources within the household to the benefit of themselves and their children. The source and stability of that income appears to play a role in influencing women's bargaining power and their overall status and well-being.[49]

On the negative side, it may have put these girls at greater risk of early sexual activity and sexual harassment and changed the traditional needs for contraceptive services, which in Bangladesh are sought typically after marriage. Moreover, Amin et al's study also points out that the girls recruited by the garment factories are often below the minimum age for child labor.[50] Entrance into paid employment at early ages can affect girls' educational attainment; education is an important source of knowledge about reproductive health. If they live with their families, these girls are also not likely to have much power to negotiate control over their earnings.

Women's occupational and environmental health may also have deteriorated as a result of trade liberalization. Employment in export processing zones (EPZs) in many countries, for instance, has been associated with high levels of machine-related accidents, dust, noise, poor ventilation, and exposure to toxic chemicals.[51] These factors create additional pressure to highly stressful work, resulting in cardiovascular and psychological disorders. In the young women who work in the EPZs, the stress can affect reproductive health, leading to miscarriage, problems with pregnancies, and poor fetal health. This has been the case of the horticultural workers in the export sector in Chile, where rates of malformation among newborns were higher among temporary workers in the industry than among workers in the general population.[52] Three studies in Mexico suggest that women working in *maquiladoras* may be more likely than other women to give birth to low birth weight babies.[53] Thus, the health hazards associated with working with chemical pesticides further dampen the positive employment effects for women,[54] although some recent studies report that progress has been made on labor conditions as a result of advocacy on the issues.[55]

Home-Based Work

Another category of female employment on the increase with trade liberalization is home-based work in which women dominate and comprise an "invisible workforce."[56] Not only do informally employed women lack formal contracts and security in their work, but they also do not have access to leave or health benefits.[57] The fact that they are not seen as "working" prevents their reproductive and occupational health needs from being considered in employment, health, or industrial policies. Thus, *chikan* embroidery workers in the north Indian town of Lucknow have long had serious back-and-eye related problems, but it was only when they were organized by the Self Employed Women's Association that these problems came on the advocacy agenda.[58] At the individual level, though home-based workers may bring in income, and this type of work may be a more viable employment option for women with small children, their access to the public domain is as limited as if they were not earning an income. This lack of access and continued controls on their mobility inhibits their access to health care as well, which in most cases tends not to be available at the doorstep, nor even within easy physical reach.

Sex Work

Several recent studies have pointed to the increase in sex work with globalization.[59] The growth of the services sector and the concomitant expansion of the tourism and hospitality industry create a demand for sex work. Unemployment, often associated with liberalization and adjustment policies, can drive women into sex work. Under or unemployment can also drive women to undertake transactional sex to buy a better quality of life.[60] Women who use sex as a tradable have multiple partners and are at greater risk of HIV/AIDS and other sexually transmitted diseases.

Part-Time and Seasonal Work

Job security arising from trade-related employment may be questionable; the increased employment opportunities may be short-lived.[61] The seasonality of non-traditional agricultural jobs for example, implies that work is available only at certain times of the year. In the case of the Chilean and South African export grape industries, women are the preferred source of temporary workers and hold a very small share of permanent jobs.[62] The subcontracting system in other sectors entails that employment is only available when the factories need a particular part or product. Women in these types of jobs are often paid by the piece, receive no incomes for out-of-season unemployment, and are not covered by employer-based health insurance plans.

Work, Migration, and Reproductive Health

Trade liberalization is associated with large-scale migrations in the last few decades.[63] In fact, the same countries that have opened up to trade in recent years have also had large-scale migration of labor from rural to urban areas. Countries in southeast and east Asia, notably, have had patterns of female-dominated migration and increased participation of women in the labor force since the 1970s.[64]

How does migration affect women's reproductive health? As noted earlier, as women move out of their homes and enter the workforce, they are exposed to new experiences, ideas, knowledge, skills, and new communities. They may also be able to move out of the family-dominated social realm into a more public realm. Often, they have control over their earnings, even though they remit some of their earnings to their homes.[65] In addition, movements into urban areas and to more developed countries bring access to reproductive technologies and services that may not have been available near their homes. Not all migration, however, is empowering. Hugo points out that migration is only empowering if it is not clandestine, if it is rural to urban, if women work outside the home and in formal jobs, and if they migrate permanently rather than temporarily.[66]

Some empirical evidence also shows that migration of women workers can be highly exploitative. Thus, contract workers migrating from Asian countries like Indonesia or Sri Lanka to countries in the Persian Gulf have few rights or access to services and enter into highly demeaning contractual arrangements. The case of Filipino domestic workers who migrate to Hong Kong and to the United States often remains invisible, either due to their precarious immigrant status or because they are under the control of their recruiting agent and employers. Hugo's work, anecdotal evidence, and newspaper reports point to long hours of work, unhygienic living conditions, sexual and physical abuse, lack of leisure, and general vulnerability of migrant women.

In countries of South Asia, male migration still predominates. For women who are left behind as their husbands migrate, the experience is often disempowering; if they live in extended families, they may lose status when their husbands are absent. If they live in nuclear families, they assume multiple roles, which increase their work burdens and remittances may be inadequate or unreliable. On the other hand, recent studies from Kerala show that women who are left as household heads can often manage the finances and gain greater power over their labor and health than if they had a husband in the home.[67]

The process of migration can put women at greater risk of sexual activity.[68] When women migrate in search of employment, they are subject to the same risks of sexual activity as women who enter paid employment for the first time, except that migrant women do not have the protection of their homes and are perhaps more vulnerable. Migrant men, seeking sex too, put themselves and their sexual partners at risk of HIV/AIDS. The provision of public services also lags migration; for instance, in Sri Lanka, the ratio of public health midwives to pregnant women per service area has increased tenfold in one EPZ, because the government has not redistributed health resources to keep up with regional migration patterns associated with the creation of EPZs.[69]

Summary

Trade liberalization brings both opportunities and risks for women's reproductive health through new employment opportunities. In the short term, women may benefit from new employment opportunities and increased income and in spite of substantial costs in terms of harsh workplace conditions, possible sexual harassment, and the "double" work burden. The long-term effects of export employment for women's reproductive health and empowerment are not known, and further study is needed.

This chapter focused on two of the possible pathways through which the liberalization of trade can affect women's reproductive health and rights. It has specified a *direct pathway* through which trade policies affect the supply of reproductive health services, and an *indirect pathway* through which trade policies and movements in goods and services affect women's demand for services indirectly through changes in their labor force participation. Although these are not the only two routes through which the linkages between trade liberalization and reproductive health are established, they nonetheless provide a starting point that can guide future research and advocacy.

As the discussion of direct pathways made clear, it will be important to monitor current multilateral negotiations and implementation of agreements once they are signed and implemented. Monitoring efforts should focus on the interrelationship between WTO agreements and the ICPD goals, as well as other international treaties or agreements such as human rights conventions that affect reproductive health and rights.[70] Ensuring coherence is a potential tool to ensure that WTO agreements do not undermine achievement of ICPD goals. It will also be important to track what sorts of reproductive health services for-profit firms are pursuing, to see whether they are concentrating in high-tech care, for example. In some countries, it may not be WTO agreements, but rather domestic regulations that determine whether foreign reproductive health providers can set up operations or invest in a given country.

Research on the impact of trade agreements would be helpful to reproductive health and economic justice advocates. For instance, studies that examine the impact of TRIPS on access to reproductive health technologies may be particularly instructive in large countries like Brazil and China, which are implementing TRIPS now, and India, which will begin implementation shortly. Industry or market studies may be important adjuncts, as well, to gain a fuller understanding of the dynamics of foreign competition in various emerging markets.

The discussion of indirect pathways highlighted many gaps in knowledge. Country and comparative studies are needed to identify the positive and negative effects of specific types of employment in different sectors on women's reproductive health problems and their access to services. Such studies may be particularly useful for policy makers, employers, and trade unions, or workers' associations because they would identify particular problems in specific places that may be amenable to intervention.

Notes

* This chapter draws on two working papers, one co-authored with Maitreyi Das and one co-authored with Guadalupe Duron, prepared in 1992–1993 as part of an exploratory project undertaken by ICRW and funded by the Ford Foundation. I am indebted to Maitreyi Das and Guadalupe Duron for their collaboration on that project. In addition, I gratefully acknowledge the assistance of Aslihan Kes in the preparation of this chapter.

1. See the Bulletin of the World Health Organization 2000 and 2001.
2. As other chapters in this volume note, globalization is a dense mix of economic, political, and social elements operating simultaneously, interactively, and unevenly in different geographical and virtual spaces.

3. R. Petchesky (2003), *Global Prescriptions: Gendering Health and Human Rights*, London: Zed Books, p. 7.
4. UNCTAD/WHO (1998), *International Trade in Health Services, a Development Perspective*, Geneva: United Nations.
5. WTO (2003), *Understanding WTO*, available: http://wstream.hq.unu.edu/presentations/wtoenglish/e-doc/understanding_e.pdf.
6. UNCTAD (2004), *Trade and Development Report 2004*, Geneva: United Nations.
7. Source: World Bank (2004), World Development Indicators, available: http://devdata.worldbank.org/dataonline.
8. D. Baker, J. Epstein, and B. Pollin (1998), *Globalization and Progressive Economic Policy*, Cambridge, UK: Cambridge University Press.
9. WTO (2004), *International Trade Statistics 2004*, available: http:// www.wto.org/english/res_e/statis_e/its2004_e/its04_toc_e.htm.
10. R. Chanda (2001), Trade in health services, *Commission on Macroeconomics and Health Working Paper Series, Paper No. WG4:5*, Geneva: World Health Organization.
11. Ibid.; As Lipson (2005) states, "In most countries, trade in health-related goods and services is a relatively minor factor affecting the availability, cost and quality of health services. The ways in which each country organizes, finances, and regulates health services are usually much more important determinants of whether countries are able to ensure the delivery of basic health care to their people, without financially burdening the poor. But trade can influence some particularly critical health goods, such as life-saving pharmaceuticals, or the availability of certain services if they are only offered by foreign-owned companies. It is these situations where trade and rules governing such trade come into play."
12. Reproductive health is a state of physical, mental, and social well-being in all matters relating to the reproductive system at all stages of life. Reproductive health implies that people are able to have a satisfying and safe sex life and that they have the capability to reproduce and the freedom to decide if, when, and how often to do so. Implicit in this are the right of men and women to be informed and to have access to safe, effective, affordable, and acceptable methods of family planning of their choice, and the right to appropriate health care services that enable women to safely go through pregnancy and childbirth, WHO (1999), *Interpreting Reproductive Health—ICDP+5 Forum*, The Hague, available: http://www.who.int/reproductivehealth/publications/RHR_99_7/RHR_99_7_abstract.htm.
13. M. Das and C. Grown (2002), Trade liberalization, women's employment, and reproductive health: What are the linkages and entry points for policy and action? *International Center for Research on Women Working Paper*, Washington DC: International Center for Research on Women.
14. G. Sen and S. Batliwala (2000), Empowering women for reproductive rights, in H. Presser and G. Sen, eds., *Women's Empowerment and Demographic Processes*, Oxford: Oxford University Press.
15. International Women's Health Coalition (IWHC) (1994), Sexual Rights, fact sheet, New York: International Women's Health Coalition.

16. Most indicators cover the medical and demographic aspects of reproductive health. Indicators are being developed to capture the sociopolitical dimensions of reproductive health but they are not available for a large number of countries. There are few indicators for reproductive rights that are agreed upon and available across countries.

17. Source: UN Statistical Database, World Development Indicators 2004 (UN) (2004), *Statistical Division—Common Database*, New York: United Nations, available:http://unstats.un.org/unsd/cdb/etc/logon.asp?rpage=%2Funsd%2 F cdb%2Fcdb%5Fadvanced%5Fdata%5Fextract%2Easp%3F&type=4), and UNAIDS Report on the Global Epidemic 1998, 2004.

18. UNAIDS (2004), A global overview of the AIDS epidemic, in *2004 Report on the global AIDS epidemic*, available: http://www.unaids.org.

19. UNAIDS/WHO (2004), *The AIDS Epidemic Update*, Geneva: UNAIDS.

20. UNAIDS (2004), A global overview of the AIDS epidemic, in *2004 Report on the Global AIDS epidemic*, available: http://www.unaids.org; G. Rao Gupta (2000), Gender, sexuality, and HIV/AIDS: The what, the why, and the how, Plenary address at the 13th International AIDS Conference, Durban, South Africa.

21. D. J. Lipson (2005), Implications of the general agreement on trade in services for reproductive health services, in Caren Grown, Anju Malhotra, and Elissa Braunstein, eds., *Guaranteeing Reproductive Health and Rights: The Role of Trade Liberalization*, Oxford, UK: Routledge Press.

22. For example, concentration of certain medical procedures in urban areas when most of the population is rural or the imposition of user fees that most cannot pay illustrate the misfit between problems (needs) and services.

23. D. J. Lipson, Implications of the general agreement on trade in services for reproductive health services.

24. As of 2003, 54 countries, nearly half of the World Trade Organization members, have made commitments to at least one of the trading modes under GATS.

25. An important GATS exemption is for purely public services—those supplied in "the exercise of governmental authority." Article I(3) defines these services as those supplied by any level of government (national, regional, local) or by nongovernmental bodies exercising delegated authority, such as regional health authorities, and requires such services be "supplied neither on a commercial basis, nor in competition with one or more service suppliers." There are some services to which these criteria clearly apply, such as the provision of health care under statutory social security plans and free medical treatment in public facilities.

26. D. J. Lipson, Implications of the general agreement on trade in services for reproductive health services.

27. C. Grown and G. Duron (2002), Guaranteeing reproductive health and rights. What is the role of the trade agreements? *International Center for Research on Women Working Paper*, Washington DC: International Center for Research on Women.

28. D. J. Lipson, Implications of the general agreement on trade in services for reproductive health services.

29. Prior to the TRIPS Agreement, a substantial number of developing countries did not adequately cover intellectual property rights for medicines and pharmaceutical products. In addition, patent coverage was highly inconsistent between some developing countries, ranging from as little as three years (Thailand) to as long as sixteen years (South Africa). These conditions generally favored the local production of less expensive generic medicines where possible. See M. Williams (2001), The TRIPS and public health debate: An overview, *International Gender and Trade Network Research Paper*, Geneva: International Gender and Trade Network.

30. Some reproductive health products—like certain forms of contraception—are off patent so TRIPS will not apply. It should also be noted that even if technology is available and affordable to women, other barriers in the health care system may prevent women from having full access to prevention and treatment of reproductive health problems. For instance, a study conducted on clinical practices related to sexually transmitted diseases (STDs) in gynecological and antenatal programs in Rio de Janeiro, Brazil, where drugs are wildly available, revealed that doctors found it difficult to disclose to married women that they had an STD, and to discuss how they contracted the infection. See K. Giffen and C. M. Lowndes (1999), Gender, sexuality, and the prevention of sexually transmissible diseases: A Brazilian study of clinical practice, *Social Science and Medicine* 48, 283–292.

31. Oxfam (2001), *Cut the Cost: Patent Injustice: How World Trade Rules Threaten the Health of Poor People*, Oxford: Oxfam.

32. F. M. Scherer and J. Watal (2001), Post-TRIPS options for access to patented medicines in developing countries, *Commission on Macroeconomics and Health Working Paper Series. Paper No. WG4: 1*, Geneva: The World Health Organization.

33. P. Maharaj and B. Roberts (2005), Tripping up: AIDS, pharmaceuticals and intellectual property in South Africa, in Caren Grown, Anju Malhotra, and Elissa Braunstein, eds., *Guaranteeing Reproductive Health and Rights*.

34. Parallel importation (Article 6) is importation, without the consent of the patent holder, of a patented product marketed in another country either by the patent holder or with the patent holder's consent. Parallel importation is often used to promote price competition between equivalent patented products, one of which is usually marketed at a lower price in other countries. The Bolar provision (Article 30) allows a generic producer to conduct all tests required for marketing approval in advance, so that a generic drug can be put on the market as soon as the patent expires. The TRIPS does not permit "stock-piling" or large-scale commercial production of the generic drug before the patent expires.
    See C. M. Correa (2000), Implementing national public health policies in the framework of WTO agreements, *Draft Working Paper No. 3*, Washington, DC: World Health Organization. WHO (2001), Globalization, TRIPS and access to pharmaceuticals; *WHO Policy Perspectives on Medicines*, 3, Geneva.

35. Commission on Intellectual Property Rights (CIPR) (2002), *The Doha Declaration, implementation of TRIPS and access to medicines*, UK: Commission on Intellectual Property Rights.

36. Another indirect pathway is through the household. For instance, changes in husband's status or in the status of other earners in the household may affect women's reproductive health and her access to services (if it is through another earner's health insurance).

37. A. Tran-Nguyen and A. B. Zampetti (2004), *Trade and Gender: Opportunities and Challenges for Developing Countries*, New York and Geneva: UNCTAD.

38. It would be interesting to explore the process of defeminization and whether the rate of defeminization has been lower in some countries (i.e., South Korea) than in others. This has implications for trends in the gender wage gap.

39. An exception to the trend of feminization of employment has been in those developing economies with less competitive manufacturing sectors, especially in Africa. As these economies have reduced tariffs on imports of labor-intensive manufactures such as clothing, women's job losses in the sector outnumber men's job losses. Many laid-off workers have been pushed into informal employment. See R. Mehra and S. Gammage (1999), Trends, countertrends, and gaps in women's employment, *World Development*, 27(3): 533–550.

40. Countries that export unprocessed primary products (e.g., ores) do not fit the stylized facts that we present here. First, exports have not expanded as a share of GDP to the extent they have in other developing economies. Also, these industries tend to be male-dominated, such that any expansion of output is likely to benefit male workers in employment and wages. Liberalization has, however, had negative effects on women's employment and income in these economies, in part through loss of manufacturing jobs, but also due to pressures on the state to reduce expenditures, resulting in a disproportionately large loss of female jobs.

41. C. D. Deere (2004), *The Feminization of Agriculture? Economic Restructuring in Rural Latin America*, OPGP 1, UNRISD, Geneva.

42. M. Carr, M. Alter Chen, and J. Tate (2000), Globalization and home-based workers, *Feminist Economics* 6(3): 123–142.

43. UN (1999), *World Survey on the Role of Women in Development: Globalization, Gender, and Work*, New York: United Nations; J. Davison-O'Connell and J. Sanchez-Taylor (1999), *Sun, Sex and Gold: Sex Tourism in the Caribbean*, Lanham, MD: Rowman and Littlefield; Carla Freeman (2000), *High Tech and High Heels in the Global Economy: Women, Work, and Pink Collar Identities in the Caribbean*, Durham, NC: Duke University Press.

44. The sex trade is also one of the fastest growing and most profitable service industries; see UN (1999), *World Survey on the Role of Women in Development*.

45. Ibid.

46. It is important to recognize that apart from women's own employment, changes in husband's employment status or that of other earners in the household may affect women's reproductive health and access to services, e.g., if husbands lose health insurance that covers all family members. However, these will not be considered further here.

47. Unfortunately, one would want to distinguish effects of trade liberalization on women's reproductive health problems and access to services by income and geographic location. However, very few studies contain information to permit analysis at this level.

48. S. Amin (2005), Implications of trade liberalization for working women's marriage: Case studies of Bangladesh, Egypt and Vietnam, in Caren Grown, Anju Malhotra, and Elissa Braunstein, eds., *Guaranteeing Reproductive Health and Rights*.

49. Lawrence, Haddad, John Hoddinott, and Harold Alderman (1997), Intrahousehold resource allocation, an overview, in L. Haddad, J. Hoddinott, and H. Alderman, eds., *Intrahousehold Resource Allocation in Developing Countries: Models, Methods and Policy*, Baltimore: Johns Hopkins Press.

50. S. Amin, I. Diamond, R. T. Naved, and M. Newby (1998), Transition to adulthood of female garment-factory workers in Bangladesh, *Studies in Family Planning* 29(2): 185–200.

51. H. Abell (1999), Endangering women's health for profit: Health and safety in Mexico's maquiladoras, *Development in Practice* 9(5): 595–600.

52. D. Rodríguez and S. Venegas (1991), *Los trabajadores de la fruta en cifras*, Santiago: GEA; S. Venegas (1993), Programas de apoyo a temporeros y temporeras en Chile, in Gomes S. and E. Klein, eds., *Los Pobres del Campo, El Trabajador Eventual*, Santiago: FLACSO/PREALC/OIT; it is important to note that these studies do not control for selection bias; it may be that other characteristics of workers in the horticultural industry are responsible for this outcome.

53. C. Denman, L. Cedillo, and S. Harlow (2003), Work and health in export industries at national borders, in Jody Heymann, ed., *Global Inequalities at Work: Work's Impact on the Health of Individuals, Families, and Societies*, Oxford; New York: Oxford University Press; B. Eskinazi, S. Guendelman, and E. Elkin (1993), A preliminary study of reproductive outcomes of female maquiladora workers in Tijuana Mexico, *American Journal of Industrial Medicine* 24: 667–676.

54. C. Dolan, J. Humphrey, and C. Harris-Pascal (1999), Horticulture commodity chains: the impact of the U.K. market on the African fresh vegetable industry, *IDS Working Paper No. 96*, Brighton, UK: Institute of Development Studies; L. A. Thrupp, with G. Bergeron and W. F. Waters (1995), *Bittersweet Harvests for Global Supermarkets: Challenges in Latin America's Agricultural Export Boom*, World Resources Institute.

55. C. Newman (2001), *Gender, Time Use and Change: impacts of agricultural employment in Ecuador*, Washington, DC: World Bank; G. Sanchez-Friedemann (November 12–13, 2004), *Assets, Wage Income, and Social Capital in Intrahousehold Bargaining among Women Workers in Colombia's Cut-Flower Industry*, paper presented at Workshop on Women and the Distribution of Wealth at Yale Center for International and Area Studies, New Haven, CT.

56. M. Chen, J. Sebstad, and L. O'Connell (1999), Counting the invisible workforce: the case of home based workers, *World Development* 27(3): 603–610.

57. R. Balakrishnan, ed. (2002), *The Hidden Assembly Line: Gender Dynamics of Subcontracted Work in a Global Economy*, Bloomfield, CT: Kumarian Press.

58. M. Das and C. Grown (2002), Trade liberalization, women's employment, and reproductive health: What are the linkages and entry points for policy and

action? *International Center for Research on Women Working Paper*, Washington DC: International Center for Research on Women.

59. V. Subramaniam (2001), The impact of globalization on women's reproductive health and rights: a regional perspective, *Development* 42(4): 145–149; U. D. Upadhyay (2000), India's new economic policy of 1991 and its impact on women's poverty and AIDS, *Feminist Economics* 6(3): 105–122; UN (1999), *1999 World Survey on the Role of Women in Development*.

60. A. Malhotra and S. Mathur (2000), *The Economics of Young Women's Sexuality in Nepal*, paper presented at the IAFFE Conference Istanbul, Turkey; N. Luke (2001), *Cross-Generational and Transactional Sexual Relations in Sub-Saharan Africa: A Review of the Evidence on Prevalence and Implications for Negotiation of Safe Sexual Practices for Adolescent Girls*, paper prepared for the International Center for Research on Women as part of the AIDSMark Project. Washington DC: International Center for Research on Women.

61. S. Ozler (2001), Export led industrialization and gender differences in job creation and destruction, micro evidence from Turkish manufacturing mector, *UCLA Working Paper*.

62. S. Barrientos (2001), *Gender, Flexibility, and Global Value Chains*, IDS Bulletin 32(3): 83–93, Brighton UK: Institute of Development Studies.

63. R. Dixon-Mueller and A. Germain (2000), Reproductive health and the demographic imagination, in Harriet B. Presser and Gita Sen, eds., *Women's Empowerment and Demographic Processes*, Oxford: Oxford University Press; S. Sassen (1998), Informalization in advanced market economies, issues in Development-*Discussion Paper 20*, Geneva: International Labour Organization.

64. G. J. Hugo (2000), Migration and women's empowerment, in H. B. Presser and G. Sen, eds., *Women's Empowerment and Demographic Processes*; Dixon-Mueller and A. Germain, Reproductive health and the demographic imagination.

65. N. Kabeer (2000), *The Power to Choose: Bangladeshi Women and Labour Market Decisions in London and Dhaka*, London: Verso.

66. G. Hugo, Migration and women's empowerment.

67. S. I. Rajan (1989), Aging in Kerala: one more population problem? *Asia-Pacific Population Journal* 4(2): June: 19–48.

68. G. Hugo, Migration and women's empowerment; UN (1999), *1999 World Survey on the Role of Women in Development*.

69. T. Hettiarachchy and S. L. Schensul (2001), The risks of pregnancy and the consequences among young unmarried women working in a free trade zone in Sri Lanka, *Asia Pacific Population Journal* 16(2): 125–140.

70. A. M. Basu (2005), Reproductive health advocacy, in Caren Grown, Anju Malhotra, and Elissa Braunstein, eds., *Guaranteeing Reproductive Health and Rights*.

In Perspective

Globalization, Trade Liberalization, and Women's Health: A Nepalese Perspective

Mahesh Maskey

In chapter 3, Caren Grown provides a global analysis of the direct and indirect pathways through which trade liberalization policies affect women's reproductive health. In this perspective chapter, my comments and analysis reflect my training as a health professional from a South Asian country engaged in political movements to ensure good health as a fundamental human right.

How globalization is perceived and defined, especially economic globalization, affects one's interpretation of its impact on reproductive health. One mainstream definition of globalization emphasizes the *flow* of information, goods capital, and people across political and economic boundaries.[1] Another definition emphasizes human *interaction* across a range of spheres, including economic, social, political, and cultural, experienced along three dimensions: spatial, temporal, and cognitive.[2] However, more precisely, the practice of economic globalization appears to have facilitated "the *shift* of control over the process of production, distribution and resource allocation to the globally integrated market controlled by a few players with vast wealth and resources."[3] For "peripheral" developing countries, globalization fuels itself on the relation of the dominance of a few and the subordination of many, and much of the resistance from developing countries against globalization is against this dominance–dependence relationship rather than against globalization, per se.[4] I believe that the process of globalization can benefit developing countries only when this unequal relationship is fundamentally transformed in favor of resource-poor nations and people.

The impact of trade liberalization has to be viewed in this context. The notion that expanding global trade is beneficial to all countries and their citizens is derived from the growth-centered mainstream trade theory. Export-oriented industries and cash crops were believed to boost employment opportunities and economic growth within individual nations. But since trade liberalization comes with a package of market deregulation, privatization, fiscal austerity, and weakened social security, the negative impact on the lives of the poor and the marginalized are more than apparent. Claims of rises in wage and employment opportunities as a result of trade liberalization have been questioned by the experience of many poor countries. Where such increases have actually taken place it is questionable whether they have led to an increased holistic well-being of poor people, the majority of whom are women.

Often overlooked by the economists and politicians is the fact that trade policies have different consequences on women and men because they each have different socioeconomic, cultural, and political status and different control over resources. When social services are cut or user fees charged, although the poor suffer in general, women usually bear a double burden: loss of education and health facilities on the one hand and increases in unpaid household labor as well as paid labor in frequently dehumanizing work environments outside the home on the other. Much of women's trade-related "gains" are characterized by "long hours, insecure employment, unhealthy conditions, low wages and often sexual harassment in export processing zones exempted by local labor laws."[5]

Privatization of health services and user fees charged by government institutions for healthcare have been direct consequences of globalization and trade liberalization policies in low-income countries with weak public sectors. A declining utilization of health services has been a common phenomenon when cost recovery schemes and user financing were introduced in these countries in the name of "Health Sector Reform," a predominantly World Bank–engineered restructuring of the health sector. In South Asia, the creation of medical markets, the gradual dismantling of public sector health institutions, and the presence of infectious diseases epidemics have been pointed out as some of the resulting health manifestations of Structural Adjustment Policies.[6] For example, in 2002, Nepal saw an increase in user fees (up to 400 percent) in the Apex Government Hospital.[7] Weak and inefficient governments in resource-poor countries are under pressure to carry out such "reforms," and it has been pointed out that aid recipient countries have to bear the international pressure of the donors, who will grant "aid" only on the condition that the recipient governments dismantle their public health and welfare systems.[8]

When trade liberalization comes with a package of "economic reforms," mere increases in employment and financial gains cannot be predictive of improved women's health. For example, in a South Asian context, unbalanced gender power relations within the household may make it difficult for women to control and use resources earned through their own labor. Therefore, the impact of trade liberalization on women has to be assessed on the real prize—their well-being and quality of life. This brings us to the issue of how we define women's health.

Women's health and reproductive rights were squarely placed on the international agenda at the International Conference on Population and Development held in Cairo in 1994. Cairo's spirit was to make reproductive rights accessible to all before the year 2015 by strengthening the primary health care system. Economic and health sector reforms, however, insinuated a reductionist approach to these concepts and recommendations. The decade of the 1990s "witnessed cuts in health budgets in the name of health sector reforms, tied to IMF and World Bank loans making it nearly impossible to make the recommendations a reality."[9] As a result, selective packages like family planning and safe motherhood (read "essential obstetric care") were gradually substituted in place of a comprehensive approach to the improved reproductive health of women and men. Such a package approach falls far short of the vision of reproductive health as defined by the WHO: the ability to have a safe, responsible, and fulfilling sex life, the freedom to make decisions related to sexuality and fertility, including when and how often to have children as well as avoid becoming ill or dying due to reproductive health problems.

Even this broader concept of reproductive health does not capture the dimension of women's health influenced by determinants that lie outside the domain of reproductive causes. For example, if we look at mortality indicators on a global scale, tuberculosis kills more women annually than all causes of maternal mortality combined;[10] and, AIDS has been found to be the largest cause of maternal deaths in South Africa.[11] Since health is determined by economic, social, educational, political, demographic, environmental, and legal systems, revisiting the Alma Ata Declaration with a focus on gender equity may be the right approach to conceptualizing and working toward the betterment of women's health instead of putting the focus on reproductive health only.[12]

Employment, Subsidies, and Privatization: The Case of Nepal

The three characteristics of trade liberalization—employment increases, cuts in subsidies, and privatization of former state-supported services—have almost become cliché. However, I have mentioned earlier that rises in employment are in contention with the experiences of developing countries. So what is happening? Assuming the data is valid, I offer two explanations.

First, globalization could be increasing jobs in export industries at the same time as it draws female workers from traditional sectors, thus resulting in the same net effect. Second, in a highly integrated and dependent economy, for example, that of Nepal dependent upon India where export industries are accompanied by hired laborers from India or Bangladesh, there may not be an increase in the Nepali female workforce. One study about Nepal states: "much of the newly generated employment has been taken over by immigrant labor, which accompanies the foreign capital coming from India."[13]

Disaggregated information may help us better visualize these easily hidden relationships between globalization and employment. Using Nepal as an example, we see that in terms of wage, employment, and livelihood, this country can be presented as a case of failed trade liberalization policies that were begun in 1985 and fully implemented by 1992. Critics have opined it as "a classic case of neo-liberal economic policies playing havoc with the social fabric of a poor developing country."[14] Rather than raising employment in the manufacture sector as expected, there was instead a drastic reduction in the number of women classified as production workers (from 18.8 percent in 1984/1985 to 1.5 percent in 1996 in rural areas, and 21.1–10.3 percent in urban areas). The number of male workers also decreased, though less drastically (12.7–7.3 percent in rural areas and 30.7–22.8 percent in urban areas) (see table 3.3).[15] During this period, both women and men had resorted to agricultural work as a source of employment.

This labor shift corresponds with the closure of almost 50 percent of 70,000 small-scale cottage industries after trade liberalization policies came into effect in 1992. These changes also reflect the "progressive destruction of indigenous industries without any replacement by alternative manufacturing system."[17] In Nepal, a total of 19.8 percent of workers have already lost their jobs due to privatized public enterprises. A vast majority of the workers are in the informal sectors unprotected by labor laws. Even in the formal sector, particularly in carpet and garment industries, contract workers are sharply increasing and 48 percent of workers in the manufacturing sector are casual laborers. In the sales and service sectors, there is an increase in male and female workers in urban areas whereas both have decreased in rural areas. Similar patterns are observed in the professional sector except that, here, female professionals have increased in the rural areas while male professionals have decreased (table 3.3).

Table 3.3 Economically active men and women in selected sectors of employment (in percent of economically active of the respective sex)

	MPHBS* (1985/86)		NLSS** (1995\96)	
	Male	*Female*	*Male*	*Female*
1. Production (manufacturing transport/communication/ordinary labors)				
Urban	30.7	21.1	22.8	10.3
Rural	12.7	18.8	7.3	1.5
2. Agriculture and forestry				
Urban	23.5	54.6	22.2	49.3
Rural	76.6	88.3	82.8	95.3
3. Sales and services				
Urban	24.1	17.3	26.9	27.5
Rural	4.2	1.3	1.9	0.4
4. Professional and technical/administrative				
Urban	7.9	3.2	9.9	7.7
Rural	2.7	0.2	2.3	0.5

Notes: * Multipurpose Household Budget Survey; ** National Living Standard Survey.

The implementation of trade liberalization policies in Nepal initially appeared to benefit the manufacturing and service sectors. The export sector represented by the carpet and garment industry (jointly 80 percent of all exports) experienced a boom in 1990. During the same period, however, agricultural subsidies were cut and the export of agricultural products declined. This resulted in Nepal importing large quantities of food grains, spending US$95 million in 1996. After 1995, the carpet sector began to show signs of decay due to negative publicity about the use of child labor and the decline of the quality of products.[18] In the garment sector, only 100 out of 1,200 registered factories are currently operational. The rise in unemployment and underemployment, the devaluation of currency, and trade deficits have become common characteristics of the Nepalese economy in the twenty-first century. Thus, from a 5 percent growth rate in the 1990s, the overall growth plunged to a negative value (−0.6 in 2001–2002) for the first time in 19 years.[19] And, economic recovery has only been further hampered by increases in military expenditure (seven fold in the 12 years since 1990) and trade deficits.

In 2000, adjusted unemployment was estimated to be 17 percent and underemployment 32 percent.[20] Decreases in employment opportunities for both male and female populations have created a huge number of rural "floating" laborers that migrate from rural areas to urban ones as well as those outside Nepal in search of jobs. Many Nepalese now work in Indian labor markets, while a substantial number of these laborers are sought by global markets for menial jobs. Human resource agencies have mush-roomed in Nepal to meet this global demand, and migrant workers are often smuggled illegally into countries, at great risk to their lives not only during the journey but once they have arrived as well.

For those who choose to stay in Nepal, the increasing unemployment for both women and men is causing a tremendous stress on gender relations. Male unemployment increases pressure upon women to find any kind of work to support the family. In the context of South Asia, although women's employment outside the household may raise the social status within the household for the women, "the household itself may be down-graded socially in the public arena,"[21] thereby aggravating the male's bruised ego or a reactive helplessness. How employment affects gender relations within the family is an area that deserves serious study in the context of countries like Nepal.

Women's Health

Discriminatory sociocultural practices, as well as inadequate health services, are major reasons for the low-health status of working women.[22] Trade liberalization appears to have aggravated these practices and inade-quacies in many South Asian countries (except for, arguably, Sri Lanka). In general, women have poor health in South Asia; Nepal is one of the two remaining countries in the world where female life expectancy is lower than that of males. In the year 2000, the Nepal Human Development Report projected the life expectancy to be 59.8 years for women and 59.3 years for men. Further breakdowns show a rather sizable disparity between rural and urban living: among women, life expectancies are 59.3 and 70.8 years for rural and urban, respectively, while men live up to 58.2 and 71.4 years, respectively.[23] Malnutrition is common and 65 percent of pregnant women suffer from anemia. Almost 27 percent of all women have a body mass index (BMI) of less than 18, indicating a relatively high level of chronic energy deficiency.[24]

In such a scenario, the net effect of trade liberalization policies on women's health may be neutral, better or worse depending upon how their gains in employment and wage are balanced by the adverse effects of pri-vatization on health services and other sectors. Women's health could be measured by several indicators to assess the impact of trade liberalization, including nutritional status, decision making on expenditure, domestic and workplace violence, sex trade, and prevalence of STIs and HIV/AIDS. Social epidemiological research is needed to throw light on these issues.

Developing alternative methods for measuring and monitoring maternal mortality in developing countries should also be a priority research area in order to measure the evolution of women's health status.

From the perspective of developing countries an urgent research question is: what happens when a crisis erupts in market economies that are related to the health and well-being of workers who are largely women? The Asian market crisis in the late 1990s showed huge cuts in worker jobs, plunging the female working population to desperate means of survival such as commercial sex work, which only heightened the spread of existing sexually transmitted infection (STI) and HIV epidemics. Recent waves of global recession have engulfed Kathmandu's export industry and a con-comitant swell in the sex trade has been noticed there. This is a relatively recent phenomenon in a country that is infamous for the trafficking of girls and women to India.

Sex trade is illegal in Nepal. Yet, it is estimated that there are 25,000 sex workers in Kathmandu alone. Cabin and dance restaurants, massage par-lors, and hotels have become flourishing centers for the local sex trade.[25] In addition, the number of street-based sex workers is also increasing. Compounding these numbers is the simultaneous rapid rise of HIV within this population, from 2.7 percent in 1996 to 17.3 percent in 2002. In a sur-vey conducted among sex workers in Kathmandu valley, 40 out of 57 respondents reported being infected with HIV/AIDS.[26] To prevent the rise of STIs and HIV/AIDS among the increasingly impoverished working population, research is desperately needed to explore the coping mechanisms of unemployed vulnerable workers in hopes of developing an alternative means of income generation.

Conclusion

The idea behind privatization and trade liberalization was to "unleash the creative entrepreneurial spirit of the industrial class and break the existing monopoly of the comprador class who thrived on their nexus with bureaucracy and politicians."[27] It was also seen as an unprecedented opportunity to catch up with the so-called advanced economies.[28] However, deregulation and removal of minimum wage policies associated with privatization appear to have succeeded only in undermining labor welfare policies in countries like Nepal in favor of businessmen and women, bureaucrats, and politicians. Critics point out the harsh condi-tional demands made by international financial institutions that may lead a country toward indebtedness, inflation, distortion of national priorities, and minimal social investment. It is likely that income inequalities driven by privatization have contributed to the current explosive political situation in Nepal. The rise of the Maoist insurgency and the violent political conflict in Nepal has been viewed as an indicator of such turmoil.[29]

Under the domination of organized bodies of finance capital such as the World Bank, IMF, and WTO, the integration of low-income countries with world markets may only promote growth alongside an unequal distribution of resources, making few people rich and many even poorer. It is true that globalization and global trade cannot be ignored in today's world. But the exploitation of cheap labor can and should be prevented and welfare of labor should be secured with strong labor laws orchestrated by a legitimate state, a state that is responsible and accountable for the health of its citizens. To begin with, rich nations and banks should refrain from imposing conditional demands on the aid they provide and the politics of debt servicing should be abandoned by writing off the debt of the least developed countries.

Such prescriptions are bitter medicines for the powers that want to preserve the dominance–dependence relationships between nations, and it is likely that the present unequal relationship will be held for a long time. However, an anti-globalization movement that was sparked in Seattle and the burgeoning movement of a world social forum in all its dimensions is a testimony to the ability for people around the world to come together to resist the vested economic interest of a grossly inequitable, capitalist form of globalization. This movement is also presenting an alternative for a different kind of globalization and global trade based on human need and cooperation across the borders.

I concede that my perspective could be viewed as one-sided. But, I believe it is difficult to have a different perspective as a native of a least developed country. As a result of globalization and trade liberalization, "the field of health care is seeing one of the greatest 'human experiments' in history" deepening the imbalance of income, power, and knowledge and wrecking the lives of millions of human beings, both men and women.[30] These deepening inequalities must be questioned and stopped, if trade liberalization is to have positive impacts on the lives of poor people around the world.

Notes

1. N. Daulaire (1999), Globalization and health, *Development* 42(4): 22–24.
2. K. Lee (2000), Globalization and health policy: A review of literature and proposed research and policy agenda, in *Health Development in the New Global Economy*, Washington, DC: PAHO.

3. M. Acharya (1998), Globalization process and the Nepalese economy: Its impact on employment and income, in M. K. Dahal, ed., *Impact of Globalization in Nepal* (pp. 26–37), Kathmandu: Nepal Foundation for Advanced Studies (NEFAS), p. 26.
4. Ibid., pp. 26–37.
5. N. Catagay (2001), Trade, gender and poverty, *UNDP Background Paper* 5, New York (available: http://www.undp.org).
6. I. Quadeer (2001), Impact of structural adjustment policies on concepts of public health, in I. Quadeer, K. Sen, and K. R. Nayar, eds., *Public Health and Poverty of Reforms: The South Asian Predicament* (pp. 117–136), New Delhi: Sage Publications.
7. M. Maskey (2002), Development of health services in Nepal: In the shadow of globalization, paper presented in the workshop "Methodological Issues Related to Critical Health Research" organized by University of Maastricht, Netherlands and JNU, India, November, 2002, unpublished.
8. G. Berlinguer (1999), Health and equity as primary global goal, *Development* 42(4): 17–21, p. 17.
9. WGNRR (2003), Primary health care and women's reproductive and sexual rights, Amsterdam: Women's Global Network for Reproductive Rights, p. 6.
10. B. Currey (2000), Maternal mortality and mother's death as development indicator, *British Medical Journal* 321(7264): 835.
11. P. Sidley (2000), AIDS is the largest cause of maternal deaths in South Africa, *British Medical Journal* 321(7274): 1434.
12. C. Mazure (2003), Case for women's health research in United States: Grassroot efforts, legislative changes and scientific development, paper presented in Yale symposium on "Globalization, Gender and Health" New Haven, CT.
13. M. Acharya, Globalization process and the Nepalese economy, pp. 26–37.
14. SAAPE (2003), Poverty in South Asia: Civil Society Perspectives, Kathmandu: South Asia Alliance for Poverty Eradication, pp. 119–146.
15. CBS/NPC/HMG (1996), Nepal living standards survey, 1995/1996, *Main Findings, Vol I&II*, Kathmandu: Central Bureau of Statistics.
16. Ibid.
17. M. Acharya, Globalization process and the Nepalese economy: (pp. 26–37), p. 33.
18. D. R. Dhala (1998), Impact of globalization in Nepal: Trade union perspective, in M. K. Dahal, ed., *Impact of Globalization in Nepal* (pp. 103–123), Kathmandu: NEFAS.
19. NPC (2003), The Tenth Plan: Poverty Reduction Strategy Paper, Kathmandu: National Planning Commission/His Majesty Government of Nepal.
20. S. P. Sharma (2004), Data provided in an interview, *Spotlight* 23(26), January 16–22, 2004.
21. M. Acharya, Globalization process and the Nepalese economy (pp. 26–37), p. 36.
22. GENPROM (2002), The linkage between women's employment, family welfare and child labour in Nepal, International Labour Organization (available: http://www.ilo.org).
23. Nepal Human Development Report 2001: Poverty Reduction and Governance (2002), *Annex 1 Human Development Monitor*, Kathmandu, Nepal: United Nations Development Program.

24. World Health Organization, *Nutrition Profile of Nepal* (available: http://w3. whosea.org/EN/Section13/Section38_2254.htm; World Health Organization, *Women's Health in Southeast Asia* (available: http://w3.whosea.org/women2/ nutrition.htm).

25. CREHPA (2003), A situational assessment of sex work in Kathmandu valley: A focused Ethnographic Study, Kathmandu (available: http://www.fhi.org).

26. Ibid.

27. D. R. Dhala, Impact of Globalization in Nepal (pp. 103–123), p. 106.

28. J. Sachs (1998), Globalization & employment, international institute for labour studies, ILO (available: http://www.ilo.org).

29. M. Acharya, Globalization process and the Nepalese economy (pp. 26–37); Dhala, Impact of Globalization in Nepal (pp. 103–123).

30. G. Berlinguer (1999), Health and equity as primary global goal, *Development* 42(4): 17–21, p. 17.

In Perspective

Gender, Health, and Globalization: An International NGO Perspective

Wendy Harcourt

Introduction

Caren Grown's chapter on "The Pathways between Trade Liberalization and Reproductive Health" presents important challenges both conceptually and politically in her analysis of trade liberalization policies and the impact of macroeconomic policy issues on the micro-reality of women's lives. This chapter is path breaking because there is such a paucity of data and lack of awareness on the topic in both the health policy and research arenas.

In this chapter, I elaborate on gender and health issues in the context of globalization from the perspective of civil society. I reflect on women's health and rights groups' gender analysis of trade and its impact on poor women, and I do so in relation to women's organizing and advocacy work surrounding global health policy debates. These debates include those generated from the World Trade Organization (WTO) since its founding in 1995, the International Conference on Population and Development (ICPD) held in Cairo 1994, and more recently the Millennium Development Goals (MDGs) as agreed in 2000 at the Millennium Summit and elaborated further in 2002 at the Doha Conference on financing development.

At the outset, I would like to clarify why I deliberately focus my comments on the impact of globalization on *women*'s health and rights. It is a strategic choice rather than any mistaken conflation of "gender" with "women." My focus on women's health and rights is couched in an awareness of the gender difference, gender bias, and gender inequalities that shape women and men's lives. I would argue it is a strategic choice to focus on the specificities of women's health when discussing trade and globalization. Recent efforts to bring in men's experiences and concerns in reproductive health debates, for example, have led to research and policy that obscure women's specific realities. It is not a question of mainstreaming "gender" into policy as it stands. Rather it is necessary to search for data that bring out the differences for women and men and therefore new frameworks that can challenge old male biases, as well as class, ethnic, and racial biases, in research and policy. Knowledge of women continues to be the hardest to come by and policy still fails to differentiate between men and women's gendered experiences, particularly among the poor. Poor women's specific need for primary health care, sexual and reproductive rights is too often marginalized from "mainstream" economic and health issues. Therefore it is important to maintain a strategic gender perspective that keeps the spotlight on the economic and social conditions that determine women's health and well-being.

The Global Trade Regime and Women's Employment and Health

An important recent article by *The Cornerhouse* compiles many civil society groups' writings on women's health in an effort to show that trade liberalization is not gender neutral.[1] Mariama Williams from International Gender and Trade Network is quoted: "Most often, international trade is seen as a technical, class-and-gender-neutral process . . . Yet, none of this can occur without the involvement of women's and men's labor. None of this can occur without the active involvement of the reproductive sector in producing food for domestic consumption, in producing and nurturing labor, and in caring for the environment."[2]

The Cornerhouse paper along with many other trade and health analysts argues that it is no longer UN agencies such as the World Health Organization or UNFPA working with the relevant ministries that determine health policy.[3] Rather it is the loans and policies of the World Bank which directly influence health policy and health systems along with the World Trade Organization. Today's trade agreements cover not only tariffs and quotas but also agricultural products, services, intellectual property rights, government procurement and overseas investment. Many of these agreements require countries to allow competition in health care, water, education and energy services, opening up the way for privatization and commercialization. These all have specific impacts on poor women's health. In a quick review of the literature from civil society groups we can point to the following impacts discussed below: agriculture, farming, health and safety in the work and home and wider environmental concerns.[4]

The World Trade Organization's Agreement on Agriculture (AoA) has been instrumental in liberalizing world agriculture with some devestating results according to the *Cornerhouse*, worsening rural poverty and deepening gender and class inequalities.[5] For many poor women farmers there are no benefits from increased production of cash crops, the primary aim of AoA, since women are largely engaged in agriculture for household or local consumption. As countries comply with WTO and cash group needs, household food security is weakened with women bearing the brunt of having to secure livelihoods and food for their families. The *Cornerhouse* study points out, for example, that large-scale agriculture reform in the Philippines has led to a massive migration of largely women from displaced families to find work in towns or overseas. The expansion of TNC-controlled commercial crop production has exacerbated women's lack of access to land, water, seeds, and other inputs.

Another concern in the agricultural sector that has direct impact on women's health, is the WTO's requirement that health and safety legislation not restrict trade. This requirement has undermined regulations governing pesticides. As a result, women working in this sector have an increased incidence of miscarriages, still births, delayed pregnancy, and birth defects. Their general health is also at risk from pesticide residues in food because of their higher levels of body fat.[6]

Domestic laws and regulations intended to protect health or the environment can be considered by WTO rulings as obstacles to trade. Poor countries are therefore obliged to change laws to comply with trade agreements. Poor women in these countries either at the workplace or in the home are therefore becoming more susceptible to harmful substances or products.[7]

Another major trade issue—the privatization of drinking water—directly impacts poor women because of their responsibilities in the household for sanitation and clean drinking water. As they are first in line in gathering and using water they are also more susceptible to water-borne diseases. Similiarly, because poor women take charge of their family's health, the intellectual property restrictions in trade agreements can restrict their access to medicines or make them more expensive.[8]

Beyond the general health issues, there are also concerns of the impact of WTO on the safety and health measures in the workplace. As Das and Grown point out, trade liberalization in Southern countries has increased paid work opportunities for many women.[9] In the year 2000, women made up between 30 and 45 percent of the manufacturing workforce in Latin America, Asia, and Africa. In the export industries of South East Asia, women make up over 80 percent of the workforce. However these women invariably have the less skilled jobs, lowest pay, and worst working conditions. They are more likely to be laid off and be affected by economic downturns. On top of health risks due to unsafe conditions in the workplace, the unpaid work within the household for women, particularly in times of economic downturn, increases along with the stress and toil and poor health conditions overall.

Even in the service sector where women take up the majority of jobs and where pay and conditions are relatively better, women are still relegated to lower pay and have little health or other security.[10] As the rules of the WTO's General Agreement on Trade in Services (GATS) push service liberalization, local providers are forced to compete with powerful transnationals undermining working conditions and long-term security.[11]

Globalization and Women's Health "on the Ground"

The overall negative impact of trade and globalization on women can be seen not only in the debates around the WTO and GATS agreements—it can also be understood in the reports from women's groups working "on the ground" to overcome the worst effects of globalization. It is here that you vividly see women are struggling in their daily lives to live and survive and resist globalization. The many stories and case studies now being compiled by gender-sensitive journalists around the world, NGOs, and social movements active in rural areas and urban slums show how women are battling it out amongst worsening living conditions, where health systems fail to reach them and poverty exposes them to multiple health risks.[12] These stories, however, rarely make it to the powerful international decision-making tables. They may become figures or accompanying charts but their stories are rarely counted among those making decisions.

For example, the life and health of migrant women, even if it is recognized just how many poor women are now migrating to ensure their family's livelihoods or to escape unbearable economic and social issues at home, are invisible in discussions on health and rights as their lives fall in between different national legislations.[13] Many migrant domestic workers are often unable to access health services or exercise their reproductive rights even in situations of abuse because of language, lack of legal knowledge, and/or restricted access to health services. In addition they can be afraid to speak out about their employer or ask for time off because of their concern for job security. Even in agencies that deal with migration, the swift changes in globalization means that many policies are outdated and do not take into consideration specific gender concerns.[14]

Grown rightly speaks about the "flow of ideas" as an important aspect of globalization. The flow of ideas among different women's health and rights groups in the last decade has been phenomenal.[15] In not only academic studies but also in what is called "gray literature" there is a wealth of information about experiences and perspectives on different women's health well-being and globalization. The studies of groups like Isis Manila, ARROW, Development Alternatives with Women for a New Era (DAWN), and Women's Global Network for Reproductive Rights (WGNRR) gather case studies by women-led NGOs dealing "on the ground" with issues as they are happening and documenting them in websites, newsletters, and advocacy reports that are strategically timed to bring attention to decision makers.[16]

Listservs and the Internet allow an important flow of information about how women are organizing to confront the health and rights problems they face. These electronic discussions, websites, and the local, national, and regional meetings through which campaigns are organized are key strategic points for dialogue and ultimately action.

Gray literature and the whole process around which it is generated is a key source of knowledge for the "global" flow of ideas on the nexus of globalization, gender, and health. It is in these exchanges that a complex picture about global and multilateral agreements and its impact on women are shared and understood.

The ICPD Cairo process is illustrative of this informal knowledge sector of women's networking, negotiation, and advocacy that has had a major impact globally as well as on the ground. The intensive process of networking, advocacy, and organizing of women's reproductive health and rights groups for the Cairo 1994 meeting as well as the ensuing +5 and +10 regional campaigns has produced a paradigm shift in population and health policy, bringing gender relations and women's rights to the center of discussions around reproductive health, challenging demography, and medical knowledge as well as the gender bias in national and international population and health policy and the statistics on which it is based.[17]

The translation and ownership of the Cairo agenda as a cornerstone policy document that impacts the lives of both women and men has been carried out not only by the United Nations, government civil servants, and politicians but also by women's groups, media groups, and local organizations. These latter agents have translated the global agreement into a reality and continue to pressure decision makers, specifically those with the purse strings, to put the Cairo agreements into action.[18]

Women's Health and Rights and the Millennium Development Goals

An interesting debate in this regard is the latest set of policy concerns by the international development community on the Millennium Development

Goals (MDGs).[19] The MDGs are a UN-wide process designed to cut poverty in half by 2015. The Goals are a set of measurable benchmarks of national efforts to eradicate extreme poverty and hunger; achieve universal primary education; promote gender equality and empower women; reduce child mortality; improve maternal health; combat HIV/AIDS, malaria, and other diseases; ensure environmental sustainability; and develop a global partnership for development.

Health and gender in these goals are officially treated as cross-cutting issues. Many civil society groups, however, are concerned that not enough is known about how to reach the MDG 3 (Promoting Gender Equality and the Empowerment of Women), MDG 4 and MDG 5 (Improving Maternal Health and Reduce Child Mortality), MDG 6 (Reversing the Spread of HIV/AIDS), and MDG 8 (Building a Global Partnership for Development), the latter being concerned in particular with trade issues and Northern countries responsibilities to provide resources to ensure the other goals are met.[20]

Women's health and right groups are concerned that the Cairo and Beijing agreements are not realistically represented in the MDGs. The framing of the MDGs, partly because they lacked a clear consultative process, seems a decade behind the gender debates and is being influenced by the U.S. government and other countries that have a negative approach to women's health and rights. They are also concerned about the use of a too technical approach—so that the economic and political reasons for why health systems fail to provide the basic health care needed to prevent maternal mortality are not tackled. Reducing maternal mortality requires funding and a reform of health systems that addresses the problems of the decimation of the public health system through privatization and structural adjustment policies. Beyond financial provisions a strong health system recovery must also include further outreach and education of the population in ways that take into account how neglected health is the "norm" for poor people—therefore health systems have to be seen as more than just delivery systems, and instead as a core social institution that can tackle the complex issues around equity, social exclusion, and gender bias.[21]

Around the MDGs, women's health and rights groups are pushing to ensure that poverty is understood as more than income poverty. They argue that to address poverty given the existing power structures radical reforms are needed. Health systems have to provide care throughout a women's life cycle starting at an early age, including antenatal care. In this sense maternal mortality and morbidity as a "health" issue has to be seen not just in relation to disease but in relation to cross-cutting concerns of "human resources for health," "ensuring access to health" and "finance for health." This approach immediately links the concerns to Goal 8 around economic, trade, and partnership and gives women the chance to be at the same table to discuss how maternal health has to be considered at the heart of the political and economic MDG discussions, not put to one side as a technical, biomedical, or a women's issue.

Proposal for Alliance Building for Research and Policy

The struggle for women's health and rights in today's global context is essentially a political one. In order to address inequalities in macroeconomic, social, and scientific agendas women's groups are collaborating with social movements striving for health and social justice. Working with the People's Health Movement, for instance, WGNRR highlights general health issues as well as the reproductive and sexual rights aspects of health. Feminist activists from around the world have attended international meetings such as the World Social Forums in recent years.[22] One recommendation would be for researchers and policy makers to seek out the knowledge of women's groups and to form an alliance with them in order to address the critical issue of removing the gender bias in academic and scientific work as well as mainstream health, development, and trade policies.

This will require dialogues among policy, academic, and women's groups working from sound knowledge and empirical evidence. Political savvy will also be needed in order to ensure that trade equity and gender equality and thereby women's health and rights are addressed in a number or areas (individual relationships, households, and communities, in health facilities and care systems, in funding priorities, and in national and international trade policies). The example of the ICPD indicates that there can be a multifaceted process that engages health professionals and researchers, advocacy groups, women's groups, other community-based movements, legislators, and policy makers. A similar process, perhaps harnessed to the Millennium Development Goals, now needs to look at the policy changes required to create an economic global environment responsive to ensuring women's health and well-being.

In this process, NGOs will no doubt continue to play a strong advocacy role both with the public and with policy makers, as well as providing much needed services (technical and informational) to women. Researchers need to be politically engaged while working alongside NGOs. Such an alliance will provide qualitative and quantitative analyses, which will record the changes in women's well-being and health issues and direct policy changes. With both parties contributing to this research/activist agenda, key policy agreements for women's health such as the MDGs, Alma Ata, and Cairo[23] agendas, can be promoted as innovative ways to collaborate, pool funding, and engage in research as well as strategic actions are also pursued.

Notes

1. The Cornerhouse (2004), A decade after Cairo: Women's health in a free market economy, *June Briefing 3.1.*
2. Ibid., pp. 15–16.
3. Meri Koivusalo (1999), World Trade Organization and Trade-creep in health and social policies, *GASPP Occasional Papers 4,* Helsinki (available: www.stakes.fo/gaspp); David Woodward (2003), Trading health for profit: The implications of the GATS and trade in health services for health in developing countries, www.ukglobalhealth.org; Kasturi Sen (2003), *Restructuring Health Services: Changing Contexts and Comparative Perspectives,* London: Zed Books.
4. There are many Websites that have gathered data on health and trade concerns see e.g., GASPP www.stake.fo/gaspp; World Development Movement www.wdm.org.uk; John Hilary's work featured on the Save the Children Website www.savethechildren.org.uk and analysis on trade and health www.cpath.org and also the series of articles in *WHO Bulletin 79/(9),* 2001 (available: http://www.who.int/docstore/bulletin). In terms of data on gender differentials in employment please see studies by Beneria and Felman (Beneria, Lourdes, and Susan Felman (eds.) (2002), *Unequal Burden: Economic Crisis, Persistent Poverty and Women's Work* Boulder, CO: Westview Press), the recent ILO report on Fair Globalization, the UNIFEM's reports on the World's Women, as well as UNDP Human Development all of which contain national tables that look at women and men's employment situation. These can be viewed on their websites (http://www.ilo.org; http://www.unifem.org; http://www.undp.org. In addition, for studies on the women's conditions in export zones see the International Gender and Trade Network website www.genderandtrade.net and studies from the 2001 UNRISD project on Globalization, Export-Oriented Employment for Women and Social Policy (http://www.unrisd.org) a study women and poverty please see Siyanda Issue 25, October 2004 (http://www/siyanda.org).
5. The Cornerhouse, A decade after Cairo.
6. L. Doyal (2004), Women, health and global restructuring: Setting the scene, *Development* 47: 2.
7. W. Harcourt (2003), Editorial: The reproductive health and rights agenda under attack, *Development* 46: 2.
8. S. Razavi, ed. (2002), *Shifting Burdens Gender and Agrarian Change under Neoliberalism,* Bloomfield: UNRISD and Kumarian Press.
9. D. Maitreyi and C. Grown (2002), Trade liberalization, women's employment, and reproductive health: What are the linkages and entry points for research and policy? Working Paper, International Center for Research on Women, Washington, DC.
10. J. Delahanty and M. Shefali (1999), From social movements to social clauses: Assessing strategies for improving women's health and labour conditions in the garment sector, *Development* 42: 4.
11. Woodward, Trading Health for Profit. S. Sexton (2001), Trading health care away? GATS, public services and privatization, *Corner House Briefing 23, July*;

B. Rodenberg (2004), Gender and poverty reduction—new conceptual approaches in international development cooperation (available: http://www.siyanda.org/static/rodeberg_genpoverty.htm).

12. W. Harcourt and K. Mumtaz (2002), Fleshly politics, women's bodies, politics and globalization, *Development* 45:1; For a review of some of these groups see Window on the World section of *Development* 45.1 (2002), which lists global and regional women's groups, see also the website of the Women's Feature Service (http://www.wfsnews.org) and DAWN (http://www.dawn.org.fi) that carry regular updates of women's experiences in the South.

13. P. Allotey (2003), Guest editorial: Is health a fundamental right for Migrants? *Development* 46: 3; L. Agustin (2003), Forget victimization: Granting agency to migrants, *Development* 46: 3.

14. See the special issue of *Development* 46.3 (2003) on migration, citizenship, identify and rights that reviews this concern.

15. R. P. Petchesky (2003), *Global Prescriptions: Gendering Health and Human Rights*, London: Zed Books.

16. The WGNRR has an extensive set of links to different groups working in reproductive rights and health, violence against women around the world http://www.wgnrr.org. See also the edition of *Development* 46: 2 (2003) on globalization, reproductive rights and health and in particular the Window on the World section, which lists women's organizations working on reproductive rights and health. (see also: S. Rowbotham and S. Linkogle, eds. (2001), *Women Resist Globalization: Mobilizing for Livelihoods and Rights*, London: Zed Books; C. Wichterich (2000), *The Globalized Woman: Reports from a future of inequality*, Perth: Spinifex Press, London: Zed Books.)

17. R. P. Petchesky, *Global Prescriptions: Gendering Health and Human Rights*; A. Cornwall and A. Welbourn, eds. (2002), *Realizing Rights: Transforming Approaches to Sexual and Reproductive Well-being*, London: Zed Books; W. Harcourt (1999), Editorial: Reproductive Health and Rights: Putting Cairo into Action, *Development* 42: 1.

18. R. P. Petchesky, *Global Prescriptions: Gendering Health and Human Rights*.

19. See www.un.org/millenniumgoals.

20. Women's International Coalition for Economic Justice (2004), Seeking Accountability on Women's Human Rights: Women Debate the UN Millennium Development Goals, New York: WICEJ (Available: http://www.wicej.org).

21. W. Harcourt (2004), *Gender and the MDGs*, Amsterdam: NCDO.

22. Women's International Coalition for Economic Justice (2004), Seeking Accountability on Women's Human Rights: Women Debate the UN Millennium Development Goals.

23. For more on the Cairo process see also the series of newsletter and articles in DAWN Informs since 2003 on the DAWN website (http//www/dawn.org.fi).

4

Globalization, Health, and the Engendering of Resistance in Everyday Life

Jerry Spiegel and Cynthia Lee Andruske

Introduction—Situating Resistance in the Era of Globalization

The term "globalization" has become commonplace in the vocabulary of the twenty-first century. However, depending on one's gender, geographic location, and position within the social hierarchy, perspectives on this phenomenon vary considerably. While global forces at play in domains such as economics, trade, work, and the environment are extensively discussed at a "macro" level, an emerging challenge for researchers has been to discern the pathways of globalization in the daily lives and health of individuals and communities.

Lee defines globalization as "the processes which are changing the nature of human action by reducing barriers of time, space and ideas which have separated people and nations in a number of spheres of action including, health and environment, social and knowledge and technology and political and institutional."[1] Although this definition refers to human action, it tends to ignore the concept of *human agency*.[2] Individuals are, after all, not merely objects to be affected by global forces, but subjects who, in turn, can affect the interplay of these forces as they carry out their social roles, resisting as well as bearing their effects.

Peoples' experience of globalization is intimately shaped by their specific circumstances and Doyal explicitly identifies gender as a critical consideration in relation to global health.[3] In particular, she argues that the effects of economic globalization on the division of labor and the distribution of resources have varying consequences on the health of both men and women. In this regard, attention has also been drawn to globalization's association with increased disparities in general[4] and a feminization of poverty in particular.[5] While gender refers broadly to "socially learned behavior and expectations that distinguish between masculinity and femininity,"[6] attention has been especially focused on the impacts of globalization on women as a particularly vulnerable group, socially, economically, and politically. This analysis presents examples of women's resistance in the face of such vulnerability.

Desai has observed that "changing gender relations . . . have engendered the discourse of global health and raised the particular concern of women's health to the forefront of discussions about health."[7] The focus of this contribution is, thus, based on Naples and Desai's contention that

> rather than view globalization as something that occurs "out there" and that is therefore distant from the everyday lives and activities of particular actors, . . . global economic and political changes are manifest in the daily lives and struggles of women and other members of communities in different parts of the world in ways that are often hidden from view in analyses of globalization that start from the perspective of multinational corporations, transnational organizations, and international political institutions.[8]

Dorothy Smith has contended that we should begin our research of the "everyday" by dissecting issues affecting individuals' daily lives, particularly examining women's gendered roles as caregivers.[9] In contrast, neo-classical labor theory examines individuals as units of analysis and focuses on the amount of *paid* work they perform in the marketplace, not the household.[10] Today, as economic trends have shifted, many women carry a double burden as paid workers in the labor market as well as unpaid caregivers in the home.

In this chapter, we concentrate on this gendered double burden, examining the care work that women perform in the home for their families and in public spaces for others. This is not to deny the significance of how role redefinitions affect men. However, as a key effect of globalization has been a commodification and privatization of broad dimensions of everyday life, this chapter specifically considers how women are acting to resist or reshape policies that may be positively or negatively created by global restructuring at a variety of levels—from formal politics to drawing "lessons around the kitchen table."[11]

To explore how resistance can be conceptualized in the context of globalization and gender, we first provide a framework for integrating the concept of human agency into our understanding of globalization and its effects on well-being and health. We then apply this framework to two quite diverse settings: the first, where the impacts of globalization have tended to marginalize women directly in the context of expanding economic globalization, in this case examining a high-income country, Canada; and the second, where impacts on a community situated outside the "mainstream" of the forces of globalization influence gender and health, in this circumstance, a very distinct low-income country, Cuba. Finally we consider the implications for how the notion of resistance can more broadly be considered in the virtually omnipresent context of globalization.

Tracing Community Impacts of Globalization: The Social Reproduction of "Care"

Discussion of the forces of globalization often concentrates on the examination of structural forces that drive and influence choices at different social levels. However, Appadurai has drawn attention to the significance of sociocultural factors by suggesting that global pressures can be traced through a distinct set of "scapes" or dimensions of interaction classified as:

- finanscapes—the flow of global capital and direction/control of economic resources;
- ideoscapes—the messages invested with political-ideological meaning that limit options;
- mediascapes—the images produced by mass media to produce meaning;
- technoscapes—the flow of technology, dictating what is technically feasible; and
- ethnoscapes—the flow of people, tourists, refugees, immigrants, guest workers, etc.[12]

While our understanding of how a wide range of social and economic determinants affect population health and well-being has mushroomed in the past decade,[13] the focus has tended to be on proximate forces, in local and national contexts. In contrast, the "scapes" framework provides a basis for considering global pressures that transcend local settings to serve as "determinants for identified health determinants."[14] As portrayed in figure 4.1, scapes provide a context for "tracing influences that can affect and constrain the options available to individuals and social groupings: laying the terrain for either homogeneity and domination by forces dictated by the power centers of globalization, or a heterogeneity and resistance, if not the development of new values through these interactions."[15]

In considering how globalizing forces act through the scapes outlined above, it is essential to more closely examine impacts on everyday life at the

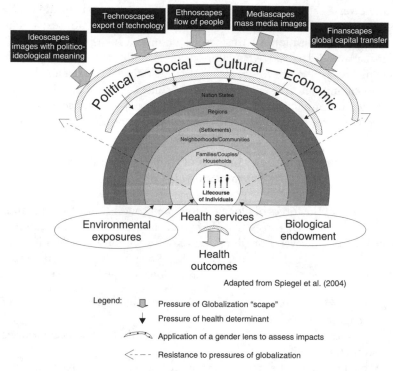

Figure 4.1   Impacts of globalization and health determinants: Integrating a gendered analysis.[16]

Note: Adapted from Spiegal et al. (2004).

community level, thereby starting from the "bottom up" to examine globalizing effects and interactions. The pressures of the *scapes* affect both high- and low-income countries resulting in altered policies that affect the work, well-being, and ultimately, the health of their citizenry in multiple areas leading to diminished government power to provide for individuals' needs.[17] The scapes, then, interact with each other at the same time as they exert pressures on various health determinants. As the diagram in figure 4.1 suggests, gender should be considered at each of these interactions in order to distinguish differentiated impacts of the scapes. Furthermore, the diagram also suggests that as the scapes exert these influences both directly and indirectly, the impact is potentially mediated and transmitted at different intermediary social levels from global to national to regional, until the individual is eventually reached. In turn, there is a potential for resistance to manifest itself at the different levels. The consequent notion of resistance, then, is one that is very much bound by the relationships established within this realm of scapes. It is also one that ultimately calls for a consideration of the *substance* of the issues at stake—not just the *form* of resistance to social forces to which one is in contact.

As individuals attempt to fulfill needs that promote health and well-being within their everyday lives, they encounter points of tension with institutions and experts that result in political struggles to interpret, fulfill, or procure ways to meet these needs, particularly, in the public domain or social spaces.[18] One way to resist or reshape opportunities is through *self-directed learning projects* as they are embedded within the social contexts and fields of our everyday lives, which are in turn influenced by multiple scapes.[19] When individuals oppose those with more power and take control of their learning to meet their needs, these learning projects often become political acts, thereby bringing them "into direct conflict with powerful entrenched interests"[20] and structures. This tendency itself challenges the impact of globalization's "ideoscapes" that foster conformity and discourage resistance, but does it within the space afforded—though not necessarily challenging the fundamental relationship that provokes the resistance.

This chapter explores this "resistance" or "reshaping" further in two very different circumstances: women on welfare in a high-income country; and resistance to marginalizing external forces in a low-income one. Both instances involve the reshaping of opportunities to allow individuals to best fit their choices and their everyday lives.

A High Income Country (British Columbia, Canada)—Women Strategizing a Transition from Welfare

One of the less visible locations of women's resistance occurs in their individual relationships with the welfare system. In this British Columbia (BC) example, examples of resistance are demonstrated in women's attempts to meet their own health needs on welfare while simultaneously caring for the health of their families and their communities.

The case study presented here is based on interviews with 23 women from 1998 to 2001 in the communities of Chilliwack and Abbotsford. The women were primarily single mothers, including three from minority groups. They ranged in age from 27 to 55 and were seeking to make transitions from welfare to paid work and education.[21] These women worked on their own behalf to strategize, resist, and reshape health and welfare policies as well as confront gendered views of women in their everyday experiences. To better understand the women's struggles and the effects of global influences on the policies that affected them, the economic and political climate within British Columbia must first be understood.

Like many areas of the world, the 1990s brought British Columbia global financial and ideological pressures that prompted a restructuring of government-provided social support programs, leading to a streamlining of social benefits and increased privatization. To respond to these forces, the provincial premier, Mike Harcourt of the social democratic New Democratic Party, reviewed the provincial economy, skills, and education of the labor force that was fast becoming polarized between those possessing highly developed human capital and those who were marginalized, unemployed, and on welfare. Through a series of Summits during the 1990s, Harcourt's government revised education, training, and welfare policies in order to move more people off welfare and into the marketplace. The revisions aimed to "train more and train better in a fiscally responsible way to better equip British Columbians with the skills they . . . require to succeed."[22]

At the time, overarching political ideas represented as policies, societal values, and popular media portrayed women without skills as unable to enter the highly technical global work spaces. The government began to label women on welfare as "problems." Many of these "problems" were single mothers who resisted the government's programs. They felt the government was steering them toward low-paying dead-end jobs, which could lead to a poorer quality of life while ignoring the important role women played as mothers and caretakers of their children. As one single mother pointed out, "I do have a job. I'm choosing to stay home. I'm raising my son. That's a job as I'm raising the next generation of citizens."[23]

Indeed, the single mothers in this study found their gendered role as mothers to be a 24-hour 365-days-a-year unpaid job, particularly since they had no partners to help with parenting, performing home chores, dealing with welfare and daycare bureaucracies, educational institutions, or other agencies. They were performing not only care-giving work, but also juggling paid work while in some cases also attempting to further their education. As one single mother said, "When my boss from my part-time job calls me with extra shifts, I must try to figure out how I can get one of my babysitters at a moment's notice. They are not always available as one is in high school, and the other has her own family. I need to work to care for my son, so I can't afford to turn down the extra work, but I can't leave him alone, so I must be creative in resolving my babysitting to ensure my son's safety." Clearly, this woman's experience illustrates that women are not, as policy makers perceived, "doing nothing."

Thus, their unpaid roles as caregivers served to marginalize single mothers from policy makers who only saw their lack of marketable skills, insufficient training, and dependency on welfare.[24] Unlike training and education provided for many men in the workplace, the government identified the employment needs of women on welfare with more gendered types of work, such as waitressing, service, and other low-paying jobs that did not require further education. By relegating women to such low-paying, part-time jobs with no or few health, medical, dental, or other benefits, and with no potential for career advancement, women on welfare who were being moved to these jobs were actually becoming even more vulnerable in many ways. For example, their health was in jeopardy due to a lack of nutritious food, adequate health benefits, and the double burden of their roles as single parents and low-wage workers.

While BC education, skills, and training polices were under revision, so were the welfare policies, social programs and benefits, and subsidies available to individuals receiving payments or attempting to transition from welfare. By 1995, when the new BC welfare policy took effect, it focused on "the growing gap between those with good jobs and those without, many of whom have become dependent on our income security system. This dependency has, in many cases, become long term. [Thus], the best form of income security . . . comes from participation in the labor market."[25] Welfare recipients, particularly single mothers, had been redefined as needing to become taxpaying citizens with jobs which would "enable members of a household to be a part of society."[26] The transition toward workforce integration, however, was hampered for many women by de facto cuts in medical, dental, and childcare support programs. As with the women relegated to low-paying jobs who also lacked in basic benefits, women on welfare found alternative ways to meet these needs, thereby reclaiming some of the control over their individual health care conditions, those of their children's as well as their communities thereby becoming social actors and strategic agents. They did so primarily through the use of social support networks and self-directed or informal learning projects.[27]

Social support networks in this case include not only the community of other women on welfare but also other government agents who these women recruited to advocate for their causes. For example, in the BC welfare system, medical and mental health professionals decided what conditions were worthy of health care time and money. As one woman explained, "The social system relies on physicians to decide what I'm allowed and not allowed. I'm sick of being tested, poked, prodded, and made ill by their diagnoses. I'll only let them go so far just to prove to them I can't work." Medical conditions had to be obvious and fit a prescribed, approved government model; if they did not, the single mothers here were questioned and immediately suspect. However, quite a few women in this study challenged government demands that doctors document and prove that they were unfit to work. A number of women had "invisible" health problems, like allergies, stomach problems, depression, or others, whose causes and existence might not be easy to diagnose. Since the problems were not easily observable, doctors tended to discount them. When one woman in this study asked her doctor to prescribe additional food benefits through a particular social program because of her irritable bowel syndrome, her doctor told her, "You need to be in a wheelchair to be getting [help from that program]."In response, this woman recruited the help of her advocate because, "I found I couldn't survive." Her advocate helped her "to fight for more money. She fought for me and did a very good job on my behalf and got me [the benefits]. It's only $100 bucks more, but it did help with food and other health costs." This woman's story shows not only individual resistance but resistance also conducted through enlisted support.

Utilizing support networks can also mean *enhancing* them. Some of the women interviewed for this case study actually sought to make greater inroads into public spaces by cultivating healthier communities. For example, one of the women interviewed actively sought to care for more vulnerable and marginalized individuals by creating educational resources on how to navigate through policies and health entitlements in order to better meet their own health needs. An immigrant herself, she established a resource center where individuals could inform themselves of their rights, government policies, and available resources. Through her own experiences as an immigrant woman on welfare, she had learned that the health needs of immigrants were not being met, nor were they even informed of their rights and entitlements. In response to this lack of knowledge, this center was intended to be "an open door. You have to care for people; otherwise, it's not going to work." More than an information center, however, she added another dimension to creating a healthy community by conducting job skill trainings for women on welfare. As she pointed out, "If I'm going to take women, I want to know when they leave they got something from here." Through these resources, she worked against the demoralization of women that she had too often seen occur at some government welfare-to-work training programs. Instead, she worked toward the empowerment of her community. "I have lived as an educational tool," she says, "by opening a road to people. I am giving them power by giving information for them to fight, not to do things for them. They learn how to do their own things."

While enhancing support networks through the establishment of a community information center, this woman also worked to enable *self-directed learning projects*, or, for example, situations in which women resisted the system and doctors' control by educating themselves about their health conditions. In one case, a woman had been misdiagnosed about her health problems and over-medicated with drugs. Finding that the drugs were making her worse, this woman decided to explore alternate and healthier forms of treatment that existed. She conducted extensive Internet and library searches to find out more about her medical conditions, thus challenging her doctor's expertise. In the end, she decided to use yoga and meditation to help her condition rather than the prescribed medication. This research enabled this woman, like others in the study, to seek and find information, ask questions, challenge policies to gain access to health care, and seek out doctors with holistic health care perspectives. Indeed, despite the reluctance of some doctors, a number of women were able to cultivate similar support networks to assist them with their health needs.

Overall, even though the women in this study may not have defined themselves as health care workers, they were, in fact, acting as creative, strategic agents to reshape policies, institutions, workplaces, and their communities in order to create healthier spaces. In the process, they navigated through different social, policy, and institutional structures that influenced their health and well-being—and encountered the scapes that were shaping their immediate environment. Simultaneously, these women shared what they learned as they resisted policies and social structures with other women on welfare. Through their resistance or reshaping of the forces acting upon them, the women developed a social policy that served to improve their own health and that of their communities.

A Low-Income Country Case (Cayo Hueso, Havana, Cuba)—Urban Regeneration Outside the Mainstream of Globalization

If globalization can be conceived of as a set of systemic relationships that shape local determinants of health and influence options for daily life and personal choice, then another expression of resistance to consider can be found in a society that lies outside the very system of globalization. In the following case study, the solidarity of resisting an external force, such as globalization itself, is the operating paradigm, albeit with gender still serving as a key transcending factor. For this analysis, we now turn to Cuba, a country noted for its high levels of health despite low levels of economic growth,[28] and more specifically, to Cayo Hueso, an urban inner-city Havana neighborhood badly in need of renovations.

The study on which this section is based was conducted by a team of Canadian and Cuban researchers in partnership with the local community. The fundamental purpose of this collaboration was to evaluate the impact of a multicomponent mobilization of resources to improve the quality of life in the community. This mobilization had been organized between 1995 and 1999 as a response to the severe economic crisis that was then being experienced. The discussion below is drawn from a sub-study that examined the role of women as agents of change during this period.[29] Before beginning the analysis, however, it is important to understand its context.

Following its 1959 revolution, the Caribbean island nation of Cuba became isolated from the emerging network of economic globalization, primarily as a result of the trade embargo enforced by the United States. From the early 1960s to 1990s, Cuba was still able to protect its national sovereignty in the geopolitical environment of the Cold War through a strategic alliance with the Soviet Union. Over this period, the internal disparities in income and living conditions that are so pronounced in many Latin American and Caribbean countries were effectively countered in Cuba through an ambitious and comprehensive transformation in the social order that promoted equity alongside universal access to health and education.

In Latin American culture (including Cuba), women's gender roles have traditionally occupied the private domain of the household, while men's roles have occupied the public sphere of the community. Motherhood has been particularly revered and indeed continues to be an important part of women's lives. Following the 1959 Revolution, however, the Cuban government established a variety of women's and community-based "mass organizations" that maintain links with the state, including the Federation of Cuban Women (FMC) and the Committees for the Defense of the Revolution (CRD). Through its subsequent actions, the Cuban government further legitimized and reinforced motherhood as a gendered role[30] and pursued other measures related to the role of women. In an effort to equalize gender roles and ensure that both men and women were sharing domestic household labor and were treated equally, the Cuban government passed the Maternity Law in 1974 and the Family Code in 1974, the political Constitution in 1976, Work Code in 1985, and other constitutional reforms in 1992.[31] The Law of Work Protection and Hygiene of 1977 and the Law of Social Security and the penal Code in 1979 protected women against dangerous employment and sexual and physical violence. Still, despite the dramatic change in the "legal" position of women in Cuban society and the economy, there was not a comparably dramatic transformation to the preexisting machismo culture and the associated gendered household division of labor, thereby creating the basis for double burdens and associated stresses and pressures.

When the Soviet Union collapsed in the early 1990s, this not only removed a key political ally for Cuba, it also prompted a dramatic (85 percent) decline in Cuba's foreign exchange earnings. This was further reinforced by an intensification of the U.S. trade embargo, harkening very difficult living conditions. This epoch is referred to in Cuba as the "Special Period"—a period most intensely felt from 1990 to 1996, although some argue it extended to the end of the decade. These changes created widespread despair throughout the country and stimulated an increase in illegal emigration, which was in turn exacerbated by an open-door policy in the United States (in ironic contrast to the restricted entry policies that greeted Haitian émigrés at roughly the same time). While there was a widespread fiscal crisis being faced by countries in the Latin American region in the 1990s that was directly associated with an interconnected global "finanscape," Cuba was even more severely affected over this period, due in large part, ironically, to its very exclusion and marginalization from the same economic globalization system. Nevertheless, a distinct characteristic of Cuba's circumstance was the policy latitude it maintained governing the response it adopted in reaction to its predicament. Thus, Cuba's exclusion from the ties of globalization, particularly its independence from neoliberal "ideoscapes" and related direct pressures, created the basis for carving a national strategy of resistance, drawing on fierce national pride, to which it rallied large sectors of the population.

During the Special Period, the Cuban government made it a priority to maintain health standards and then to continue to improve them.[32] An important part of the country's adaptive strategy was to decentralize some levels of decision making from a previously heavily centralized model. At the local community level, this provided a space for participation in the newly created Popular Councils (for Peoples Power), a more immediate order of governance within each municipality. In Central Havana, one of Havana's 15 municipalities, and the country's most densely populated area with 170,000 inhabitants in a relatively small area, there were 5 such units. Our study community, the Popular Council of Cayo Hueso, was a long established neighborhood with a population of approximately 38,000. Within Cayo Hueso, an innovative organizing center the *Taller de Transformación Integral del Barrio* (Integrated Neighborhood Transformation Workshop) had just been established at the time of the Special Period to enhance local abilities to work with other municipal, provincial, and national inter-sectoral councils related to the Healthy Cities' Movement[33] (an example of a global "ideoscape" that did establish a presence on the island in this period). This facilitated the community's ability to determine, define, and prioritize their health needs in order to take collaborative community action.[34] Other Cuban communities subsequently established similar structures based on this model.

A particularly challenging matter to address in the capital city of Havana was housing, a need that had been relatively neglected due in part to a relative emphasis on improving living conditions in other parts of the country.[35] In this context, provincial and municipal governments, non-governmental organizations such as UNICEF, government organizations, community activist, and the neighborhood's *Taller* coordinated efforts to mobilize the plan for urban regeneration of living conditions and well-being in the community.[36] In the following analysis, we examine the gendered roles of women in the efforts to promote community health and how their role represents an actively mobilized "resistance" to the Special Period and the circumstances causing it, which were primarily perceived as being externally imposed.

Through 28 interviews conducted with formal and informal community leaders as well as participation in community workshops, it was observed that the women in the community played the leadership role in organizing community support for the physical labor conducted by workers from various government ministry enterprises to repair houses and neighborhood infrastructure.[37] As expressed in a community meeting "this [the Cayo Hueso Project] was not a construction project, it was a community in action, a mobilization of people." Still, the roles adopted by women in the community tended to conform to traditional caring roles: "We enthusiastically received the construction workers and we gave them a lot of attention—pop, lunch, sometimes we made them salads . . . we cleaned up the construction waste, we created the "Marianas" and when the workers finished we would go to clean"; . . . "I had the responsibility of carrying out cultural activities with the neighborhood children each time they were going to complete a street and we gave them gifts . . ." reported one 55-year-old woman in Cayo Hueso.[38]

Based on the intense and dense community networks, the *Taller* provided a strong volunteer network for recruiting and notifying others via word of mouth about activities and meetings to identify, discuss, problem-solve, and plan actions to resolve community issues. Women used the *communitarias* and *Talleres* as physical, local landmarks to provide credibility for community residents as well as meeting places for foreign collaborators providing much needed financial assistance for local projects. The *Talleres* also served as a gathering place for residents to partake in *diagnosticos* to identify community issues, problem-solve, elicit solutions, and take action with input from residents ranging from children to seniors. In these activities, the women of Cayo Hueso took leading roles to transform and regenerate their urban community in conjunction with the support of the Cuban government and other organizations.

To promote urban regeneration, the people focused on cultural, artistic, and sports capacities and strengths of the people that could be developed and shared without major financial expenditures while group activities promoted individual and community psychological health, potentialities, sociability, economic development, and environmental care of plants and animals. One initiative focused on using environmental brigades to improve physical spaces by creating community gardens for green space for children to play and others to enjoy. Community gardens became very important for the local economy and for planting food to supplement the residents' diets and medicinal plants. Another phenomenon occurred where women began teaching informally to promote the importance of these green spaces. In essence, this was a form of self-directed learning expanded to the community level. As Brookfield would point out, self-directed learning of this type is often political, and it is a catalyst for individuals to regain power and control over their everyday lives. Put in the context of the global influences that created the Special Period, this seems to have held true in Cayo Hueso's case of urban regeneration for community health.

As the women involved in the Cayo Hueso project became politically engaged, using their community networks to promote urban regeneration through community mobilization, they identified themselves as the "mothers of the community"[39] similar to what Collins discusses as "other mothers"[40] and Naples identifies as "activist mothers."[41] In fact, the strategies and the mechanisms the women utilized in the community revitalization activities reflected their gendered roles as mothers, caretakers, and nurturers of their families and households and, ultimately, the community of Cayo Hueso. By examining women within their everyday lives in this period of economic crisis, we were able to observe how women's roles influenced the type of work they performed in Cayo Hueso to create a healthier community. In spite of economic restraints created by the Special Period, the women in Cayo Hueso were able to oppose conditions that created scarce community resources. In this way, their volunteer community roles created a social, civic, physical, and greener environment in their community ultimately promoted a healthier community. As a result, a renewed neighborhood pride emerged and these projects promoted social responsibility to and for the community through their active participation in all aspects of the initiatives.

The despair that was rampant in Cuba during the Special Period had been particularly acute in inner-city districts such as Cayo Hueso that were badly in need of improvements to living conditions. So, in essence, the government action taken together with the active involvement of community members, particularly the volunteer labor of women was a strategic expression of resistance with great meaning at the time. For members of the community, what was at stake was preservation of values that were held dear in response to a crisis situation in addition to a literal improvement of living conditions.

Conclusions

Although Cayo Hueso, Cuba, and Abbotsford and Chilliwack, BC, Canada present very different settings for considering resistance in the context of globalization, gender, and health, an examination of the two cases allows for a broad exploration of the issues at stake. In particular, they provide an opportunity to assess the usefulness of the "scapes" framework that was introduced to help understand the nature of globalization and its impacts. While our case studies focused almost exclusively on gender in relation to women, it is worthwhile to reflect on how approaches to broader issues of gender and health could be addressed.

In the BC case, we clearly delineate how a set of global, fiscal, and ideological pressures have resulted in national and provincial government social program and economic restructuring, which, coupled with various cultural and technological trends, have created and restricted gendered options for a marginal population of women on welfare who lived in the context of a changing demographic environment. It is clear that there was virtually no resistance at play from the very levels of government that were conveying the essentially globally influenced pressures. While the women in the study essentially responded individually in their resistance, they also established loose collective interactions, and have even broadened their resource capacities in their response, facilitated by global development in communication technology. In other case studies illustrating restructuring that occurs in response to global pressures in British Columbia, we have observed profound gendered effects on men as well. This is manifested, for example, through declines in male-dominated, high-income, primary-resource exploitation industries such as forestry alongside a shift to lower-paying service sector positions, producing significant direct and indirect effect to both one's earning power, social role, and position within family relations.

While the BC case is in many ways quite representative of how globalization exerts impacts that are then manifest locally through a series of gendered interactions, the Cuban case presents a rather distinct circumstance to consider. For a variety of reasons, the pressures of globalization have been sharply resisted by the Cuban state, which through further political interactions has produced an isolation that has intensified the impacts of restricting economic development options. In terms of the figure 4.1 framework diagram, global finanscapes and ideoscapes coupled with a sharp national resistance have provoked an even further isolation and economic crisis. This same separation however, has reinforced the resolve to resist even further, and adopt policies that would be strongly rejected by neoliberal orthodoxies, such as Cuba's persistent commitment to protect and strengthen health systems and public services amid a severe fiscal crisis. For individuals who then must suffer the brunt of the consequences in their everyday life, the options in the community of Cayo Hueso were (a) to resist the national and local policies; (b) pursue illegal emigration as an extreme but plausible strategy (that was repeatedly pursued); (c) recede from any involvement; or (d) join forces with the local campaign to resist the pressures that the community was undergoing, in the context of the national pride and defiance "ideoscape" produced nationally.

The view of resistance in the Cayo Hueso case deviates from conventional approaches that tend to consider resistance solely in relation to more proximate political and social forces. Some, in fact, may be very reluctant to even consider community mobilization in collaboration with government involvement with anything other than considerable skepticism. Nevertheless, a perspective that dismisses the notion of the state playing a positive role is in fact quite consistent with neoliberal views of the state that relegate such supportive activities to "civil society," implicitly assuming that it is not the state's role to do this. To a large degree, this is precisely one of the "ideoscape" poles (i.e., that certain political options should not even merit consideration), and hence, such a position cannot be accepted as an analytical perspective that is open to examining globalization pressure and the resistance to this. In the Cuban case, what is truly remarkable, after all, is that in a decade when health systems across the globe were subject to serious cutbacks in response to fiscal restructuring, it is Cuba, a country with one of the sharpest economic declines, that managed to retain and even reinforce its capacities. That certain strata of the population would support such a policy orientation is accordingly quite conceivable, regardless of any other considerations; the fact that this defies the conventional global approach further suggests that the application of the concept of "resistance" may indeed be especially appropriate. Beyond this consideration, however, there is still ample need to explore persisting internal contradictions, such as machismo gender roles despite the adoption of formal legal rights for women. Ironically, in Cuba today, the expansion of tourism is now heightening the systematic impacts of globalization.

In both the Canadian and Cuban cases presented, then, the consideration of the impacts of globalization at an everyday level provides insights that are not readily discernible from a macro review of policy. The use of scapes promises to be a vehicle that can allow a consideration of many influences that can have a bearing on both impact and resistance. These cases move well beyond "disease specific" approaches to understanding global health and instead explore the impacts and relationships of global factors that affect health by setting the very context for more proximate health determinants.[42]

This chapter has represented an attempt to bring women's "hidden" unpaid health work into the public discourse—not leave it "between the institutional spheres"[43] as it challenges forces imposed by the finanscapes, ethnoscapes, technoscapes, mediascapes, and ideoscapes. The focus has been to start with the everyday as problematic and to examine women's gendered roles, the impact global forces have on their health needs, and how women resist or seek to fulfill their needs in spite of the structures created through social relationships and global forces as scapes. As the gendered roles of caring and the marginalization from the "marketplace" become less demarcated between men and women, the implications can transcend a pure focus on "women" per se, thus considering broader gendered implications.

To better understand the relationship and linkages between globalization on health and women's gendered roles through their unpaid care work, and between informal and social learning in maintaining, renewing, and regenerating the health of communities, more research needs to be undertaken. To do this, women at the grassroots level, community organizations, social networks, health professionals, and adult educators all need to work together to explore these issues and relationships impacted by global forces.

Notes

1. K. Lee (2000), Globalization and health policy: A review of the literature and proposed research and policy agenda, in A. Bambas, J. A. Casas, H. A Drayon, and A. Valdes, eds., *Health & Human Development in the New Global Economy: The Contributions and Perspectives of Civil Society in the Americas* (pp. 15–41), Washington: Pan American Health Organization, p. 19.
2. P. Bourdieu (1977), *Outline of a Theory of Practice*, Cambridge: Cambridge University Press.
3. L. Doyal (2000), Gender equity in health: Debates and dilemmas, *Social Science & Medicine* 51(6): 931–939; L. Doyal (June 2003), *Understanding Gender, Health and Globalization: Opportunities and Challenges*, paper presented at the Gender, Health, and Globalization Conference at Yale University.
4. G. Cornia and J. Court (2001), *Inequality, Growth and Poverty in the Era of Liberalization and Globalization*, retrieved August 27, 2004 from http://www.wider.unu.edu/publications/policy-brief.htm.
5. S. Razavi (1999), Gendered poverty and wellbeing: Introduction, *Development and Change* 30(3): 409–433; N. Craske (2003), Gender, poverty and social movements, in S. Chant and N. Craske, eds., *Gender in Latin America*, London: Latin American Bureau.
6. V. S. Peterson and A. S. Runyan (1999), *Global Gender Issues*, Boulder, CO: Westview Press, p. 5.
7. M. Desai (June 2003), Gender, health, and globalization: A critical social movement perspective, paper presented at the Gender, Health, and Globalization Conference at Yale University, p. 1.
8. N. A. Naples and M. Desai, eds. (2002), *Women's Activism and Globalization*, New York: Routledge, p. vii.

9. D. Smith (1987), *The Everyday World as Problematic: A Feminist Sociology*, Toronto: University of Toronto Press.

10. S. Butler and S. Seguino (1998), Gender and welfare reform: Redefining the issues, *Journal of Progressive Human Services* 9(2): 51–82.

11. L. Dobson (2001), At the kitchen table: Poor women making public policy, in N. J. Hirschmann and U. Liebert, eds., *Women and Welfare: Theory and Practice in the United States and Europe* (pp. 177–190), New Brunswick, NJ: Rutgers University Press.

12. A. Appadurai (1990), Disjuncture and difference in the global economy, *Theory, Culture & Society* 7: 295–310.

13. R. G. Evans and G. L. Stoddart (2003), Models for population health: Consuming research, producing policy? *American Journal of Public Health* 93(3): 371–379.

14. J. M. Spiegel, R. Labonte, and A. Ostry (2004), Understanding "globalization" as a determinant of health determinants: A critical perspective, *International Journal of Occupational and Environmental Health* 10: 360–367.

15. Ibid., p. 361.

16. Ibid.

17. K. Lee, S. Fustukian, and K. Buse (2002), An introduction to global health policy, in K. Lee, K. Buse, and S. Fustukian, eds., *Health Policy in a Globalizing World* (pp. 3–17), Cambridge: Cambridge University Press, p. 14.

18. N. Fraser (1989), *Unruly Practices: Power, Discourse and Gender in Contemporary Social theory*, Minneapolis, MN: University of Minnesota Press.

19. S. Brookfield (1993), Self-directed learning, political clarity, and the critical practice of adult education, *Adult Education Quarterly* 43(4): 227–242; R. G. Brockett and R. Hiemstra (1991), *Self-Direction in Adult Learning: Perspectives on Theory, Research, and Practice*, London: Routledge.

20. Brookfield, Self-directed learning, political clarity, and the critical practice of adult education, p. 237.

21. C. L. Andruske (2003), *I'm not Sitting on the Couch Eating Bonbons!: Women's Transitions from Welfare to Paid Work and Education*, unpublished doctoral dissertation, University of British Columbia, Vancouver, BC, Canada.

22. British Columbia Institute of Technology (1993), Premier's summit on skills development and training: Skills development and training: Summary of proceedings, Victoria, BC: Queen's Printer, pp. 5–6.

23. Andruske, *I'm not Sitting on the Couch Eating Bonbons!: Women's Transitions from Welfare to Paid Work and Education*, p. 53.

24. Ibid.

25. British Columbia, Social Program Renewal Secretariat (1995), *British Columbia Premier's Forum: New Opportunities for Working and Living: Report from the Forum*, Victoria, BC: Queen's Printer, pp. 1–2.

26. British Columbia, Advisory Council on Income Assistance (April 1995), *The Second Report of the Minister's Advisory Council on Income Assistance*, Victoria, BC: Queen's Printer, p. 9.

27. Brookfield, Self-directed learning, political clarity, and the critical practice of adult education.

28. J. Spiegel and A. Yassi (2004), Lessons from the margins of globalization: Appreciating the Cuban health paradox, *Journal of Public Health Policy* 25(1): 96–121.

29. A. Fernandez (2003), *Building Better Communities: Gender Roles, Resources and Gendered Processes of Urban Regeneration in Cayo Hueso, Havana, Cuba*, unpublished Master's thesis, University of British Columbia. Vancouver, British Columbia, Canada; A. Yassi, N. Fernandez, A. Fernandez, M. Bonet, R.B. Tate, and J. Spiegel (2003), Community participation in a multisectoral intervention to address health determinants in an inner-city community in Central Havana, *Journal of Urban Health* 80(1): 61–80.

30. Fernandez, Building better communities: Gender roles, resources and gendered processes of urban regeneration in Cayo Hueso, Havana, Cuba.

31. Ibid.

32. Spiegel and Yassi, Lessons from the margins of globalization: Appreciating the Cuban health paradox.

33. http://www.euro.who.int/eprise/main/WHO/Progs/HCP/Home.

34. Yassi et al., Community participation in a multisectoral intervention to address health determinants in an inner-city community in Central Havana.

35. Ibid.; Spiegel & Yassi, Lessons from the margins of globalization: Appreciating the Cuban health paradox; R. B. Tate, M. Fernandez, A. Yassi, M. Cañizares, J. Spiegel, and M. Bonet (2003), Change in health risk perception following community intervention in Central Havana, Cuba, *Health Promotion International* 18(4): 279–286.

36. Spiegel et al., Understanding "globalization" as a determinant of health determinants: A critical perspective; Yassi et al., Community participation in a multisectoral intervention to address health determinants in an inner-city community in Central Havana.

37. Fernandez, Building better communities: Gender roles, resources and gendered processes of urban regeneration in Cayo Hueso, Havana, Cuba.

38. Yassi et al., Community participation in a multisectoral intervention to address health determinants in an inner-city community in Central Havana.

39. Fernandez, Building better communities: Gender roles, resources and gendered processes of urban regeneration in Cayo Hueso, Havana, Cuba, p. ii.

40. P. H. Collins (1994), Shifting the center: Race, class, and feminist theorizing about motherhood, in D. Bassin, M. Honey, and M. Kaplan, eds., *Representations of Motherhood* (pp. 56–74), New Haven: Yale University Press.

41. N. A. Naples (1992), Activist mothering: Cross-generational continuity in the community work of women from low-income neighborhoods, *Gender & Society* 6(3): 441–463.

42. R. Labonte and J. Spiegel (2003), Setting global health research priorities, *British Medical Journal* 326: 722–723; Spiegel et al., Understanding "globalization" as a determinant of health determinants: A critical perspective.

43. D. Smith (1987), *The Everyday World as Problematic: A Feminist Sociology*, Toronto: University of Toronto Press, p. 69.

In Perspective

Gender, Health, and Globalization in the Middle East: Male Infertility, ICSI, and Men's Resistance*

Marcia C. Inhorn

Introduction

Since the 1978 birth in England of Louise Brown, the world's first test-tube baby, in vitro fertilization (IVF) has spread around the globe, reaching countries far from the technology-producing nations of the West. The same is true of intracytoplasmic sperm injection (ICSI), a variant of IVF designed in Belgium and first used successfully in 1992 to overcome intractable male infertility. The rapid globalization of both IVF and ICSI to the far reaches of the globe is abundantly apparent in the 22 nations of the Muslim Middle East, where a private assisted reproductive technology (ART) industry is flourishing. There, ART centers have opened in small, petro-rich Arab Gulf countries such as the United Arab Emirates and Qatar, as well as much larger but less prosperous North African nations, including Morocco and Egypt. As of 2003, Egypt boasted nearly 50 ART centers, outstripping its high-tech neighbor Israel, with its 24 ART centers.[1] Interestingly, the tiny neighboring country of Lebanon has nearly 15 ART clinics for a population of less than 5 million, constituting one of the highest per capita concentrations of ART centers in the world. In most of these ART centers, both IVF and ICSI are now performed. As I argue in this chapter, the newer reproductive technology, ICSI, has led to both local resistances and social transformations, which are the very result of its globalization into this region of the Muslim world.

The Local in the Global

As with all forms of global technology transfer, ARTs are not transferred into cultural voids when they reach places like Egypt and Lebanon. Rather, local considerations, be they cultural, social, economic, or political, shape and sometimes curtail the way these Western-generated reproductive technologies are both offered to and received by non-Western subjects. Thus, the assumption on the part of global producer nations that ARTs—as value-free, inherently beneficial medical technologies—are "immune" to culture and can thus be appropriately transferred and implemented anywhere and everywhere is subject to challenge once local formulations, perceptions, and actual consumption of these technologies are taken into consideration.

Indeed, the global spread of ARTs provides a particularly salient but little discussed example of what anthropologist Arjun Appadurai has termed a "technoscape," or the "global configuration, also ever fluid, of technology, and the fact that technology, both high and low, both mechanical and information, now moves at high speeds across various kinds of previously impervious boundaries."[2] Appadurai reminds us that this movement of technologies around the globe is both a deeply historical and inherently *localizing* process. In other words, globalization is not enacted in a uniform manner around the world, nor is it simply culturally homogenizing—necessarily "Westernizing" or even "Americanizing" in its effects. The global is always imbued with local meaning, such that local actors, living their everyday lives at particular historical moments in particular places, mold the very form that global processes take.

This acknowledgment of the importance of locality in the global dispersion of modern biotechnologies has been a theme of much recent work in gender, globalization, and health, particularly in the anthropology of reproduction. In *Conceiving the New World Order: The Global Politics of Reproduction*, Faye Ginsburg and Rayna Rapp argue that the global technoscape through which new reproductive technologies spread is an uneven terrain, in that some nations and regions within nations have achieved greater access to these fruits of globalization than others.[3] Ginsburg and Rapp have employed the term "stratified reproduction" in an attempt to get at these transnational inequalities, whereby some are able to achieve their reproductive desires, often through recourse to globalizing technologies, while others (usually poor women of color around the globe) are disempowered and even despised as reproducers. However, as Ginsburg and Rapp are quick to point out, the power to define reproduction is not necessarily unidirectional—flowing from the West, with its money and technology, to the rest of the world. Rather, "people everywhere actively use their cultural logics and social relations to incorporate, revise, or resist the influence of seemingly distant political and economic forces."[4] Thus, it is important to ask how Third World recipients of global technologies resist their application, or at least reconfigure the ways in which these technologies are to be adopted in local cultural contexts.

Middle Eastern Resistances to ICSI

The goal of this chapter is to highlight the local reactions and resistances to the introduction of a global reproductive technology—namely, ICSI—in the Middle Eastern region in 1994. Over the past decade, ICSI has proven to be a fairly revolutionary means of overcoming male infertility, a condition that contributes to more than half of all cases of infertility globally, but which is generally untreatable by conventional medical means.[5] With ICSI, infertile men with very poor sperm profiles—even azoospermia, or lack of sperm in the ejaculate—are now able to produce biological children of their own. As long as a single viable spermatozoon can be retrieved from a man's body, including through painful testicular aspirations and biopsies, this spermatozoon can be injected directly into the ovum under a high-powered microscope. This "microscopic injection" essentially "forces" fertilization to occur from otherwise nonviable sperm. For infertile men with otherwise healthy fertile wives, ICSI has provided a long sought-after solution to childlessness, and has, in fact, led to the creation of thousands of healthy ICSI babies worldwide. Furthermore, ICSI has decreased the reliance on sperm donation and adoption as alternatives to family formation.

It is important to point out that both sperm donation and legal adoption are prohibited by Islamic law throughout most of the Middle Eastern region.[6] In the absence of these alternatives, might Middle Eastern men be particularly willing to use ICSI to overcome their infertility? The answer to that question is both "yes" and "no." Placing ICSI in local cultural context in the Muslim Middle Eastern region necessitates highlighting the resistances to this biotechnology, some of which are based on the stigma of male infertility itself, as well as moral anxieties surrounding the use of ARTs in general.

Yet, the increasing popularity of ICSI—and, with it, the "outing" of male infertility as a male reproductive health problem—has led to new and surprising forms of resistance to be documented in this chapter. As I argue here, men are resisting the traditional gender scripts that implore them to divorce their reproductively aging wives. In ART centers in Lebanon, for example, infertile men whose wives are too old to undergo the ICSI procedure are accepting donor eggs in order to preserve their marriages to the wives they love. For Muslim men, this act of love is socially transgressive and thoroughly resistant, for reasons that are described in this chapter. Thus, this chapter seeks to highlight how the globalization of ICSI to the Middle Eastern region has engendered resistance to ICSI itself, based on stigma and other local arenas of constraint, as well as resistance to traditional gender scripts, which could not have happened without the globalization of ICSI to this part of the world. In other words, the globalization of ICSI to the Middle East has engendered dual, and somewhat opposing, forms of male resistance, with implications on men's and women's lives and well-being that are profound.

Male Infertility, Stigma, and Resistance

To understand Middle Eastern men's resistances to ICSI—particularly in the mid-1990s when the technology was first introduced into the region—it is necessary to understand the stigma surrounding male infertility. Indeed, studies from around the world have shown male infertility to be among the most stigmatizing of male health conditions.[7] Such stigmatization is clearly related to issues of sexuality. Male infertility is popularly, although usually mistakenly, conflated with impotency, as both disrupt a man's ability to impregnate a woman and to prove one's virility, paternity, and manhood.[8]

Little, if any, social scientific research has explicitly focused on the subject of male infertility among Middle Eastern men. Yet, Middle Eastern men may also suffer over their infertility, for a number of important reasons. First, on a social structural level, men living in pronatalist Middle Eastern communities are expected to have children, as reflected in the relatively high marriage and fertility rates across the region.[9] Middle Eastern men achieve social power in the patriarchal, patrilineal, patrilocal, endogamous extended family through the birth of children, especially sons, who will perpetuate patrilineal structures into the future.[10] "Intimate selving" in Arab families involves expectations of "patriarchal connectivity,"[11] whereby men assume patriarchal power in the family not only with advancing age and authority, but through the explicit production of offspring, who they love and nurture, but also dominate and control. Thus, in this region of the world, which "with some truth, is still regarded as one of the seats of patriarchy,"[12] men who do not become family patriarchs through physical and social reproduction may be deemed weak and ineffective and may be encouraged to take additional wives in order to contribute to the patrilineage and to prove their masculine virility.[13] In addition, a repeating theme in the growing literature on Middle Eastern masculinities is one of homosocial competition between men in the realms of virility and fertility, which are typically conflated.[14] Thus, the experience of male infertility for a Middle Eastern man can only be imagined as an extremely threatening and emasculating condition, particularly in a region of the world where so-called hegemonic masculinities[15] are homosocially competitive and men work hard to sustain their public images as "powerful, virile" patriarchs.[16]

My own studies, particularly in Egypt but also in Lebanon and Arab America, suggest that this may, in fact, be the case.[17] In Egypt, for example, few men in my study were willing to tell anyone, including their closest family members, that they suffered from male infertility. Male infertility was described variously as an "embarrassing," "sensitive," and "private" subject for the Egyptian male, who would necessarily feel *ana mish raagil*—"I am not a man"—if others were to know that he was the cause of a given infertility problem. Because of the association between infertility and threatened manhood, men's wives were generally expected to participate in a two-person cult of silence regarding the male infertility, which usually meant that women shouldered the blame for the infertility in public, as well as the responsibility for treatment seeking. Feeling humiliated and emasculated by their infertility, many men preferred to keep this stigmatizing health condition secret, refusing to seek treatment or to squander their hard-earned money on an uncertain ICSI attempt.

ICSI and Local Moral Resistance

Indeed, ICSI is an expensive technique (at local rates of about US $2,000–$5,000 per cycle), easily accessed only by middle- to upper-class elites in most Middle Eastern countries.[18] Yet, it may represent the only hope for Muslim men to overcome their infertility. Why? In the Sunni Islamic world, contemporary Muslim religious scholars, following mandates originally set forth in the Islamic scriptures, have effectively disallowed alternative modes of family formation for infertile couples, including third-party donation of sperm, eggs, embryos, or uteruses as in surrogacy.[19] For this reason, third-party donation is illegal in most Sunni-dominant Middle Eastern countries, including Egypt, where it is simply not practiced in ART clinics.[20]

Yet, it is important to point out the exception to the rule, which has affected the practice of IVF and ICSI in two Middle Eastern countries, namely Iran and Lebanon, as well as in Arab America. At the end of the 1990s, Iran's Ayatollah ᶜAli Hussein Khamanei, the supreme jurisprudent of the minority Shi'a sect of Islam, issued a *fatwa*, or religious ruling, approving of both egg and sperm donation for infertile Shi'ite couples, under certain conditions. Egg donor programs were subsequently initiated in Iran and in some of the clinics in Lebanon that cater to large Shi'ite populations.

Despite the permissive *fatwa* ruling, the notion of third-party gamete donation-and particularly the use of donor sperm—still does not meet with social acceptance among the vast majority of infertile Muslims, be they Shi'ite or Sunni. Clearly, the strong social prohibitions against sperm donation, which I found in both Egypt and Lebanon among Sunni and Shi'ite men alike, can be traced to patrilineal kinship ideologies and Islamic scriptural beliefs, which privilege patrilineal continuity and the importance of men's biological paternity. Or, to put it in the words of Egyptian and Lebanese male informants, a child produced from donor insemination (DI) "will not be my son." The questionable nature of such a DI child is reflected in Ayatollah Khamanei's own ruling: Namely, a DI child can be raised by, but not inherit from, its infertile social (as opposed to biological) father. Indeed, in 2003, sperm donation was officially outlawed by the Iranian parliament, thereby overturning Ayatollah Khamanei's *fatwa* ruling.[21]

Given these religious understandings and strong prohibitions against the uses of donor sperm, ICSI remains the only hope for most infertile Middle Eastern men. Yet, ICSI itself engenders a range of moral anxieties among Middle Eastern Muslim men, who may fear (un)intential sperm "mixing" and "mix ups" in Middle Eastern IVF laboratories.[22] In addition, infertile men also worry about the stigma that might surround their child if its "test-tube origins" were revealed, due to the popular societal assumption that a test-tube baby might be the product of donor gametes. Thus, the stigma and secrecy surrounding male infertility are compounded by the "technological stigma" of IVF/ICSI itself, which continues to be morally questionable because of lingering assumptions that something *haram*, or religiously sinful, is going on through the mixing of donor gametes in ART laboratories.

When I returned to the Middle East in 2003 to conduct a study of male infertility and ICSI in Lebanon, some of this moral stigma had lifted, showing that local reactions to biotechnologies may evolve over time. Whereas many infertile men were deeply reluctant to speak with me about their infertility problems, reflecting the ongoing emasculation associated with this condition,[23] the ART clinics in Lebanon were nonetheless overwhelmingly catering to male infertility cases (at least 60–70 percent of all patient couples), reflecting the increasing social acceptance of male infertility as a medical condition that could be solved through resort to ARTs.[24] Furthermore, much of the technological stigma surrounding ICSI had dissipated, with far fewer men worrying about sperm mixing than they had in my earlier study in Egypt. Thus, in the Middle East over the past decade, ICSI has "come of age" as a technology that can help to solve the otherwise intractable and socially unacceptable condition of male infertility. Indeed, it could be argued that ICSI has helped to bring male infertility "out of the closet" in the Middle East. In clinics in Lebanon, for example, many men stated in interviews that male infertility is a medical problem, "like any other medical condition," and thus "has nothing to do with manhood." In short, ICSI has medicalized what was once a social condition, by offering a medical solution to the social problem of childlessness. In so doing, it has also salvaged infertile men's masculinity, allowing Middle Eastern men to conform to traditional gender scripts that equate manhood with fatherhood.

Resistance to Traditional Gender Scripts

However, ICSI has also allowed Middle Eastern men to transgress traditional gender scripts in other ways. In fact, ICSI—along with the new donor egg programs emerging in Shi'ite areas of the Middle East—is leading to quite remarkable social transformations, characterized by Muslim men's resistance to the traditional gender norms that allow (even encourage) men to divorce or marry polygamously in cases of childlessness.

As Mounira Charrad argues in *States and Women's Rights: The Making of Postcolonial Tunisia, Algeria, and Morocco*, Islamic personal status laws throughout the Muslim world lead to the essential "fragility of marital bonds."[25] As she explains, "Far from fostering the development of long-lasting, strong emotional ties between husband and wife, the law underplays the formation and continuity of independent and stable conjugal units. This shows in particular in the procedure to terminate marriage, the legality of polygamy, and the absence of community property between husband and wife."[26] With regard to infertility, Charrad notes that the legality of polygamy allows a man to marry a second wife in the hope of having heirs, particularly sons. However, she also notes that despite Western stereotypes of widespread marital polygamy, polygamy is statistically insignificant in most Middle Eastern countries, practiced by only a few, generally less than 2 percent.

Despite the personal status laws permitting divorce and polygamy, a committed marriage is a highly valued and normatively upheld institution throughout the Middle East. While allowing for divorce, Islam clearly extols the virtues of marriage, regarding it as *Sunna*, or the way of the Prophet Muhammad. Thus, Middle Easterners are among the "most married" people in the world,[27] with well over 90 percent of adults marrying at least once in a lifetime. Divorce rates are also relatively low, half the 50-percent rates found in the United States.

Furthermore, marriages in the Middle East are definitely evolving toward a companionate ideal, or what I have termed "conjugal connectivity."[28] In my book *Infertility and Patriarchy: The Cultural Politics of Gender and Family Life in Egypt*, I draw upon anthropologist Suad Joseph's[29] provocative work on "patriarchal connectivity" in the Middle East—or the ways in which patriarchy operates through both male domination *and* deeply enmeshed, loving commitments between Arab patriarchs and their female and junior family members. According to Joseph, socialization within Arab families places a premium on connectivity, or the intensive bonding of individuals through love, involvement, and commitment. In the Arab world, family members are generally deeply involved with each other, expecting mutual love, exerting considerable influence over each others' lives, prioritizing family solidarity, and encouraging subordination of members' needs to collective interests. Persons are thus embedded in familial relational matrices that shape their deepest sense of self and serve as a source of security when the external social, economic, and political situation is uncertain, as is the case in much of the Arab world.

While Joseph's research focuses on the Arab family, my own work focuses on the couple, a social dyad for which there is no term in Arabic. Extending Joseph's analysis, I suggest that the loving commitments of patriarchal connectivity, which are socialized within the Arab family, also operate in the marital sphere. In my own work in Egypt and more recently Lebanon, I suggest that both men and women, including poor men and women, are negotiating new kinds of marital relationships—relationships based on the kind of loving connectivity experienced and expected in families of origin, but that has heretofore been unexpected and unexamined within the conjugal unit. That conjugal connectivity is true even among *infertile* Middle Eastern Muslim couples attests to shifting marital praxis and the importance of love, mutual respect, and the sharing of life's problems even in the absence of desired children. Despite widespread expectations within the Middle East that infertile marriages are bound to fail—with men necessarily blaming women for the infertility and divorcing or replacing them if they do not produce children, especially sons— such expectations may represent indigenous stereotypes based on the aforementioned features of Islamic personal status law described by Charrad.[30] As I would argue instead, the success of so many infertile marriages in the Middle East bespeaks the strengthening of conjugal connectivity in resistance to patriarchy, which is being undermined.[31] Indeed, the tremendous growth of ARTs clinics in this region of the world over the past two decades bespeaks the deep feelings of love, loyalty, and commitment experienced by many couples, including *both* husbands and wives in childless marriages.

However, it is important to note that the globalization of ICSI to the Middle Eastern region has also posed new marital possibilities for men— and new marital vulnerabilities for women—with consequences on women's lives that are potentially profound.[32]

Namely, middle-aged infertile men are generally married to middle-aged women—the latter of whom may have "stood by" their infertile husbands for years, even decades in some cases, but may have grown too old to produce viable ova for the ICSI procedure. In the absence of adoption or of any kind of egg donation, infertile Muslim couples with a reproductively elderly wife face four difficult options: (1) to remain together permanently without children; (2) to legally foster an orphan, which is rarely viewed as an acceptable option; (3) to remain together in a polygamous marriage, which is rarely viewed as an acceptable option by the women themselves; or (4) to divorce so that the husband can have children with a younger wife.

Because of the Sunni Islamic restrictions on the use of donor eggs, at least some Muslim men *are* choosing to divorce or take a second wife, believing that their own reproductive destinies lie with younger, more fertile women. However, in my research in both Egypt and Lebanon, the first option has proven to be *much* more common—namely, infertile husbands and their forty-something wives often love each other deeply, and remain together in long-term marriages without producing any children. Thus, divorce is not the immediate consequence of infertility that it stereotypically is portrayed to be, including in the new era of ICSI.

Indeed, these technologies seem to be giving infertile couples, both Sunni and Shi'ite Muslims, new hope that their infertility problems can be overcome, thereby increasing sentiments of conjugal love and loyalty. For example, in Lebanon, where egg donor programs are now in place in some ART clinics, new marital scenarios are beginning to emerge as infertile husbands, particularly those of the Shi'ite faith, are beginning to accept the idea of donor eggs. Because Islam allows polygyny, or the taking of more than one wife, egg donation is being conceptually conflated with polygyny, whereby the egg donor becomes like a second wife to the husband. The growing acceptance of this practice in the complicated, multisectarian religious landscape of Lebanon has brought with it the possibility of new marital imaginaries still unthinkable in the more homogeneous Sunni Islamic environment of Egypt, where egg donation is firmly banned.

In short, the globalization of ICSI and donor egg technologies to parts of the Shi'ite Muslim world has fundamentally altered understandings of the ways in which marriages can be saved through the uses of ARTs. The "adventurous" attitude on the part of the otherwise conservative, male Shi'ite religious leaders toward third-party donation has led to a potential transformation in gender relations among infertile Muslim couples, who are clamoring for donor eggs in IVF clinics in Lebanon. Furthermore, in multi-sectarian Lebanon, the recipients of donor eggs are not necessarily only Shi'ite Muslim couples. Indeed, some *Sunni* Muslim patients from Lebanon and other Middle Eastern Muslim countries (as well as Christians couples of all sects) are quietly "saving their marriages" through the use of donor gametes, thereby secretly "going against" the dictates of Sunni Muslim orthodoxy.

Conclusion

The globalization of ICSI to the Middle East has been accompanied by local, moral, and gender responses that are rapidly evolving and that have major implications for women's well-being and security. Although the Sunni Muslim ban on third-party donation may be particularly disadvantageous to women—as some infertile men begin to replace their reproductively elderly wives in order to try the newest variant of ICSI with younger, more fertile women—divorce is not the inevitable consequence of infertility that it is stereotypically portrayed to be. Rather, as my research has shown, patriarchy is being undermined by infertile couples themselves, who are often choosing to remain in long-term, loving marriages, even in the absence of children.

In general, the tremendous growth of the ART industry in the Muslim Middle East is a testament to loving commitments, and particularly to men's resistances to traditional gender scripts that allow them to divorce or take additional wives. Furthermore, with the arrival of ICSI and now donor egg technologies in the region, many men have now overcome their initial resistances to these morally ambiguous technologies. They have also begun to rethink the meaning of male infertility and its connection to masculinity in their lives, as these technologies offer hope of medical solutions to the social problem of emasculating childlessness.

As ARTs such as ICSI become further entrenched in the Muslim world, and additional forms of global reproductive technology become available, it is important to interrogate new local moral dilemmas, as well as new manifestations of love and conjugal connectivity, that are likely to arise in response to this variant of globalization. Indeed, researchers interested in globalization and reproductive health need to prioritize the study of new reproductive technologies in multiple global sites, assessing how such technologies affect *both* men and women as reproductive partners. Policy makers, furthermore, should question issues of access to these technologies—especially when, as in the case of male infertility, ARTs represent the only means of overcoming this intractable male reproductive health condition.

Ultimately, the case of ICSI—and the particular local responses that this global reproductive technology have engendered among men and women in the Middle East—reminds us of the importance of understanding the meaning of the "local in the global." This is a lesson that extends well beyond ICSI. In fact, it may apply to *all* new health technologies as they make their way around this large and locally varied globe.

Notes

* This chapter is based on nearly twenty years of multi-sited research on the globalization of assisted ARTs to the Middle East. Working in Egypt, Lebanon, and Arab America, I have conducted qualitative, ethnographic interviews with infertile Middle Eastern men and women, now totaling nearly 400 patient couples. I want to express my gratitude to these individuals for sharing their reproductive and marital lives with me, as well as to the physicians who have helped me with my study in seven different Middle Eastern ART clinics. This research was generously supported by the National Science Foundation and the U.S. Department of Education Fulbright-Hays Program. I also want to thank Kari Hartwig, for inviting me to participate in this seminal volume.

1. S. M. Kahn (2000), *Reproducing Jews: A Cultural Account of Assisted Conception in Israel,* Durham: Duke University Press.
2. A. Appadurai (1996), *Modernity at Large: Cultural Dimensions of Globalization,* p. 34. Minneapolis: University of Minnesota Press
3. Ginsburg and R. Rapp eds. (1995), Introduction, *Conceiving the New World Order: The Global Politics of Reproduction,* Berkeley: University of California Press (pp. 1–18).
4. Ibid., p. 1.
5. A. Kamischke and E. Neischlag (1998), Conventional treatments of male infertility in the age of evidence-based andrology, *Human Reproduction* 13(suppl. 1): 62–75.
6. D. Meirow and J. G. Schenker (1997), The current status of sperm donation in assisted reproduction technology: Ethical and legal considerations, *Journal of Assisted Reproduction and Genetics* 14: 133–138; M. C. Inhorn (2003a), *Local Babies, Global Science: Gender, Religion, and in vitro Fertilization in Egypt,* New York: Routledge.
7. G. Becker (2000), *The Elusive Embryo: How Women and Men Approach New Reproductive Technologies,* Berkeley: University of California Press; G. Becker (2002), Deciding whether to tell children about donor insemination: An

unresolved question in the United States, in M. C. Inhorn and F. van Balen, eds., *Infertility Around the Globe: New Thinking on Childlessness, Gender, and Reproductive Technologies*, Berkeley: University of California Press (pp. 119–133); Inhorn, *Local Babies, Global Science: Gender, Religion, and in vitro Fertilization in Egypt*; M. C. Inhorn (2004a), Middle Eastern masculinities in the age of new reproductive technologies: Male infertility and stigma in Egypt and Lebanon, *Medical Anthropology Quarterly*, 18: 162–182.

8. R. E. Webb and J. C. Daniluk (1999), The end of the line: Infertile men's experiences of being unable to produce a child, *Men and Masculinities* 2: 6–25.

9. Population Reference Bureau (2004), *World population data sheet*, Washington, DC: Population Reference Bureau.

10. M. M. Charrad (2001), *States and Women's Rights: The Making of Postcolonial Tunisia, Algeria, and Morocco*, Berkeley: University of California Press; M. C. Inhorn (1996), *Infertility and Patriarchy: The Cultural Politics of Gender and Family Life in Egypt*, Philadelphia: University of Pennsylvania Press; C. M. Obermeyer (1999), Fairness and fertility: The meaning of son preference in Morocco, in R. Leete, ed., *Dynamics of Values in Fertility Change*, Oxford, UK: Oxford University Press (pp. 275–292); L. Ouzgane (1997), Masculinity as virility in Tahar Ben Jelloun's fiction, *Contagion: Journal of Violence, Mimesis, and Culture* 4: 1–13.

11. S. Joseph ed. (1999), *Intimate Selving in Arab Families: Gender, Self, and Identity*, Syracuse, NY: Syracuse University Press.

12. M. Ghoussoub and E. Sinclair-Webb (2000), Preface, in M. Ghoussoub and E. Sinclair-Webb, eds., *Imagined Masculinities: Male Identity and Culture in the Modern Middle East* (pp. 7–16), London: Saqi Books, p. 8.

13. Inhorn, *Infertility and Patriarchy: The Cultural Politics of Gender and Family Life in Egypt*.

14. K. A. Ali (2000), Making "responsible" men: Planning the family in Egypt, in C. Bledsoe, S. Lerner, and J. I. Guyer, eds., *Fertility and the Male Life-Cycle in the Era of Fertility Decline* (pp. 119–143), Oxford, UK: Oxford University Press; Ouzgane, Masculinity as virility in Tahar Ben Jelloun's fiction.

15. R. W. Connell (1995), *Masculinities*, Berkeley: University of California Press.

16. Ouzgane, Masculinity as virility in Tahar Ben Jelloun's fiction, p. 4.

17. Inhorn, *Infertility and Patriarchy: The Cultural Politics of Gender and Family Life in Egypt*; M. C. Inhorn (2002), Sexuality, masculinity, and infertility in Egypt: Potent troubles in the marital and medical encounters, *The Journal of Men's Studies* 10: 343–359; Inhorn, Middle Eastern masculinities in the age of new reproductive technologies: Male infertility and stigma in Egypt and Lebanon; M. C. Inhorn (2003b), "The worms are weak": Male infertility and patriarchal paradoxes in Egypt, *Men and Masculinities* 5: 236–256.

18. Inhorn, *Local Babies, Global Science: Gender, Religion, and in vitro Fertilization in Egypt*.

19. Ibid.; Meirow and Schenker, The current status of sperm donation in assisted reproduction technology: Ethical and legal considerations; G. I. Serour (1996), Bioethics in reproductive health: A Muslim's perspective, *Middle East Fertility Society Journal* 1: 30–35.

20. Inhorn, *Local Babies, Global Science: Gender, Religion, and in vitro Fertilization in Egypt.*
21. S. Tremayne (May 2005), The moral, ethical and legal implications of egg, sperm and embryo donation in Iran, paper to be presented at University of Michigan.
22. Inhorn, *Local Babies, Global Science: Gender, Religion, and in vitro Fertilization in Egypt.*
23. Inhorn, Middle Eastern masculinities in the age of new reproductive technologies: Male infertility and stigma in Egypt and Lebanon; M. C. Inhorn (2004b), Privacy, privatization, and the politics of patronage: Ethnographic challenges to penetrating the secret world of Middle Eastern, hospital-based in vitro fertilization, *Social Science and Medicine* 59: 2095–2108.
24. Inhorn, Middle Eastern masculinities in the age of new reproductive technologies: Male infertility and stigma in Egypt and Lebanon.
25. Charrad, *States and Women's Rights: The Making of Postcolonial Tunisia, Algeria, and Morocco.*
26. Ibid., p. 35.
27. A. R. Omran and F. Roudi (1993), The Middle East population puzzle, *Population Bulletin* 48: 1–40.
28. Inhorn, *Infertility and Patriarchy: The Cultural Politics of Gender and Family Life in Egypt.*
29. S. Joseph (1993), Connectivity and patriarchy among urban working class Arab families in Lebanon, *Ethos* 21: 465–484.
30. Charrad, *States and Women's Rights: The Making of Postcolonial Tunisia, Algeria, and Morocco.*
31. Inhorn, *Infertility and Patriarchy: The Cultural Politics of Gender and Family Life in Egypt.*
32. Inhorn, *Local Babies, Global Science: Gender, Religion, and in vitro Fertilization in Egypt.*

In Perspective

Globalizing Gendered Resistance: Moving Beyond the Individual*

Gillian Lewando-Hundt

As illustrated by Spiegel and Andruske and Inhorn in their respective chapters in this volume, gendered resistance to effects of globalization are experienced at both the individual level and among couples and families. In this chapter, I draw examples of resistance from within communities and social movements. In this analysis, I feel a conceptual framework for the development of a gendered analysis of resistance to issues within the process of global restructuring should include men and women, as Doyal suggests in her chapter in this volume.[1] The framework should also enable analysis of the interactions between globalization, health, and gender at macro, meso, and micro levels in looking at resistance as expressed by both individuals and social movements. This is an approach that draws on ideas of the interplay between structure and agency as often expressed in relation to globalization and modernity.[2]

It may not be clear that the coping strategies described in Spiegel and Andruske's chapter are resistance unless one understands resistance as surviving and navigating space to maneuver and express agency within complicated social structures.[3] The expression "kitchen table resistance" is used to signify the sites of resistance as being within the home, or, in their chapter, in the informality of the domestic sphere in Canada and among women organizing within their neighborhoods in Cuba.

Marchand sets out a conceptual framework that frames gender as operating on three levels: symbolic, physical, and social.[4] Within this framework, global restructuring leads to boundary rearticulation and renegotiation; and resistance occurs at the interstices of these boundaries.

There are multiple practices, strategies, and sites of resistance, including the home, places of employment, streets, and the Internet.

My own work as an applied medical anthropologist has involved researching health issues in the Middle East, South Africa, and Kenya in addition to the United Kingdom. The resilience and resistance of people I have worked with and lived among in these different settings is striking and has demonstrated to me that there are multiple practices, strategies, and sites of resistance as Marchand argues. The global restructuring of spheres of action, such as in the domain of health, has provided opportunities and threats that have led to new forms of resistance and resulted in the emergence of different patterns of gender relations. These are often expressed not just by individual strategies of resistance but by social movements within which women and men become active. I illustrate this with two very different examples. The first involves the social movement of antimilitarism that continues to be an expression of women's resistance to military conflicts. The second explores the way in which both women and men as individuals and within the social movements of evangelical churches in South Africa deal with the misfortune and affliction of stroke.

Women in Black as a Gendered Social Movement of Antimilitarism

In 1989 during the first Palestinian Intifada of 1988–1994, I demonstrated with Women in Black in Beersheva, Israel. At that time, this was a small, national group of mainly Jewish Israeli women who would stand silently at major intersections in Israel on Fridays as people left work for the weekend. They/we would wear black and hold signs on which were written, in a variety of ways and languages, "Stop the Occupation," and "Withdraw from the Palestinian territories." In this provincial town of about 150,000 people, we almost never reached double figures in size. Our average age was quite high; some of us were grandmothers, others had young to adult children, and few of us were below 35 years of age. There was one woman who had been active in the Black Sash, another in the Resistance in France.

We stood on an island in the middle of a four-lane road. Opposite us would be a counterdemonstration of men waving Israeli flags from the Party for Arab Transfer out of Israel (led by an Israeli retired general since assassinated, ironically nicknamed "Ghandi"). There would be two policemen there to protect us, who, ironically, would chat to the male demonstrators throughout the hour. Derogatory statements were often shouted out by the men across the road, and people in passing cars often spat on us. The anti-demonstrators' placards had the following choice phrases amongst them:

"The Left is poison in the heart of Israel."
"Hitler should have finished you off."
"May you wear black all your lives for your sons and husbands."
"Why aren't you at home, cooking for the Sabbath?"
"Arafat's prostitutes."

Supporters of our views would wave and occasionally give a thumbs-up or hoot. Occasionally, a male sympathizer would bring cold drinks. However, colleagues from work or acquaintances with different views would pretend not to see us. The spontaneous reactions of the drivers shouting through their open windows in the heat of the day was an emotional split-second reaction and their fury was directed at the demonstrators in terms of their sex, their domestic role, the historical past, and the political present.

This was a social movement of resistance that was developed by women whose own sons and husbands, or those of their friends and peers, were being called upon to perpetuate the occupation or were being court-martialed and imprisoned for refusing to serve. Women in Black eventually joined up with other peace groups both within Israel and internationally and began to represent a new social movement of gendered political resistance during a time of political renegotiation. The protests were both physical (women protesting at a public intersection) as well as socially symbolic in terms of time, place, and dress.

Since Women in Black has become an international movement of women for peace, different groups hold regular vigils in many countries in Europe, the United States, and Latin America (http://www.womeninblack.org). For example, there is a regular demonstration in London on Wednesday evenings at the statue of Edith Cavell, opposite the National Portrait Gallery. Far from being a one-issue movement, these women have protested the continuing conflict in Iraq, and prior to that, Bosnia. In addition, women of this international movement travel as human shields and campaign internationally not only through vigils, but also by virtual means: books, films, weblists, and weblogs.[5] There is a community of practice and interest, of public action and private debate that crosses virtual, international, social, and physical boundaries.

The related movement in Israel today of "Maksom Watch" in which Israeli women stand at checkpoints to monitor and report on the behavior of Israeli soldiers is another example of how women as part of the anti-militarism movement are not only demonstrating for peace but monitoring the behavior of men and women in the military. These checkpoints are sites of confrontation, humiliation, harassment, and sometimes, fatal delay for sick patients requiring medical treatment at hospitals beyond the checkpoint. They may involve difficult decisions involving the balancing of security issues with humanitarian issues particularly in the case of ambulances transferring people for emergency or tertiary care and there are many documented cases of human rights abuses.[6] They make daily movements an undertaking of extreme difficulty through an informal policy of road closure and separation.[7]

How would one say that this social movement of antimilitarism is related to health? It is an act that relates directly to the physical, mental, emotional, and social well-being of people in countries where there is ongoing conflict. In her monograph, Cockburn looks at three sites of women's resistance: Ireland, Israel/Palestine, and Bosnia/Herzegovina.[8] In the latter, the women set up a women's therapy center for survivors of abuse. They also publicly resisted military interventions in which men were often unwilling actors. Their example illustrates resistance that is social, political, and symbolic, a phenomenon that occurs at many sites locally, nationally, and internationally.

Sites of Resistance for Coping with "xistroku" and "xifulana" in Rural South Africa

Another area of study that has drawn my attention to global restructuring, gender, and health is more recent research in rural South Africa where I explored the meaning and impact of strokes in households. As part of the health transition from infectious disease to noncommunicable disease, cardiovascular disease is emerging in older people as a major problem in sub-Saharan Africa. In the study site, the subdistrict of Agincourt in Bohlablelo district, stroke is the major cause of death of people over 35.[9] The burden of coping with the misfortune of stroke in households has had a gendered impact, and several different types of social movements have offered support and sites of resistance to stroke survivors and their families in dealing with this affliction.

The Southern Africa Stroke Prevention Initiative (SASPI) was a multi-disciplinary study bringing together epidemiology, anthropology, and medicine. The anthropological component of the study focused on the community understandings of health and illness and patterns of health care–seeking behavior as well as the impact of strokes on households. The medical findings included a high prevalence of strokes and a lack of secondary prevention to inhibit recurrence.[10]

An ethnographic assessment in 6 villages involving 105 interviews and 35 semi-structured interviews with stroke survivors and their caretakers offered some insight into the way in which the Shangaan people living in these villages close to the Mozambican border deal with and resist misfortune and afflictions such as sudden weakness down one side of the body. The research revealed pluralistic understandings of illness and health-seeking strategies.[11] People in the area perceived illnesses as being of two main types: *xilungu* (Western, white) and *xintu* (traditional, African). The former is a category for natural physical illness while the latter denotes physical symptoms with social explanations.

During illness-ranking exercises, both types were named by people. Some illnesses were recognizably biomedical, such as HIV or tuberculosis, and others were conditions that had social causes. Stroke (*xistroku*) was recognized as a natural physical illness that occurs suddenly, possibly resulting in weakness down one side of the body and possibly linked to high blood pressure ("high blood"). It was also recognized as being a possible manifestation of *xifulana*—when an individual gets a dry or swollen limb as a result of others wishing misfortune upon her/him.[12] Explanations of these differences are described by various key informants below:

> Xifulana is similar to stroke because if affects the body parts and they both stop blood from flowing in other parts of the body. But the difference is that xistroku is not a human- caused illness whereas xifulana is. (Male healer)

> I think there are similarities between xistroku and xifulana. By this, I mean a person not being able to use one part of his body. Stroke is also when one part of your body is weak. (Young man)

> Weakness or dryness on one side is a natural illness. Xifulana is caused by human-beings. They both cause dryness, are painful and there is little use of the affected part. (Woman)

There was a general agreement that when a condition is both physical and social then "double treatment" is required from the hospital or private and public clinics for the physical (*xistroku*) as well as from healers (*inyangas* and *sangomas*) and/or pastors and prophet healers in the African Independent Churches (AICs) for the socially induced affliction of *xifulana*.[13] The practice of medical pluralism was described by one woman:

> Your hands and legs would be dry and might lead to one being crippled and you may have a swollen stomach. Others might experience headaches. Normally the clinic can cure headaches. If after the treatment, you see no change, then you start to suspect it is xifulana and then you consult traditional healers . . . clinics are for natural illness but there are illnesses that are caused by human beings that a clinic cannot treat successfully. (Woman)

Respondents often described *xifulana* as being caused by jealousy. For example, someone may be jealous of another's ability to pay school fees for their children or to choose when to eat breakfast, lunch, or dinner. *Xifulana* is believed to be transmitted by stepping on a "trap," an object laid in your path with "your name on it," intending to hurt you:

> "Xifulana is caused by hatred and jealousy. Like the fact that you are educated and my children are not. I might become jealous of that."
> "People just set a trap; you step on it and xifulana attacks."
> "For example, I see this house is well decorated and in my house I don't even have a tin to decorate. I may be tempted to do it. Or if your child drives a car and mine does not own a car." Group discussion with women in a burial society—3 speakers.

In the acute phase of stroke manifestations, individuals visited the clinic, hospital, or private doctors. But almost all of them also visited traditional healers or prophets. Both healers and prophets try to cleanse them of the affliction by cutting the flesh to remove the polluted blood or by using enemas to cleanse the body. Other treatments included the use of herbs and prayer. The healers invoke the ancestors and the prophets, Jesus, and the Holy Spirit. Many of the stroke survivors attended church services held by the Zion Christian church or the International Pentecostal churches. These churches focus on healing in their services and offer social support to the afflicted. The largest of these African Independent Churches was the Zion Christian Church whose headquarters were in the province. The resistance to *xifulana* manifested as a *xistroku* (stroke) was therefore conducted by utilizing plural healing; and the burden of ill health was largely borne by the family members, the local churches, and healers.

These people in Limpopo province request both clinical and social diagnostics of their stroke-like symptoms and actively seek their containment in order to maintain their physical, mental, and social well-being. The growing burden of cardiovascular disease is part of the health transition as well as the restructuring of global health through changes in lifestyle. Dealing with the burden of stroke also has a gendered effect as the burden of care for stroke survivors is borne by women in the home: wives, sisters-in-law, daughters, and granddaughters. Healers can be both male and female, though pastors, prophets, and doctors are primarily male. The impact of global restructuring on the physical manifestation of cardiovascular disease in this setting does not seem to differentiate in terms of gender, but there is a socially gendered impact in terms of gender roles and attitudes. Resistance to poverty, social divisions, and illness is expressed through the use of healers, prophets, and churches to explain, come to terms with, and sometimes overcome both individual and social misfortune.

Conclusion

As Doyal states, global restructuring manifests itself in fragmented and often contradictory dimensions of global change that affect the health of individuals and local communities.[14] It clearly affects individuals and restructures relationships in households. However, resistance is not only expressed by individuals but also by social movements within communities and across societies. Some of these are both simultaneously local and global, such as evangelical churches and women's antimilitarism. Resistance to personal, social and political events can be seen as fostering health in terms of preventing social isolation and sometimes mitigating the effects of misfortune or abuse. An exploration and increased understanding of the dynamics and structuring of these multiple sites of resistance would illuminate how global restructuring results in new modes of gendered resistance through social movements, both long established and more recent, as well as how these may enhance the health of the participants.

In terms of specific research recommendations, we must work to better understand how global restructuring fosters new social movements and sites of resistance locally and globally; how mental health can be enhanced by individuals expressing resistance through social movements; and how global restructuring affects the health transition in terms of communicable and noncommunicable illnesses and their management. In terms of specific policy recommendations, consideration and support for informal health care and social movements in supporting the resistance and resilience of women and men experiencing the multiple effects of global restructuring would greatly enhance social cohesion and mitigate social exclusion in many settings.

Notes

* The study in South Africa was funded by the Wellcome Trust, Health Consequences of Population Change Panel 2001–2003, Grant no: 06476/Z/01/Z.

1. L. Doyal, Understanding gender, health and globalization: Opportunities and challenges, in I. Kickbusch, K. Hartwig, and J. M. List, eds., *Globalization, Gender, and Health in the 21st Century*, New York: Palgrave Macmillan.
2. A. Giddens (2003), Runaway World: How Globalization is reshaping our lives, London and New York: Routledge.
3. J. Spiegel and C. L. Andruske (2005), Globalization, Health, and the Engendering of Resistance in Everyday Life in this book.
4. M. H. Marchand (2003), Challenging globalization: Toward a feminist understanding of resistance, *Review of International Studies* Special Issue(29): 145–160.

5. C. Cockburn (1998), *The Space Between Us, Negotiating Gender and National Identities in Conflict*, London: Zed Books.
6. Bt'selem: The Israeli Information Centre for Human Rights in the Occupied Territories. (June 2001), *No Way Out, Medical Implications of Israel's Siege Policy*, www.btselem.org; Bt'selem: The Israeli Information Centre for Human Rights in the Occupied Territories. (March 2002), *Wounded in the Field: Treatment and Firing at Ambulances by IDF soldiers in the Occupied Territories.* www.btselem.org; Bt'selem: The Israeli Information Centre for Human Rights in the Occupied Territories. (December 2003), *Harm to Medical Personnel: the Delay, Abuse and Humiliation of Medical Personnel by Israeli Security Forces.* www.btselem.org; Bt'selem: The Israeli Information Centre for Human Rights in the Occupied Territories. (January 2004), *Case Study 18 Abuse of Palestinians at the Sarra Checkpoint, Nablus District 27–31 December 2003*, www.btselem.org.
7. Bt'selem: The Israeli Information Centre for Human Rights in the Occupied Territories. (August 2004), *Forbidden Roads: The Discriminatory West Bank Road Regime*, www.btselem.org.
8. Cockburn, *The Space Between Us, Negotiating Gender and National Identities in Conflict.*
9. K. Kahn, S. M. Tollman, and J. S. S. Gear (1999), Who dies from what? Determining causes of death in South Africa's rural northeast, *Tropical Medicine & International Health*, 46: 433–441.
10. G. Hundt, M. Stuttaford, and B. Ngoma (2004a), Prevalence of stroke survivors in Rural South Africa: Results from the Southern Africa Stroke Prevention Initiative (SASPI) Agincourt Field Site, *Stroke* 35: 627–632; G. Hundt, M. Stuttaford, and B. Ngoma (2004c), The social diagnostics of stroke like symptoms: Healers, doctors and prophets in Agincourt, Limpopo Province, South Africa, *Journal of Biosocial Sciences, special issue on Mental Health in Complex Emergencies* 36: 433–443.
11. G. Hundt, M. Stuttaford, and B. Ngoma (2004b), Hypertension in stroke survivors and secondary prevention of stroke in a rural South African population: Results from the Southern Africa Stroke Prevention Initiative (SASPI) study, Agincourt Field Site, *International Bulletin of the World Health Organization* 82 (7): 479–558.
12. Hundt, Stuttaford, and Ngoma, The social diagnostics of stroke like symptoms.
13. Ibid.
14. Doyal, Understanding gender, health and globalization: Opportunities and challenges.

5

Women, Health, and Globalization: A Critical Social Movement Perspective*

Manisha Desai

The identification and international spread of SARS (Severe Acute Respiratory Syndrome) in early 2003, made it is easy to see the globalization of health and disease. But what the intense media coverage of SARS shows, as Paul Farmer notes eloquently in his article on "SARS and Inequality" in *The Nation*,[1] is one of the most troubling aspects of global health policies in the last decade, namely the hijacking of health as a means for global trade and economic growth. Were SARS not so prevalent in regions vital to global trade (China, Taiwan, and Hong Kong), would it be receiving the same attention?

One aspect that has received no attention is the epidemic's gender dimension. Fortunately, the discourse on SARS will soon be engendered. This attention to gender in the global health arena is primarily a result of women worldwide connecting their community activism around health issues to the transnational level, first through the International Women's Decade from 1975 to 1985 and then in the 1990s through "linkage politics" via the various UN world conferences on human rights, population, social development, and the environment.

An examination of the international women's health movement (IWHM)[2] constitutes the focus of this chapter. I argue that the changing of gender relations, as manifested in the rise of this movement, have engendered the discourse of global health and raised the particular concern of women's health to the forefront of discussions about health. At the same time, because of the IWHM, the globalization of health and disease has altered gender relations, as is evident in many innovative examples of

HIV/AIDS service delivery leading to community-level changes in norms and practices of gender inequality.

The IWHM, however, has not been so successful in engendering national and local policies nor in raising budgets for women's health. This is primarily a result of an unfortunate historical conjunction. Ironically, the engendered global health discourse coincided with the worldwide adoption of neoliberal policies all through the 1990s, such as Structural Adjustment Programs (SAPs), which served to undermine its effectiveness in terms of women's well-being and health.

I begin with a brief review of the context in which the IWHM emerged, then discuss its impact on the global health discourse. I then highlight how, despite these successes, the gains have been limited by the SAPs. Finally, I examine recent efforts of the IWHM in coordination with the People's Health Movement (PHM) to challenge these neoliberal health policies and return to the concept of Primary Health Care (PHC) and Health for All (HFA).

The International Women's Health Movement

Health has long been considered a cross-border issue and attempts to protect the health of subjects and citizens within certain territories also have a long history from the quarantines during the plague epidemic of the Middle Ages to the various colonial health policies that in its civilizing mission disciplined or destroyed various "native" healing and health practices.[3] But health as an international issue began to take shape first with the League of Nations and then more specifically with the development of the United Nations and its specialized agencies such as the World Health Organization (WHO) and the United Nations Fund for Children (UNICEF).

Initially, the international health focus was on developing norms and standards of technical knowledge, spreading expertise about treatment and prevention around the world, and developing programs geared toward the needs of developing countries. These international efforts followed one of two approaches, either (1) they focused on specific diseases and its eradication like smallpox, polio, and other such efforts or (2) they supported general health care.[4] Both these approaches saw gender only in terms of women's reproductive health, primarily as targets of population control policies.

The international health regime was state-centered and worked from the top down, focusing primarily on the role of medical experts or, as far as women were concerned, the role of contraceptive technology. As Manderson and Whiteford argue, too often the international health regime developed plans as though there were a level playing field around the world, leading to obstacles in its implementation.[5] Gendered and cultural local realities were rarely given any primacy in this regime.

These realities of the international health regime's attention (or lack thereof) to women's health were first challenged by the second wave of the feminist movements that were emerging in all parts of the world. In the United States and the West, radical feminists sought to reclaim women's bodies and sexualities; and self-help groups emerged in which women learned to perform self-exams. The publication of *Our Bodies Our Selves* by the Boston Women's Health Book Collective was one of the landmark developments in the women's health movements.[6] Women's collective organizing and self-education about their health also challenged the ando-centric medical establishments and their appropriation of women's skills and knowledge which, though devalued when performed by women, were valued once professionalized and institutionalized.

Most scholars see the emergence of the IWHM from these radical feminist groups in the United States and Western Europe.[7] However, around the same time, there were women in other parts of the world also develop-ing a critique of the dominant health perspective based on their participa-tion in community health and development projects as well as activism in the liberation theology movements in Latin America and other radical student and peasant movements in India, China, and the Philippines. For example, when India became independent in 1947, it embarked on an innovative, mixed economic model that prompted the development of primary health care centers in every rural area. In China, "bare-foot doctors" were also a response to meeting people's needs in rural areas.

It was this work in Asia that inspired the 1978 concept of primary health care presented in the Alma Ata Declaration of the World Health Assembly. PHC was seen as the key strategy for achieving Health for All by the year 2000. This strategy was based on the understanding that to meet basic health care needs, policies and programs have to address the under-lying economic, political, and social disparities that lead to poor health. The principles that it encompassed were: "universal access and coverage on the basis of needs; comprehensive care with an emphasis on disease prevention and health promotion; community and individual involve-ment and self reliance; intersectoral action for health; and appropriate technology and cost-effectiveness in relation to available resources."[8] These principles reflected the basic-needs approach of development in the 1970s.

Feminists, both radical and liberal, in the United States and Europe were not as familiar with these development discourses as they were oriented toward the developing countries. This was to change with the declaration of the International Woman's Year in 1975 and subsequently the International Women's Decade (IWD) from 1975 to 1985. This is the first time that women activists, not just governmental representatives, from different countries met at the NGO Forums that were held simultaneously with the three Women's World Conferences at Mexico City in 1975, Copenhagen in 1980, and Nairobi in 1985. The Forums became expected locales for activists and grassroots workers to debate as well as share meanings and strategies. These contentious events became more accommodative in Nairobi, due in part to its location. There, Third World women outnumbered Western women; white women were critiqued in the United States by women of color and had become more class and race conscious; and the interactions over the decade meant that all women were developing knowledge about women's issues in other parts of the world and becoming less provincial and more open to other perspectives.[9] Violence against women was the key issue around which consensus developed.

It was in this process of interaction with Third World Activists that the IWHM in the West, which had primarily focused on reclaiming sexuality and abortion rights, began to consider population issues. This focus was facilitated by the scandals of the 1970s when contraceptives such the Dalkon Shield and Depo Provera that were banned in the United States were dumped in the Third World; and sterilization abuses in India and China rationalized by the state as population policies came to light.[10]

In these early years the IWHM in the West and the Third World focused on consciousness-raising and mobilizing outside traditional policy channels. They worked primarily to create linkages between women's health groups around the world, sharing information and learning about women's health issues.[11] Groups like ISIS International and the International Women's Tribune Center were formed in 1974 and 1975, respectively, to act as avenues of gathering and disseminating information, holding workshops, and linking groups. In 1978, the Women's Global Network for Reproductive Rights was formed with similar aims.

At its initial stage, the IWHM had a limited impact on reproductive policies since they worked outside the population policy framework and very few activist groups attended the first two population conferences sponsored by the United Nations in 1974 and 1984. This changed in the mid-1980s as a result of the transnational networks that had developed during the International Women's Decade (IWD) and of the new, more transnational identity of the IWHM. In addition to the networks developed during the IWD, the IWHM activists also gained valuable knowledge and understanding of how to influence the UN system and policy debates. Most importantly, the IWHM formed epistemic communities of policy professionals and activists from around the global to pursue issues of common interest.

The 1980s were a decade of right-wing governments in the United States and Europe and many of women's rights were under attack. During the Reagan years there was a cut in the U.S. funding for the International Planned Parenthood and the UN Population Fund. Thus, the international arena became a more attractive site of action. Furthermore, the UN conferences and foundations provided resources for the Preparatory Committee meetings (Prep-Coms) held immediately prior to the formal meeting where women from different regions could meet beforehand to shape the agenda of the conference. All of this meant that the IWHM became very active in the UN arena in the 1990s.[12]

The 1990s were also the decade of several important UN conferences around human rights, the environment, social development, and included the 4th World Conference on Women in Beijing. The women's lobby was the most vocal at these conferences as they planned innovative strategies to gain visibility for their issues. But the most important gains of this period included the linking of women's rights to human rights. This meant redefining human rights to include rights violated by non-state actors such as violence against women,[13] and broadening the definition of reproductive rights from family planning and "safe motherhood" to include issues of sexuality, gender relations, and economic status. Also new institutional actors emerged such as the International Women's Health Coalition in 1984 and the International Network on Feminist Approaches to Bioethics (FAB) in 1992.

Thus, the Cairo declaration linked the social and economic empowerment of women to their reproductive rights. This success of women's issues is tied to what Mayhew and Watts call "linkage politics,"[14] that is, they sought credibility and funding for women's issues by linking them to issues already high on the international agenda such as peace, human rights, and economic development. For example, at the Nairobi conference, gender violence was seen as an obstacle to peace as it was seen as an obstacle to human rights for all in Vienna. That such linkages are necessary only highlights how secondary women's issues are in and of themselves. However, in adopting this accommodating stance, the IWHM has made some gains.

One gain was the major call of the Cairo conference that was the "rights of all people to reproductive health, special attention to women's empowerment and clients' needs, repudiated reliance on contraceptive services as the tool achieving demographic targets."[15] Using 22 projects in 18 countries, Haberland and Measham illuminate the efforts of policy makers, program managers, health workers, advocates, and clients in translating the Cairo declaration. The most important changes they found were that both India and China abolished or modified policies that were hostile to women's rights and freedom of choice; decision makers were increasingly willing to include sexuality as a legitimate part of reproductive health; there was acceptance of a wider range of reproductive services than just those related to family planning; and there were efforts to address economic and social inequalities pertaining to women affecting their empowerment as health consumers, equal partners in sexual relationships, and important members of their families and communities in decision making.

Another gain has been the wider range of contraceptive choices in China despite the continuation of the one-child policy. In South Africa the government is working with a women's health organization to improve the public health system that was geared toward apartheid. There are numerous examples of health care staff at all levels, engaging in intensive workshops to examine their own attitudes and behaviors about sexuality and women's rights to change their internalized scripts as well as those of consumers. In the Philippines, a simple analytic tool of asking women their health care needs has reshaped the agenda and programs of the providers. In Turkey, programs have included men in pregnancy, delivery, and postpartum recovery.

Unfortunately, despite these gains, there were other hurdles to leap. As I discuss in the next section, the SAPs of the 1990s wrought havoc on women's health.

Structural Adjustment and Its Undermining of Women's Health

In the 1980s and 1990s, despite the gains made by the IWHM, there was a big shift in the international perception of health from a humanitarian issue to an issue of economic growth and security.[16] This meant the emergence and importance of new political actors in the international health arena such as the World Bank, the International Monetary Fund (IMF), and the World Trade Organization (WTO). These new actors have completely redefined the discourse on health as evident in World Bank's 1993 report titled, "Investing in Health Care."

The report emphasizes two strategies: the "introduction of market forces into the health care sector and the allocation of public resources according to criteria of technical and instrumental efficiency."[17] As Laurell and Arellano argue, "the practical outcome of this orthodox neo-liberal logic is health care reorganization that implies state withdrawal from the financing and provision of health services and a reorientation of public institutions toward selective assistance, in a scheme reminiscent of antiquated models of charity for the poor . . . a modern version of the 19th century charity."[18] Navarro has called this domination of the neoliberal discourse in the health arena "intellectual fascism."[19]

So we have two contrasting developments. On the one hand, health is defined by health activists and the IWHM as an issue of rights. On the other, governments pressured by the World Bank and IMF define it as an issue of security linked to economic and political development.[20] As a result, if health is taken to mean a "state of complete physical, mental, and social well-being," as defined by the WHO, then women's health has deteriorated in all respects in the era of global trade.

The main recommendation of the World Bank's health reforms was privatization of health care to be understood as: introduction of user charges in state health facilities, especially for consumer drugs and curative care (the rationale was that the rich would be made to pay, thus leaving the government free to pay for community services and public health for the poor); promotion of third-party insurance such as sickness funds and social security; promotion of private facilities and clinics; and decentralization of planning, budgeting, and purchasing for government health services.[21]

Such privatization recommendations are surprising in Third World countries where the people already assume a greater share of health care burden than in the First World countries. In the latter, especially Scandinavian countries, governments assume over 90 percent of health expenditure. By contrast, in sub-Saharan Africa and Asia, governments only contribute about 52–57 percent toward the total health budget.[22] Such universal recommendations did not take into consideration the differential impact within countries by gender or other social factors. Hence, national policies are now being set at the international level with little understanding of local realities.

One of the impacts of privatization of health reforms in Third World countries has been a cut in public health services, particularly primary care, and the increased use of nongovernmental and private voluntary organizations to deliver services.[23] In Africa, NGOs provide between 25 and 94 percent of health services. For example, 25 percent of hospital care in Ghana is private, while in Zimbabwe, 94 percent of services for the elderly are privatized, and in Uganda and Malawi, 40 percent of all health services are privatized. Privatization has greatly reduced government-funded primary care, thus limiting access to health care for the poor, particularly among women. In some cases, health care is completely inaccessible to poor women. When poor women have to pay for health care from their meager earnings, they do so for their children but not for themselves.

Thus health reforms have made women even more vulnerable healthwise. In the United States the linking of health care to employment has meant that women who are unemployed or work part-time have no health care. The introduction of managed care in the United States and the crisis in socialized medicine in Western and Northern Europe has meant a decline in the availability of health care for women. Women are expected to make up the cuts in public services by providing unpaid care at home and in the marketplace. One of the sharpest measures of women's deteriorating health can be seen in Eastern European countries undergoing transition. The UNICEF-sponsored MONEE Report found that while life expectancy declined in 22 countries of the region after 1989, 15 of those countries began to rebound by 1999. Seven did not, continuing to have lower life expectancy rates in 1999 than pre-1989. In Russia, women lost 2.1 years.[24] In addition to life expectancy, the maternal death rates in these countries are higher than in Europe generally.[25]

In the mid-1990s, the World Bank came under severe criticism from governments and health movements around the world. In response to this criticism, the bank made a more layered recommendation distinguishing between low-income, middle-income, and formerly socialist countries. It now advises governments to provide some health care and, in low-income countries, it recommends at least a clinical package consisting of perinatal and delivery care, family planning, sick children's care, and care for diseases like tuberculosis and sexually transmitted diseases.

Thus, women's right to health is limited to their reproductive health during their child-bearing age. Violence against women, which affects women's and girl's health at all ages, while recognized by the World Bank as a threat to their health, has received very little attention. Yet, despite the focus on child-bearing years, women's reproductive rights have been curtailed.

In countries like China and India, with very high populations, the government has enforced strict family planning.[26] Because of the traditional preference for male babies in both these countries, parents have resorted to selective abortions of female fetuses or even infanticide of girl babies to have a son. The governments in both countries have tacitly ignored these practices to ensure population reduction.

In Eastern Europe, there has been deterioration in the reproductive health of women since the post–Cold War transition as access to prenatal care has weakened. In Russia, at 52 deaths per 100,000, maternal mortality rates are six to seven times higher than those in the United States or Europe.[27] As much as one-third of those deaths are related to complications from abortions. In 1997, the average abortion rate in the region was three abortions for every birth,[28] more than twice as high as rates in the United States.[29] More than simply a physical phenomenon, abortion also affects women's emotional health. High abortion rates may reflect its acceptance and availability in these countries, but it also reflects a lack of access to family planning and contraceptives.

The population conference in Cairo in 1994 emphasized the need for countries to empower women as the best means to control their populations, yet most national governments have taken very few steps to do so. The rise of religious fundamentalisms has also curtailed women's reproductive rights by limiting access to family planning and abortion in the United States and some countries in Eastern and Western Europe.[30]

Cuts in public expenditures on health have meant that fewer people have access to family planning and sexually transmitted diseases (STD) clinics, which has facilitated the spread of STDs and HIV. Cuts in health care expenditures have meant fewer screening facilities, lack of condoms, gloves, and disposable syringes, all of which are crucial to the prevention of the spread of diseases. Finally, cuts in budgets have also meant fewer outreach programs in the community to educate women about the disease.

Given this global effort to compromise women's health, and despite the engendering of the global health discourse, the IWHM has sought a new strategy of going back to its movement roots and using the networks made during the IWD and the 1990s to launch a campaign for Health for All by collaborating with the People's Health Movement.

The IWHM and the People's Health Movement

While the above realities and the inequalities in the global health arena are being acknowledged by everyone, including the World Bank, "Missing from this literature are analyses of how and why the social inequalities within and among our societies are generated and reproduced, and how the socioeconomic and political forces responsible for this situation are affecting the quality of life of our population."[31] The aim of the People's Health Movement is to highlight this analysis and to recommit to Primary Health Care and Health for All.

The People's Health Movement (PHM) is an "international network of organizations and individuals that came together in 2000 to re-ignite the call for Health for All Now!"[32] The goal of the PHM is "to re-establish health and equitable development as top priorities in local, national and international policy-making, with comprehensive primary health care as the strategy to achieve these priorities." Its main aim is to begin with the work done by people's health movements around the world to develop long-term and sustainable solutions to health problems.

Toward this end, in December 2000 it held a People's Health Assembly (PHA) in Bangladesh. This PHA—the first of its kind—was a unique gathering. Unlike the WHO Health Assemblies, this one involved people in village and district meetings, national events, and regional workshops to prepare for the global gathering in Bangladesh. The purpose of this Assembly was to bring together policy makers, activists, and professionals to develop a People's Charter for Health and to strategize about ensuring that Health For All would become a reality rather than remain a laudable goal. The Assembly took place in a community health center in Bangladesh where the accommodations were modest and where people had a chance to talk about their concerns regarding health. Over 1,400 people from 92 countries attended this inspiring assembly.

The preamble of the resulting People's Charter For Health, which drew upon the Alma Ata Charter of Health For All, reads as follows:

> Health is a social, economic and political issue and above all a fundamental human right. Inequality, poverty, exploitation, violence and injustice are at the root of ill-health and the deaths of poor and marginalized people. Health for all requires that powerful interests have to be challenged; that globalization has to be opposed; and that political and economic priorities have to be drastically changed. This Charter builds on perspectives of people whose voices have rarely been heard before, if at all. It encourages people to develop their own solutions and to hold accountable local authorities, national governments, international organizations and corporations.[33]

What is crucial about this movement is that women's issues are central to its charter and women's networks and activists are key actors and decision makers in it. This is a direct result of the successes of the IWHM during the 1980s and 1990s. Following the Assembly, the PHM has launched two important campaigns. The first campaign, coordinated by the Women's Global Network for Reproductive Rights, is the Women's Access to Health. From 2003 to 2005 the campaign will center on primary health care for all people everywhere, "taking into account, in theory and practice, women's reproductive and sexual health needs."[34] May 28, 2003 was declared the International Day of Action for Women's Health. The three-year campaign's slogan is "Health for All—Health for Women." In 2003, the Campaign was primarily directed at national governments: "Governments Take Responsibility for Women's Health."

The other campaign that PHM launched in 2003, to celebrate the twenty-fifth anniversary of the Alma Ata Health For All Declaration and to remind the international health community of its commitment, was a year-long global campaign reviving Alma Ata's vision of a holistic approach to health care, which addresses the social, economic, and political determinants of health, rather than the World Bank's selective and privatized health care for a few. The campaign occurred in over 92 countries from where delegates came to attend the first People's Health Assembly in Bangladesh. A focus of the campaign was to promote the worldwide adoption of the People's Charter for Health, which they claim constitutes the largest consensus document on health since the Alma Ata declaration of 1978.

Research and Policy Recommendations

To conclude, if globalization is understood as changes in spatial, temporal, and cognitive boundaries, then all these have an impact on health.[35] We have new spatial configurations of health and disease in all countries; temporally, the SARS epidemic demonstrates how microbes travel faster across the globe as does information about monitoring, reporting, controlling, and treating diseases. In terms of the cognitive dimension, there have been contradictory effects. On the one hand, more knowledge is shared, as exemplified by the PHM and the success in articulating health as a human right rather than as a means to ensuring a more productive workforce; and there are more possibilities of adopting standards of health and workplace and environmental safety. On the other hand, however, messages of consumption based on U.S. lifestyles and standards of beauty also become global, which can have devastating health effects around the world.

In this global context, as Garrett notes, the international players in the health arena, especially the World Bank and the IMF have "betrayed the trust" on an unparalleled global dimension.[36] This calls for a renewed research and policy focus by all actors, state/movements/NGOs/UN, interested in realizing health as a human right for all. To this end, we need more research in the following areas. First, we must understand how states faced with SAPs can enact health policies that ensure funding for public health systems oriented to meeting health for all. In this regard, the experience of gender and people's budgets being enacted in Brazil and South Africa might provide useful ground for formulating research questions and policies. Second, more research is also needed on how the success of the discursive shift regarding health as a human right in the UN system can be translated into real redistributive policies that will ensure its realization.[37] This would also involve conducting an in-depth analysis of how the IMF and World Bank were able to enact "health reforms" that contradicted the health as a human right position of the United Nations and its many "mega conferences" and what this disjuncture between global institutions means for health and other social justice policies. The structural problems of the current global institutions that prevent them from implementing their various rights-based declarations and commitments would also be analyzed. Finally, we must learn how various social movements and NGOs working on different aspects of economic and social rights can forge coalitions that formulate monitoring mechanisms and processes to ensure that various local, national, and global institutions put people over profits, elevating the right to health (along with rights to education and a living wage) over the right to trade and property.

As Anne Donchin concludes, ". . . we need to hear stories of transformative strategies that have worked—stories by women near the centers of power—and by those at the margin. Only through such continuing dialogue can we hope to interject feminist concerns into the dominant discourses and practices that define the norms of medicine and health care delivery services."[38]

Notes

* Adopted from previous article in *Development*, 47: 36–42, June 2004, Copyright permission, Palgrave Macmillan.

1. P. Farmer, SARS and Inequality, *The Nation*, March 25, 2003.
2. I use Melucci's definition of a social movement. For him movements are ongoing constructions of collective action and identity, always in progress. They are fragmented, heterogeneous constructions including a diverse set of organizational forms, ideologies, and identities. They are continually reconstructed through diffuse, decentralized subterranean networks. They aim to bring about social change based on myriad strategies and ideological positions. What makes such fragmented heterogeneous activity a movement is the self-identification with a larger web of feminist activism. See A. Melucci (1999), *Challenging Codes: Collective Action in the Information Age*, Cambridge, UK: CUP.
3. S. Prasad (2003), Sanitizing the domestic: Cleanliness and care in nationalist discourses on health and hygiene in early 20th century Bengal, paper presented at the 4th Transnational Workshop at the University of Illinois at Urbana-Champaign.
4. O. Gomez-Dantes (2001), Health, in J. Simmons and C. D. Chantal, eds., *Managing Global Issues: Lessons Learned* (pp. 392–423), Washington, DC: Carnegie Endowment for International Peace.
5. L. Manderson and L. Whiteford (2000), "Health, Globalization, and the Fallacy of the Level Playing Field," in L. Manderson and L. Whiteford, eds., *Global Health Policy, Local Realities* (pp. 1–19), Boulder: Lynne Rienner.
6. M. M. Ferree and B. Hess (1985), *Controversy and Coalition: The New Feminist Movement*, Boston: Twayne Publishers.
7. A. Higer (1999), International Women's Activism and the 1994 Cairo Population Conference, in M. Meyer and E. Prugl, eds., *Gender Politics in Global Governance* (pp. 122–141), New York: Rowman and Littlefield.
8. D. Sanders and M. Chopra (2003), Globalization and the Challenge of Health for All: A View from sub-Saharan Africa, in K. Lee, ed., *Health Impacts of Globalization: Towards Global Governance* (pp. 105–122), London: Palgrave and Macmillan.

9. M. Desai (2002), Transnational Solidarity: Women's Agency, Structural Adjustment, and Globalization, in N. Naples and M. Desai, eds., *Women's Activism and Globalization: Linking Local Struggles and Transnational Politics* (pp. 15–33), London: Routledge.

10. A. Higer, International women's activism and the 1994 Cairo population.

11. Ibid.

12. R. Petcheksy (2003), *Global Prescriptions: Gendering Health and Human Rights*, New York: Zed Books.

13. M. Desai (1999), From Vienna to Beijing: Women's human rights activism and the human rights community, reprinted in P. Van Ness, ed., *Debating Human Rights: Critical Essays From U.S. and Asia* (pp. 184–196), London: Routledge; J. Joachim (1999), Shaping the human rights agenda: The case of violence against women, in M. Meyer and E. Prugl, eds., *Gender Politics in Global Governance* (pp. 122–141), New York: Rowman and Littlefield.

14. S. Mayhew and C. Watts (2002), Global rhetoric and individual realities: Linking violence against women and reproductive health, in K. Lee, K. Buse, and S. Fustukian, eds., *Health Policy in a Globalizing World* (pp. 159–180), Cambridge, UK: Cambridge University Press.

15. N. Haberland and D. Measham (2002), Introduction, in N. Haberland and D. Measham, eds., *Responding to Cairo: Case Studies of Changing Practices in Reproductive Health and family Planning* (pp. 1–21), New York: The Population Council.

16. O. Gomez-Dantes (2001), Health, in J. Simmons and C. D. Chantal, eds., *Managing Global Issues: Lessons Learned.*

17. A. Laurell and O. Arellano (2002), Market commodities and poor relief: The world bank proposal for health, in V. Navarro, ed., *The Political Economy of Social Inequalities: Consequences for Health and Quality of Life* (pp. 191–208), Amityville: Baywood Pub. Co., p. 192.

18. Ibid. p. 194.

19. V. Navarro (2002), A historical review (1965–1997) of studies on class, health, and quality of life: A personal account, in V. Navarro, ed., *The Political Economy of Social Inequalities: Consequences for Health and Quality of Life* (pp. 1–9), Amityville: Baywood Pub. Co.

20. I. Kickbusch (2003), Global health governance: Some theoretical considerations on the new political space, in K. Lee, ed., *Health Impacts of Globalization: Towards Global Governance* (pp. 105–122), London: Palgrave Macmillan.

21. M. Turshen (1994), The World Bank and Family Planning, *Women's International Public Health Network News* 1: 16–17.

22. World Health Organization. (2005), Annex Table 5: Selected national health accounts indicators: measured levels of expenditure on health, 1997–2001, *World health report 2004.*

23. Kickbusch, Global health governance: Some theoretical considerations on the New Political Space.

24. MONEE Project. (2001), *A Decade of Transition*, IRC.

25. MONEE Project. (2001), *Women in Transition*, IRC.

26. M. Desai (2002), Transnational Solidarity: Women's Agency, Structural Adjustment, and Globalization, in N. Naples and M. Desai, eds., *Women's Activism and Globalization: Linking Local Struggles and Transnational Politics.*

27. W. Kingkade (1997), *International Brief, Population Trends: Russia*, U.S. Department of Commerce, Economics and Statistics Administration, Bureau of the Census.

28. T. Parfitt (2003), Russia moves to curb abortion rates. *The Lancet* 362 (9388): 968.

29. J. DaVanzo and C. Grammich (2001), *Dire Demographics: Population Trends in the Russian Federation* (available at: http://www.rand.org/publications/MR/MR1273/).

30. R. P. Petchesky (2003), *Global Prescription: Gendering Health and Human Rights*, London and New York: Zed Books.

31. V. Navarro (2002), Introduction, in V. Navarro, ed., *The Political Economy of Social Inequalities: Consequences for Health and Quality of Life* (pp. 1–9), Amityville: Baywood Pub. Co.

32. People's Health Movement (available at: http://www.phmovement.org).

33. People's Health Movement, *People's Charter for Health* (available at: http://www.phmovement.org/charter/pch-english.html).

34. People's Health Movement, *A Call for Action: Campaign on Women's Access to Health* (available at: http://www.phmovement.org/campaigns/women/index.html).

35. K. Lee (2003), *Globalization and Health: An Introduction*, London: Palgrave Macmillan.

36. L. Garrett (2000), *The Betrayal of Trust: The Collapse of Global Public Health*, New York: Hyperion.

37. M. Desai (1999), From Vienna to Beijing: Women's human rights activism and the human rights community, reprinted in P. Van Ness, ed., *Debating Human Rights: Critical Essays From U.S. and Asia*; Shaping the human rights agenda: The case of violence against women, in M. Meyer and E. Prugl, eds., *Gender Politics in Global Governance.*

38. A. Donchin (2001), Introduction, in R. Tong, G. Anderson, and A. Santos, eds., *Globalizing Feminist Bioethics: Crosscultural Perspectives* (pp. 1–9), Boulder: Westview.

In Perspective

Gendered Cures for Global Health Initiatives in Africa

Josephine Nhongo-Simbanegavi

Introduction

Manisha Desai's contribution on the international women's health movement raises important points regarding the performance of international initiatives aimed at improving gender relations and raising the standard of women's health.[1] I would like to follow up two very pertinent issues that she raises: (1) historical aspects of globalization and (2) international and local policies and agendas in discordance. I consider these two issues to be very critical in helping us assess the potential of international health movements to renegotiate gender relations in Africa and to place the continent's peoples in a better position to contribute to, as well as benefit from, global health initiatives.

While Desai's chapter focuses largely on contemporary forms of globalization, she recognizes that the phenomenon has a long historical dimension spanning over several centuries. So in looking at the current relationship between globalization and Africa, it is pertinent for our analysis to incorporate precolonial, colonial, as well as postcolonial globalizations. Such a background analysis is a major factor in explaining why international health programs have often missed their targets when it comes to Africa.

The second issue I would like to raise that relates to Desai's chapter is her very insightful observation that international policies and agendas are often at variance with local and national ones. She identifies the gap between them as requiring mediation and sees this as a major challenge for the success of global initiatives. She underscores that as a constraint on the performance of initiatives such as the International Women's Health Movement (IWHM) of the late 1970s and early 1980s, and I consider it important to extend such an analysis to the period before and after the IWHM.

To address the current debate in connection with Africa, not only is it desirable to understand the issues of health from an African perspective, it is necessary. One such factor, and one that requires our serious interrogation, is the status of traditional African health or healing systems relative to Western ones. We need to explore this in the context of global power relations. More specifically, those involved in the formulation of health policies for the continent have to deal with the problem of access to health facilities and a lack of provisions for the majority of African populations, especially in relation to those groups living on the margins of African society. Marginalized communities consist mainly of victims of poverty, political strife, cultural exclusion, and those prejudiced by the continent's unequal developmental patterns. As an economic entity, Africa is divided into small islands of wealth and vast seas of poverty. To understand the distributional challenges health initiatives face in that part of the world, gender is one of the main tools of analysis. Such an analysis would enable us to understand potential gendered health disparities both at the policy level as well as on the ground, where a gendered analysis would measure the potential and actual rate of success or failure for various health policies and their impacts.

While some common patterns can be discerned, the process of identifying these African perspectives should not underestimate challenges presented by the continent's vastness. No one African experience can fully and effectively speak for others. I point this out because, for a long time, it has been a very contentious issue with most Africans. The tendency in some circles has been to form opinions about the whole continent on the basis of very limited interactions with just a handful of Africans, or worse still, on the basis of unverified and poorly understood news reports. Intervention programs fashioned on the basis of such reductionist assessments have the potential to create great harm and achieve very little. For that reason, it is important to identify the specific position of each of the countries targeted for international initiatives.

Apart from simply identifying the major health issues, we need to explore how gender relations in different countries on the continent mediate these issues. As globalization also affects each country and society in a different way, health issues must also be examined with respect to differing experiences of global influences.

Traditional Health/Healing Systems and Western Medicine

For the majority of African countries, Christian missionary ventures preceded colonization, and they thrived under it. Mission stations came to constitute major sites of struggle between the European colonizers and their reluctant African hosts. In the battle to conquer the elusively understood African soul, colonial missionaries extended their activities beyond the confines of the spiritual into the day-to-day lives of the indigenous peoples. Apart from being contenders in the area of religion, European colonizers also adopted strategies to wrestle African health and education from traditional practitioners. As instruments of colonial globalization, the missionary ventures created significant conflicts between preexisting health and healing systems and the newly emerging European systems. While the latter demonized the former, traditional health practitioners resisted the invasion of their space by Christian missionaries, and a major battle soon ensued, initially over the souls of the Africans, and later over their bodies.

One of the major strategies the newly arrived Westerners adopted was to use church sermons to declare traditional medico-religious practices as worthless. However, more energy and resources were required to convince the Africans that the tested methods their ancestors had relied on for centuries were less effective than Western remedies. To secure that unlikely victory, the missionaries campaigned for the criminalization of traditional African health practices. This venture was more successful, as it merely required them to secure the signature of the colonial administrator. Under that new dispensation, traditional healers were gradually pushed to the margins of medical practice, into the service of the very poor and die-hard "pagans".

Initially designated as witches, traditional healers' very existence was later denied through the passing of witchcraft suppression legislations in most of the conquered territories.[2] Such were some of the earliest effects of global restructuring. That scenario prevailed in the colonial period and beyond it. Up to now, the field of traditional African medicine is still haunted by the effects of colonial harassment. In global health discourse, African medicines or health remedies are still considered primitive and unscientific. In that sense, the continent is largely viewed as a recipient rather than a producer of medical knowledge.

Apart from interrogating the above in the context of global power relations, we also need to understand the gender dimensions and implications from these relations. This is critical in helping us identify the points of intervention to resuscitate African health systems and give them due space to play their role in the battle against global challenges such as HIV/AIDS. It is important to note that historically, women were major players in traditional African health and healing systems. Even under precolonial patriarchal systems, in all their excesses, African society had always recognized the importance of women's contributions toward health delivery and healing. To that effect, traditional societies gave women space to practice their trade as herbalists and as religious figures. While both genders played equally important roles in the areas of general adult medicine and in the fields of sexual and spiritual health, the areas of what Western medicine designates as obstetrics and gynecology, firmly belonged in the women's terrain. Women also dominated the field of child health, or what modern medicine refers to as pediatrics.

Knowledge relating to the gender of traditional medical practitioners is important in helping us see that women held a significant proportion of the knowledge that colonial agents sought to undermine through their deliberate sabotage operations. Attempts to recover that knowledge should not lose sight of the fact that women were central rather than peripheral players in that exercise. Just as the distribution of traditional or indigenous health knowledge was gendered, so should the policies that seek to facilitate its recovery in the present time. It is no coincidence that the fields where women traditionally dominated are the areas hardest hit by the current health crisis on the continent. Performance and delivery in these fields deteriorated with the status of African women under colonialism.

Gender is also a very useful paradigm in the interrogation of the colonial health systems that submerged traditional African ones. The generation of Western medical knowledge has traditionally been a male preserve, although the delivery of its services has been largely dependent on women who dominate in nursing and community health care. In recent years, the number of female doctors has risen. However, there has been no proportional growth in relation to women's contribution to medical research. Male doctors spend more time in research and in private medical practice, having off-loaded their public hospital duties onto the female doctors. For Africa, the pattern in the colonial era, whereby men dominated the production of Western medical knowledge while women took care of the delivery of health services seems to prevail still. There is no evidence that the pattern has significantly changed. What does that mean for Europe's former colonies on the continent?

As highlighted earlier, female health and child health are some of the hardest hit areas. Africa's health challenges have been increasingly assuming a female characteristic, both in terms of the distribution of illness as well as in terms of health care delivery. At the same time, research and the generation of prescriptions or solutions to the continent's health problems is a male-dominated process. That discrepancy exacerbates Africa's health crises. It is true that these dynamics are also reflected in the West. However, one cannot fail to see that they are most desperately felt on the African continent where they have been accentuated by structural adjustment programs. We can trace their development from the earlier globalization that came to Africa through colonialism, to the current one, which is a brainchild of the Bretton Woods institutions.

International and Domestic Agendas

This brings me to the other major point I want to follow up from Desai's contribution; that is, the need to address the discrepancy between local or national agendas and the form and content of international health initiatives. This is an issue that relates to the common practice by African governments to sign international conventions without bothering to review their domestic legal instruments that they might reflect or promote those internationally declared commitments.

Zimbabwe's case provides useful insights in that respect. Zimbabwe, like many others in Africa, joined the international family and signed the much-discussed Convention to End All Discrimination Against Women (CEDAW). However, Section 23(3) of the domestic constitution still allows for women's discrimination in the area of family law, as this aspect of one's life is subject to the dictates of "custom." To legalize such discrepancies, Section 111(b) of the country's constitution expressly states that international instruments that Zimbabwe ratifies do not necessarily become part of domestic law. Zimbabwe is not alone: similar discrepancies can be found in the constitutions and statutes of other African countries. Differently and imaginatively packaged, they invariably have the same effect: that of compromising women's legal status and leaving them exposed to gender-based violence and discrimination.

A document compiled by united Zimbabwean women's groups highlighted such laws as providing the legal and constitutional framework for practices that seriously compromise women's health. According to the document they had produced for the failed constitutional review exercise of 1999, the women demanded a removal of the constitutional clauses that sealed their fate as female citizens subject to "custom." Speaking as a country-wide coalition of women's groups, they observed that the current constitution undermined their capacity to address the problems of maternal mortality and illness, reproductive diseases, erratic contraceptive use by women with little control over their fertility, denial of sexual rights, and exposure to sexually transmitted diseases, coerced sex in the home and in the workplace.[3] In relation to women's general health, the coalition highlighted the incidence of malnutrition for women in poor households, especially given the cultural norms that favor feeding male members of the family at the expense of their female counterparts, the heavy workloads and poor working conditions that many women endure, mental health problems, exposure to HIV/AIDS, violence, and generally poor access to health services.[4]

The examples provided in the cited document demonstrate without doubt the wide gap between the form and content of international gender laws (and by extension health policies), and the lived experiences of women in some of the countries that sign those laws. At the same time, that document shows that when women are directly engaged, their input on what needs to be done is very clear and specific—a far cry from the thinking in certain circles that Africa's male leadership has all the answers to the continent's health problems. The compilation of such a document by a coalition of women's groups is a tremendous story about African women's organizational capacity and their ability to select from a wide variety of options what best suits them.[5] This has critical implications for international organizational strategies.

There is a need to take into account the fact that those government-focused international forums inviting delegates to converge at a European or North American venue may not be the most effective ways of reaching out to grassroots women in Africa. Such a "northern-based" gathering is more likely to be attended by African men and the problems highlighted above are likely to continue unabated. The "man" question in international relations[6] will remain unresolved. On the other hand, if international organizations moved out of their ivory towers in Europe or North America and headed south for such meetings, they would be more likely to make contact with grassroots organizations where women dominate. That would enhance chances to mediate the gap between the international and the domestic. It is both a global relations issue as well as a gender one.

The Need for Refocused Gender Awareness

It is encouraging to note that current efforts to confront the HIV/AIDS epidemic in Africa recognize the critical position of women. However, this awareness only extends to their positions as the major victims of infection and as the main caregivers in the face of Africa's collapsing health institutions. In other words, there is a strong awareness of the feminine orientation of the current challenges. The focus of international health initiatives has therefore been to *teach* women about the disease. On the occasions that the women's voices have been sought, it has only been for the purposes of rendering the "donor community" conscious of their "plight." One cannot deny that such exercises are important and necessary. However, the next question we need to ask is: when are these women going to be considered experienced enough (if not knowledgeable) about their diseases to begin to teach the "international community" something about those medical challenges? With the long experience of infection, and all those "clinical" hours they have spent with HIV /AIDS patients going through the various stages of the disease, when are we going to acknowledge these women's expertise on the subject and refocus our gender awareness? Given the roles women used to play in traditional healing systems, and given the depth of the medical knowledge they held then, would we not like to give these women a different kind of attention now?

To address the above question, it is also necessary to learn from the women's initiatives. We are only too aware of how the latest instruments of globalization have impacted the limited health infrastructure that existed in Africa prior to the phenomenon of structural adjustment programs. Women have responded by returning to traditional knowledge systems. Frustrated by the prohibitive costs of Western medicine and the uncertainty of a continued supply, many African health practitioners are putting more emphasis on indigenous remedies. Their prescriptions are a combination of traditional herbs and indigenous foods, all the things that were once degraded as primitive and inferior. Success in recovering that vital medicinal knowledge, and in promoting the production of those indigenous foods, will very much depend on the gender awareness we are willing to inject into our health actions. Already, women's trading networks are critical channels through which this vital knowledge is transmitted within and across the boundaries of several African countries. Health organizations, whether local or international, should follow the directions that the women are currently charting. In this way, the gender and global discrepancies will be addressed, and in the process, the major health challenges will be confronted.

Notes

1. M. Desai (2003), Gender, health, and globalization: A critical social movement perspective, paper presented at the Gender, Health, and Globalization Conference at Yale University, June 20–22, 2003.
2. The legislation criminalized the act of accusing someone as a witch rather than the practice of witchcraft. In that sense "witches" did not exist. In Zimbabwe such a law came into existence just nine years into the colonial period *Witchcraft Suppression Ordinance*, 1899. In the case of colonial Zimbabwe, the subject of the importance of incorporating African methods to confront African illnesses and sickness was bravely tackled by the late Michael Gelfand who became the first professor of African medicine at the then University of Rhodesia. He published widely on the subject. A critical study of European medicine and diagnosis for African illnesses also exists in relation to colonial Malawi.

See M. Vaughan (1991), *Curing Their Ills, Colonial Power and African Illness*, Cambridge: Polity Press.

3. Zimbabwe Women's Resource Centre and Network (ZWRCN), Reproductive Health. *Fact Sheets*, pp. 19–20.

4. ZWRCN, Health, *Fact Sheets*, pp. 25–26.

5. The women consulted a variety of materials from other constitutional processes on the African continent, e.g., Uganda, Tanzania, Kenya, Zambia, South Africa.

6. See M. Zalewski and J. Parpart, eds. (1998), *The "Man" Question in International Relations*, Boulder: Westview.

In Perspective

Globalization, Gender, and Health: A Perspective on Latin American Sexual and Reproductive Health

Liliana Acero

Introduction

Sexual and reproductive health has been a privileged domain of social and gender stratification at both country and international levels for centuries. With globalization, an international division of labor between countries and genders manifests more openly: new types of sexual and reproductive health resources are transferred to the North and have an unequal impact on the negotiation of gender power in the North and South. The way to socially reproduce generations, including caring for children, meeting subsistence needs and ensuring socialization, does not only vary with time, but also between income levels and geographic locations. Globalization has had a direct bearing on stress and disease within this reproductive stratification, especially among the most vulnerable women in the Third World.

This chapter sets out to briefly comment on some of the implications for Latin American populations at the intersection between globalization, gender and health, focusing on sexual and reproductive health patterns in certain countries. First, some international and regional policies that impacted Latin America are addressed and quantitative trends are described for two countries. Then, the overall international and local driving forces of local health reforms are described to illustrate their effects on women and gender, where possible. Finally, specific cases—especially that of Norplant in Brazil—are summarized to show the importance of local civil society action in shaping health and gender. The chapter ends with a note on gaps in research and policy at the intersection of globalization, health, and gender.

The Main Impacts of International Policies

The model of globalization led by the policies of the International Monetary Fund (IMF) and the World Bank, has posed particular problems for gender and health in Latin America. In the 1990s, the international shift from demographic control concerns into reproductive rights within population studies, impacted Latin American gender and overall health policies. A number of United Nations Conferences in the 1990s—addressed within Desai's chapter in this volume—developed substantive programs on social equality, justice, development, and peace, women's rights and sexual and reproductive rights that had a strong regional impact.[1]

Three main positions were taken by Latin American scholars who represented different constituencies: that of the UN population specialists, mainly at the UN Population Fund (UNFPA), the World Health Organization (WHO), and the Pan-American Health Organization (PAHO); that of the women's movement; and that of the pro-natalist movement and the Vatican.[2] First, the Economic Commission on Latin America and the Caribbean (ECLAC) reframed the population policy to meet its original demographic goals[3] of applying the concept of "unsatisfied demand": showing how rights sometimes cannot be exercised due to lack of information and material resources, especially among the most vulnerable female groups. Secondly, the position held by the International Women's Health Coalition was that women should be seen as social subjects within population policies and female rights to decision making should be recognized.[4]

The Latin American and Caribbean Women's Health Network[5] followed the Cairo Program of Action with six diagnostic themes for the 1990s, around which the women's movement reorganized activities: female sexual abuse, male responsibility in reproductive health, women's organizations participation in decision making, quality of reproductive health services, incomplete abortions, and adolescent access to reproductive health. They emphasized research, policy, and action and suggested that specific topics, such as pregnancy, birth, and sexual identity, be addressed through gender comparisons.

Sexual and Reproductive Health

Despite the initiatives described earlier, rights to sexual and reproductive health are still incompletely researched and exercised in Latin America.

Table 5.1 Relevant indicators on female sexual and reproductive health: Chile/Argentina for 2002*

Reproductive health indicator	Chile	Argentina
Use of contraceptives	—55.6% of urban women & 53.6% of rural women users (IUD's, 67.1%; pills 29.9%) —82.3% of people (W&M) claim disinformation on methods	Between 44% and 60% of women users, (modern methods only 30%) —High inequity of access to methods for both W&M
Adolescent fertility rates	13.7% of total births within the 15–19 years-old age-cohort	Higher (2.9%) than national one of (1.3%)
Abortion	Between 150,000 and 160,000 estimated per year	Between 450,000 and 500,000 estimated per year (sub-registry estimated at 50%)
Maternal deaths	—Reduction in maternal deaths from 2.7 × 1,000 in 1960, to 0.3 in 1997) —1/3 of cases caused by unsafe clandestine abortions	—Rates of 0.35 × 1,000 deaths in 2000 (compared to an average 1.2 × 1,000 1985–1995) —30% of cases caused by unsafe clandestine abortions
Sterilization	Banned by law, but practiced by 5.9% of urban and 8.9% of rural women (1997)	Banned by law, but practiced sparsely (1)
HIV/AIDS	Increasing feminization (15.2 times between 1991 and 1999)	Fourfold increase in disease between 1991 and 1994 (qualitative estimates indicate feminization)
Sexually transmitted diseases	60% of STDs borne by women	Qualitative estimates show increases in STDs, including chlamydia
Breast and cervix cancer	Both represent 2.4% of total female deaths	Breast cancer represents 20.6% of female deaths from tumors
Old age	Higher female life expectancy (78.3 years average—compared to 75.8 between 1985 and 1990) with no quality service for menopause/old age	Lack of adequate allopathic or alternative support for women's menopause or old age

Note: * Data corresponds to 2002 for both countries, unless otherwise indicated in the table; (1) Surgical sterilization in Brazil is a major trend. It is the primary method of contraception used by women between ages 15–49.

Table 5.1 presents selective indicators based on two countries and one gender.[6] However, they reflect broader general Latin American trends.

Table 5.1 shows that, overall, women have improved their reproductive health in the last two decades, especially in terms of maternal mortality and the use of contraception. However, their frequent use of abortion, high levels of sexually transmitted diseases (STDs), especially among the poor, and diseases related to the reproductive organs, as well as high percentages of adolescent births (as illustrated by the earlier and selected case studies[7]) show that differential access to information and services as well as inequality in the distribution of economic and health resources are hindering both genders in the lower-income brackets. For example, in Chile, only 10 percent of public hospitals admit men in the birthing room and the father is present in only 19.9 percent of births.[8] Stereotypes among gender categories permeate contraception.[9] Females are still the main contraceptive users. Men, especially those older and middle-aged, tend to refuse to use condoms and poorer females bear the highest burden of the lack of adequate contraception, that is, high abortion rates, STDs, and the feminization of HIV/AIDS. These structural changes are to be better understood in the light of: (a) globalization trends that provided an incentive for a series of local health reforms, and, (b) the pressure of local and international women's movements.

Gender in the Health Reforms

The need for health reforms in the region became apparent when the move to more democratic regimes in Latin America in the 1980s demanded the reform of the State, the inclusion of marginalized populations, and a higher quality of health care in the context of financial shortage. Efficiency and quality improvement as the goals of IMF and World Bank policies influenced the aims and goals of the health reforms by promoting or financing them. World Trade Organization agreements on trade in services also became a local incentive for efficiency in health delivery.[10]

The implementation of these changes depended largely upon the previous characteristics of the social protection system (health care system and social security), which varied greatly between countries in the region. For example, some countries spent 18 percent of their GDP on social policies while others spent no more than 8 percent; and 20–90 percent of the region's population was covered by social security.[11] Still, the health reforms have largely resulted in the displacement of the institutional and political contexts in health care from the central to the local level, and from the public to the private sector. Further, strategies were implemented differently across countries. For example, while Brazil originally followed a bottom-up strategy strongly influenced by civil society, Argentina and Mexico implemented a top-down strategy led by government bureaucracies.

All the health reforms took place in the context of neoliberal policies of trade liberalization and structural adjustment programs (SAPs), which had already brought about strong cutbacks in local government expenditures on social, health, and education policies. The enactment of these policies increased poverty levels significantly, drawing larger parts of the population below the poverty line and increasing unemployment rates[12] (in the order of 25–30 percent and even higher among young age-cohorts in lower-income levels[13]). As Desai's chapter argues, the growing international women's health movement, "has not been as successful in engendering national and local policies and in raising expenditures on women's health,"[14] partly because this new health discourse has arisen in the context of neoliberal policies of structural readjustment.

These health reforms have been critiqued from a gender perspective for a number of reasons. First, in the model of primary health care, prevalent prior to the reforms, primarily young mothers already played a key role as voluntary health monitors at the community level. On the one hand, these women helped to improve the types of national health indicators mentioned earlier, as well as allowing women to negotiate greater autonomy vis-à-vis their partners through their involvement in community work. On the other hand, it strengthened women's gendered attributes as health assistants. A similar model shapes the new health strategies in the reforms, where this female role has largely gone unquestioned.

Second, as the delivery of public services decreased and/or became partially paid for, new autonomous social networks developed in order to address the most urgent health problems of poor populations. Women took the lead in health prevention and self-help for chronic diseases, even in cases of government-initiated health-promotion strategies.

Third, a greater responsibility for health care was externalized to households and families. In many cases, this was based on the false assumption that households were formed by nuclear families. It disregarded the extent to which social relations have been changing in Latin America toward an increase in single-parent and one-person households among the old and the young, the feminization of the workforce, the decrease in extended families, the aging of the population, and so on. For example, in Chile between 1970 and 1992, extended families, where women usually play large roles in health care, had decreased from 47.4 percent of households to 23.4 percent. In 2000, already 35 percent of Chilean women, between 18 and 60 years old, were employed and women above 60 years old represented around 10 percent of the population.[15]

Fourth, there are a number of new health-related activities at the intersection of the domestic and the institutional systems carried out mainly or solely by women. Today, time-consuming encounters with the institutional system are required for a number of activities, including the regular care of children, the home-care of the sick, the care-givers' own health care, care of the chronically ill and of people with sustained disabilities, as well as meeting new requirements for hospitalization that are due to the reduction in hospitalization times and the increase in in-hospital tasks, for example, meals and drugs provision.

The contradictions present in these phenomena are hardly invisible. There is a greater demand upon women's time to perform health-related activities and less availability of real time to do so. This overburdens the already "double working day" of employed women (although some level of sharing in domestic chores between genders can be seen, especially related to food preparation and weekend activities).[16] Moreover, some women see their possibilities of integration into the labor market dwindle due to their role as caretakers. For those already poor, this in turn perpetuates the cycle of poverty. And, for those living alone, a model based on domestic health becomes totally inadequate. If a single person falls ill, there is little access to institutional and domestic support. In turn, men who are displaced from the labor market by economic crisis or recession, or who are no longer the primary household income providers, frequently resort to domestic or street violence or addiction.[17] Not surprisingly, then, epidemiological profiles show increases in the proportion of the mentally ill and related syndromes of mental distress in both sexes: depression in females, alcoholism in men. For example, in Chile, depression accounted for 5.1 percent of disease burden in 1996 and alcoholism for 4.7 percent; and both are the second leading cause of disease in that country. If posttraumatic stress disorders were included, mental health–related ailments would total 7.3 percent of Chilean women's disease burden.[18] These figures are often directly related to stress generated by impoverished economic conditions, increases in productivity levels to compete in a global world, and a rise in domestic violence. The latter is largely a consequence of poverty-inducing globalization as well as of changing gender roles in the household—while male roles remain relatively static, the more active public presence of women results in a shifting of the balance of household dynamics.

The Local Women's Movement: The Case of Norplant in Brazil

With these critiques in mind, what have been the avenues opened for the social and women's movement around health? Paradoxically, in the context of reform, increasing reliance upon domestic and community-level involvement has also led to the empowerment of women and the renegotiation of gender roles through newfound links between NGOs and the State.

Following the implementation and failure of international reform policies, private, nationally, and internationally funded NGOs associated with health or women's issues blossomed in many countries, occupying the gap left by the privatization and decentralization of health services as well as the cutbacks in public service deliveries. Many of their followers regrouped in the Latin American and Caribbean Health Network (RSMLAC) or in the Association for Women's Rights in Development (AWID), the latter comprised primarily of socially involved academics. Also, new international social movements with a strong Third World—and Latin American—presence united around a deep critique of existing globalization strategies met repeatedly in Porto Alegre, Brazil,[19] to participate in Anti-globalization Social Forums. Here, "Health for All," as discussed in Desai's chapter[20] in this volume, was one of the leading concerns in the development of alternative health reform strategies.

The new role played by NGOs and community-level organizations was crucial in such circumstances as the civil society debates and actions that led to the interruption of the clinical trials for the contraceptive Norplant in Brazil.[21] Norplant, an under-skin hormonal device for long-term contraception, surgically implanted and removed, had proved to have uncomfortable and even dangerous side-effects in developed and developing countries.[22] Yet, UN Population Fund's global policies for the international implementation of contraception favored the controlled trials of Norplant in Brazil, as did the government. In response, the evaluations and critiques developed by feminist academics and women's organizations voiced both domestically and at international forums, incited a public debate on sexuality and reproduction. It was held through both the printed and broadcast media, and it went beyond the application of Norplant: traditional gender roles in sexuality were publicly discussed and questioned; the suffering of women using certain forms of contraception became apparent; women's rights to know about medical interventions to their bodies and general difficulties in using informed consent for marginal populations were all openly illustrated by this case.

NGOs played an important role in the dissemination of alternative information on Norplant and led the opposition through specific publicizing strategies. Eventually, public disagreement pressured the government to review its decision, and questionable trials were interrupted.

On Research and Policy

There are many more undocumented examples of local struggles related to globalization, gender, and health that have been minimally researched compared to Norplant or to the practices of female sterilization. These include the use of pharmacogenics, inter-country genetic/reproductive tourism and trafficking, trials of drugs banned in developed countries, the claims of the disabled and the elderly around pension funds and health coverage, and the demands of midwives/traditional and alternative practitioners against the global medicalization of health and mental health.

There are also few inter-country comparisons within Latin America and between developed and developing countries on topics where linkages between globalization, gender, and health are explicitly drawn. In an increasingly globalized world, the intersection of these constructs is a new field in both research and policy.

Relevant surveys on gender and health, useful for comparative research, are either incomplete, as for drug addiction by gender, age, and type of substance, or do not allow strict inter-country comparisons, as for non-standardized and longitudinal data of HIV/AIDS. To date, local case-study work has proven to garner the richest analysis of gender identities, notions of motherhood, parenthood, and women's reproductive rights.[23]

Engendering policymaking, in spite of the initiatives of international organizations, has not permeated local government bodies on a daily basis, especially at the municipal level. In some cases, local social/health movements have promoted more gender-equality than local policies designed specifically to address particular issues, as in SOS—Brazil which works against domestic and sexual violence. For advocacy groups and international and academic forums to develop equity-based and sustainable policy-making in gender, globalization, and health, new regional social practices must be more systematically studied from an international perspective.

Notes

1. Most especially: The IV World Conference on Women (Beijing, 1995 and Beijing Five plus and Ten plus); The World Summit on Social Development (Copenhagen, 1995), the International Conference on Population and Development (Cairo, 1994), and the World Conference on Human Rights (Vienna, 1993). M. Desai (2003), Gender, health, and globalization: A critical social movement perspective, paper presented at the Gender, Health, and Globalization Conference at Yale University, June 20–22, 2003.
2. For example, CELADE and ECLAC (1993) sought a regional productive transformation with equity: economic growth within globalization together with redistribution policies, to diminish social gaps internal to different countries.

3. ECLAC/CELADE (1993), *Población, Equidad y transformación productiva*, Santiago de Chile: ECLAC/CELADE.
4. International Women's Health Coalition, IWHC (1994), Women's Voices 94, in *Women's Declaration on Population Policies*, New York: IWHC.
5. Brazil, Colombia, Nicaragua, Peru, Chile.
6. Table data based on PAHO, "Gender, Health and Sexual and Reproductive Rights of women in the context of Reform," various articles, Santiago, April 2002 CEDES (2002), "Salud y derechos sexuales y Reproductivos en Argentina," *Notas informativas* N1, April 2002, Buenos Aires: Argentina, CEDES. CELADE (1997), Boletín Demográfico, Year 20, N 20-22, Santiago de Chile: CELADE; J. Werneck, F. Carneiro, and A. Rotania, Autonomy and procreation: Brazilian Feminist Analyses, In *Globalizing Feminist Bioethics: Crosscultural Perspectives*, ed. Tong, R. with Anderson and Santos (pp. 114–134) Boulder: Westview Press, 2000.
7. For example: T. Valdés, and M. Busto, eds. (1994), *Sexualidad y reproducción: Hacia la construcción de derechos*, Santiago de Chile: CORSAPS/FLACSO Editores.
8. MINSAL (2001), *Transversalización de la perspectiva de género en las políticas de reforma de Salud en Chile*, Santiago de Chile: Ministry of Health.
9. There is some evidence in case-study work that trends are changing among young married couples in different income brackets, where open discussions on contraception are more frequent: L. Acero, et al. (1991), *Textile Workers in Brazil and Argentina: A Study of the Interrelationships between Work and Households*, Tokyo: The United Nations University; L. Acero (1997), Conflicts between demands in new technologies and women's households: Female work and training needs in Argentina and Brazil, in S. Mitter and S. Rowbotham, eds., *Women Encounter*, Technology (pp. 135–152), London: Routledge and Kegan; MINSAL (2000), Estudio Nacional de Comportamiento Sexual, *Primeros Análisis*, Santiago de Chile: Ministry of Health, National Commission for HIV.
10. S. Fleury, S. Belmartino, and E. Baris, eds. (2000), *Reshaping Health Care in Latin America: A Comparative Analysis of Health Care Reform in Argentina, Brazil and Mexico*, Ottawa: IDRC.
11. C. Mesa-Lago (1978), *Social Security in Latin America: Pressure Groups, Stratification and Inequality*, Pittsburgh: University of Pittsburgh; According to the author, in 1990, the health expenditure per capita on social security was US 167.8 in Argentina, 26.4 US in Brazil, and 38.8% in Mexico.
12. At present, in Argentina they are as high as 56% in some Provinces (*Journal Página* 12, from July 26, 2004 and July 28, 2004, quoting INDEC (INDEC [2004], *Boletín Indicadores de Desocupación*, Buenos Aires: Argentina: Ministerio de Economía).
13. L. Acero (1996), Programa de Acción Social para Grupos Vulnerables: Documento sobre Jóvenes Vulnerables, *Final Report*, Buenos Aires/Washington: Secretary of Social Development and the Inter-American Bank of Development.
14. M. Desai, Gender, health, and globalization.
15. PAHO (2002), Gender, Health and Sexual and Reproductive Rights of Women in the Context of Reform, Various articles, Santiago de Chile: PAHO.

16. A study I carried out with a thousand textile workers' households in Brazil and Argentina in the early 1990s—and a follow up in the mid-1990s (Acero, 1991; 1997) showed that while female workers performed on average four hours of domestic tasks on the average week day, men did less than one hour during the week and about two to three on the weekend, compared to six to eight among women. The younger age cohort had a slightly fairer division of household labor, but men still did not much participate in health care work, except for the purchase of medication and some health-related paperwork.

17. PAHO, Gender, Health and Sexual and Reproductive Rights of Women in the Context of Reform; S. Larraín, et al. (1993), *Estudio de prevalencia de la violencia intrafamiliar y la situación de la mujer en Chile*, Santiago de Chile: ISIS Internacional; J. Olavaria, ed. (2001b), *Hombres: identidad/es y violencia, 2 Encuentro de Estudios de masculinidades: identidades, cuerpos, violencia y políticas públicas, UAHC/FLACSO*, Santiago de Chile: FLACSO.

18. M. Concha and X. Aguilera, et al. (1996), *Carga de enfermedad*, Santiago de Chile: Ministry of Health.

19. Also in India, in 2003.

20. M. Desai, Gender, health, and globalization.

21. S. Correa (1994), Power and Decision: The social control of reproduction, in *Norplant in the Nineties: Realities, Dilemmas, Missing Pieces* (pp. 287–309), Cambridge: Harvard School of Public Health; C. Barroso and S. Correa (1995), Public servants, professionals and feminists: The politics of contraceptive research in Brazil, in F. Ginsburg and R. Rapp, eds., *Conceiving the New World Order* (pp. 292–306), Berkeley: University of California Press.

22. It was being promoted for population control, especially among poor women. In developing countries, the information provided by medical teams during clinical trials was so poor that, it did not allow a real informed consent process, especially as this contraceptive could not be voluntarily self-removed. Moreover, developing country clinical trials provided scarce resources for surgical removal of Norplant and for the training of health experts and promoters.

23. For example: J. Olavarría (2001a), *¿Hombres a la deriva? Poder, trabajo y sexo*, Santiago de Chile: FLACSO. Pantelides and Botta, eds. (1999). *Reproduction, Health and Sexuality in Latin America*. WHO, Geneva: Ed. Biblos. T. Valdés and A. Faúndez, (1997), *Diagnóstico de Salud Reproductiva en Chile*, Santiago de Chile: fondo de Población de Naciones Unidas- Fundación Ford. Red de Salud de las Mujeres Latinoamericanas y del Caribe (RSMLAC) (2000), Mujer, Sexualidades, Derechos, *Cuadernos Mujer-Salud /5*, Santiago de Chile: RSMLAC.

6

A Comfortable Home: Globalization and Changing Gender Roles in the Fight against HIV/AIDS

Joanne Csete

Introduction

HIV/AIDS is the disease of globalization par excellence. It has thrived as a pandemic in the era of globalization in part because it is driven by factors that are the defining traits of globalization, including rapid international movement of goods and capital, migration of labor, deepening income disparity and poverty, and economic and political transitions at the end of the Cold War.[1] Increased migrant labor, a booming international trade in sex, and trafficking of persons are features of globalization, with all the HIV risk that these entail. The fall of the Soviet Union brought the opening of trade routes for the opiates of south central Asia as well as massive unemployment and desperation, leading to unprecedented increases in drug use and in the numbers of women and children in the sex trade. A globalized world appears to provide a comfortable home for an AIDS pandemic that shows few signs of slowing.[2]

HIV/AIDS is also a crucial manifestation of the interaction of globalizing forces and changing gender roles.[3] Elucidation of the links among HIV/AIDS, gender relations, and globalization is a neglected element in the analysis of the HIV/AIDS pandemic. There is growing recognition that HIV/AIDS is a disease of marginalization and poverty virtually everywhere.[4] There is a further belated recognition that the subordination of women and girls has been a primary driving factor in the spread of

HIV/AIDS,[5] but little analysis of HIV/AIDS in the context of globalization and globalization-linked changes in gender roles and relations. The role of the gay rights movement in the development of the response to HIV/AIDS in North America is well documented, but the impact of globalization and changing gender roles on AIDS among gay and bisexual men outside North America is little understood.

This chapter considers the interactions of factors linked to globalization, HIV/AIDS and changing gender roles by examining these questions: (1) how has globalization changed gender roles or perceptions of them that may lead to greater (or lesser) vulnerability to HIV/AIDS; and (2) how has HIV/AIDS as a globalized phenomenon affected gender roles? From an analysis of these issues, suggestions for policy and research are offered.

There is no single definition of "globalization" that is likely to satisfy all who would decry its consequences or praise the opportunities it brings. "Globalization" generally refers to intensively increased flows of capital, information, traded goods, services, and people resulting from unbridled (or relatively unbridled) capitalism and assisted by advances in information technology. In context, "gender roles" is often as difficult to define as globalization. For the purposes of this chapter, in addition to the usual range of biological and social factors that contribute to notions of gender roles and relations, I consider progress in gender relations to encompass the reduction of the frequency or likelihood of gender-linked human rights abuses.

Gender and the Evolution of HIV/AIDS

Though many experts already pronounce HIV/AIDS the worst epidemic in history, the epidemic is nearer its beginning than its end. The commonly used figure of about 30 million lives, mostly of young adults, claimed so far by AIDS is probably an underestimate, not least because the people most affected by AIDS tend to be difficult to count.[6] Sex workers, gay and bisexual men, injection drug users, prisoners, migrant workers, and sometimes women and girls—that is, those hit hardest by the disease—are often relatively hidden on the margins of society.

In more mature AIDS epidemics, the disease tends to become more prevalent among women and girls than men and boys. Hence, we have the situation in Africa where well over 50 percent of persons living with HIV/AIDS are women and girls.[7] It is clear that women's and girls' principal vulnerability to HIV/AIDS is a function of their lack of power in sexual decision making. There is also a physiological element to their vulnerability as HIV is transmitted more easily from men to women than vice versa, and young women and girls are exceptionally vulnerable.[8] Untreated sexually transmitted diseases (other than HIV/AIDS) are a risk factor for HIV transmission, and STDs of women are more likely than those of men to be asymptomatic, and thus untreated.[9]

But power relations probably trump these physiological factors in explaining, for example, the much higher rate of HIV prevalence among girls than boys that has been documented in numerous African and Caribbean countries.[10] Wherever women and girls are unable to control the terms of their sexual relations, they are vulnerable to sexually transmitted diseases, including in long-term unions. There seem to be few cultures in which it is socially unacceptable for men to have sexual partners outside marriage or other long-term unions. In addition, in many countries, unequal property, inheritance and divorce laws, and discrimination in labor markets cement women's economic dependence on men and limit their option to leave dangerous unions.[11] Sexual violence and abuse, which virtually always affect women disproportionately, put them at direct risk of HIV/AIDS.

Gay and bisexual men are still closely identified with HIV/AIDS, even where same-sex behavior is not a principal means of HIV transmission. The construction of HIV/AIDS as a "gay disease" has profoundly influenced social perceptions of homosexual and gay identity. In spite of the AIDS-related policy victories of the gay rights movement in North America and Western Europe, gay and bisexual men are vilified and their sexual behavior criminalized in many countries.[12] This demonization of gay and bisexual men in society and the law, often reinforced by popular associations of homosexuality and AIDS, also itself constitutes a major risk factor for HIV/AIDS as sexual minorities are marginalized and driven away from AIDS-related information and services.

Human Rights Watch staff members have interviewed thousands of persons around the world who live with HIV/AIDS or are at very high risk for contracting it. It is catastrophic that so little has been done to translate into legal and policy protections this growing analysis of women and sexual minority vulnerability to HIV/AIDS. Geeta Rao Gupta rightly points out that it is equally catastrophic that, similarly, so little has been understood about the vulnerability of heterosexual men, especially young men, to HIV/AIDS.[13] Young men, in her analysis, often face pressure to engage in unsafe sex or sex with multiple partners as a "proof" of masculinity. A deeper understanding of the interaction of globalization and changing gender roles with HIV/AIDS may suggest new policy and program directions for fighting both AIDS and gender inequities.

Globalization, Gender Roles, and HIV/AIDS

Globalization, Women's Economic Status, and Gender-Linked Abuse

If the subordination of women is a key element of undermining their sexual autonomy and increasing their risk of HIV/AIDS, it is pertinent to explore ways in which elements of what we call globalization may contribute to that subordination. Altman posits that the principal impact of globalization on women's social roles is likely to be a rapid diffusion of ideas that challenge constraints to women's autonomy and sexual freedom, as well as new acceptance of alternatives to traditional family structures.[14] He cites, for example, the efforts of Japanese women to break free of arranged and repressive marriages and to initiate divorce and sexual harassment complaints. But these progressive forces of globalization have been countered in many parts of the world by the increased feminization of poverty and other factors that put women and girls at HIV risk.

The rise and in some cases fall of the Asian "tigers," the decline of the Soviet Union, the continued global neglect of Africa, and the various displacements and conflicts that accompany these features of globalization have obviously transformed the global economy. The shift of factory jobs to the developing world has meant a rapid increase in women and girls in the formal workforce in many parts of the world as well as into a wide range of informal-sector jobs.[15] With globalized capital chasing low-wage economies, it is not surprising that these new workplaces for women are so often characterized by poor wages, poor working conditions, and lack of protection from abuse.

Though many of women's new economic "opportunities" may open them to sexual abuse and risk of HIV/AIDS, these risks are probably most pronounced for migrant workers and, obviously, for workers in the sex trade. As the feminization of poverty has gone global, women and girls in the millions have migrated from their home countries or within their countries to pursue livelihoods in factories, the households of the well-off, and the sex or "entertainment" industry.[16] Neither the magnitude of labor migration nor the importance of women and girls in it is small. The non-governmental organization (NGO) Coordination of Action Research on AIDS and Mobility (CARAM) estimated in the late 1990s that women accounted for 60 percent of migrant workers from the Philippines and two-thirds of migrant workers in Indonesia.[17] CARAM cites an airport survey in Sri Lanka showing that 84 percent of migrant workers there were women and, of these, 94 percent were domestic servants.

Trafficking of persons for labor or sex can be important in fueling HIV/AIDS. The trafficking of human beings obviously did not begin in the era of globalization, but it has undoubtedly increased and been facilitated by the borderless economies and by the internationalization of information flows associated with globalization.[18] The trafficking industry thrives on increasing poverty and reduced economic opportunity in developing countries and the newly independent states, features of the new global economy.

The case of Ukraine is particularly revealing with respect to women and HIV/AIDS. Ukraine has the highest rate of HIV prevalence in Europe, and, as in Russia, the AIDS epidemic is growing there with frightening speed.[19] The fall of the Soviet Union brought enormous and rapid increases in unemployment and poverty. Both women and men were suddenly without the jobs and benefits they enjoyed under the Soviet system and some of the adjustments to this situation have disfavored women. There has been a resuscitation of traditional stereotypes about women's inability to perform certain kinds of work and widespread discrimination against women in the labor market.[20] Job advertisements explicitly exclude women or exclude women not conforming to certain norms of appearance or attractiveness. Employers also use the long maternity leave established in the Soviet period to justify discrimination against women. The increased flow of Ukrainian women into sex work locally and increased trafficking of Ukrainian women for sex are practically inevitable in this environment, with all their implications for the continued stoking of HIV/AIDS.[21] Globalization of black markets in sex and drugs in the former Soviet Union has greatly facilitated this traffic.[22]

Besides sex trade work, migrant workers in household jobs and other trades are often also at very high risk of HIV. Migrant domestic workers often live and work in relative isolation with little social support.[23] Women who are migrant workers may find themselves in situations where they are unable to refuse sex because of investments made in gaining their foreign jobs (employment middlemen, agents, bribes at the border, etc.), even if they are not bonded laborers.[24] Women migrant workers may also find that they are unable to earn a living wage in a new country without trading sex. In addition to situations of coercion, Fernandez emphasizes that migrant women (or men) are usually young adults separated from their families and often struggling with loneliness.[25] Voluntary sex occurs without the benefit of HIV and STD prevention services, from which migrants are often excluded.

HIV/AIDS risk among migrant workers has been widely documented. Hugo's review of this literature highlights that among migrants HIV infection is most closely associated with work in the sex trade (obviously);[26] temporary labor to relatively isolated sites such as settlements, plantations, or private homes; jobs involving constant travel such as trucking; and jobs involving rural-to-urban migration—in short, the jobs of the new global economy. In 2001, half of the estimated 8,000 Sri Lankans living with HIV/AIDS were returned migrant workers, a high percentage of them domestic workers recently returned from Middle Eastern countries. In the Philippines, nearly one-quarter of people officially registered as HIV-positive in 1995 had worked overseas.

Human Rights Watch documented physical and sexual abuse of migrant workers in the homes of international business executives and officials of international organizations in the New York and Washington D.C. areas, including of women whose visa status did not permit them to leave the job without facing deportation.[27] These stories strikingly feature abuses of Third World women in the homes of the international elite who are the well-dressed and well-spoken "best and brightest" of globalization.

In short, employment and livelihood possibilities for women and girls in the globalized economy are heavy in the kinds of occupations that expose them to sexual abuse and exploitation and therefore HIV. Though this exploitation is widespread, it has figured little in analyses of HIV/AIDS. In spite of opening some economic doors for women and girls, the new global economy provides little hope for livelihood opportunities that are less associated with risk of sexual abuse and coercion and more with fair wages and humane working conditions.

Globalization, HIV/AIDS, and Gender-Linked Violence

Statistics on rape and other gender-linked violence are notoriously unreliable. Though it is difficult to prove, there is some evidence that sexual violence has become more widespread and frequent in tandem with globalization. The case is perhaps best made with respect to conflicts that are features of post–Cold War politics, such as the wars in the Democratic Republic of Congo, the former Yugoslavia, and Sierra Leone, where sexual violence was (or, in the case of Congo, is) rampant and used as a weapon of war.[28] The Congo war, in which an estimated three million people have died,[29] is driven in part by global demand for natural resources, including coltan, an essential mineral in the manufacture of cell phones.[30] In eastern Congo, Human Rights Watch documented horrific and violent rape and sexual slavery perpetrated by numerous military factions at a scale that was effective in terrorizing the population. In some cases, the resulting population movements enabled greater exploitation of natural resources by the warring factions.

Beyond war, the dislocations and impoverishment of millions, as well as changing gender roles in the new global economy, may be linked to a higher frequency of rape. Commenting on the epidemic of sexual violence in post-apartheid South Africa, Simpson and Kraak suggest that violence is a vehicle through which men assert their sense of self and identity as their power bases have been eroded by declining traditional values in an increasingly globalized society.[31] While there is widespread recognition of the importance of rape as a cause of HIV transmission in parts of Africa, only South Africa has a policy on HIV prevention services for rape survivors, and many countries have wholly inadequate rape laws.[32] Women who request condom use of their rapists in some countries in Africa and other regions are judged to have given consent to sex.[33]

Sadly, the evidence is mounting that HIV/AIDS is both a consequence and a cause of sexual violence. Much has been made of the belief in some parts of the world, notably parts of Africa, that sex with a virgin has curative powers with respect to AIDS. But the more rational targeting of young girls for sex because, other things being equal, they are less likely to be HIV-positive is probably much more widespread.[34] As Altman notes, this AIDS-related pursuit of young girls for sex shows itself in the global sex trade with increasing profitability of sex trafficking of young girls from rural areas for whom it is relatively easy to assert their HIV-negativity or virginity.[35]

Women known to be HIV-positive have been subjected to violence and even death. The case of Gugu Dlamini, a South African woman beaten to death after she revealed publicly that she was HIV-positive, is well known.[36] Domestic violence against women living with HIV/AIDS at the hands of their husbands or long-term partners is reportedly widespread in parts of Africa but certainly not confined to Africa.[37] In this regard, urgent attention should be paid to the globalization of public health policies on AIDS and HIV testing. The U.S. Centers for Disease Control and Prevention (CDC) recommends "opt-out" HIV testing for pregnant women in the United States—that is, women presenting for prenatal care will be tested for HIV unless they have a good reason not to be.[38] A similar policy for some countries in Africa has been promoted strongly by CDC staff in Nairobi, Kenya, with the strong public health justification that identification of HIV-positive pregnant women will allow health facilities to administer the short course of antiretroviral drugs that can reduce the risk of mother-to-child transmission of HIV.[39] Little consideration has been given to the consequences of a situation in Kenya where, on a massive scale, women but not men would be officially identified as HIV-positive. It is impossible to imagine that violence against women would not increase in these circumstances.

Globalization and Responses to Gay and Bisexual Men: The Impact on HIV/AIDS

As noted earlier, the political success of the gay rights movement in mobilizing around HIV/AIDS may be measured in legal and policy protections for people with AIDS and those at risk in North America, notably in the area of confidentiality of testing and HIV status. Many of these protections were taken up in international recommendations about HIV/AIDS and human rights.[40] Some observers credit the AIDS-related successes of the gay rights movement with breakthroughs in the promotion of positive images of gay male sexuality as well as the opening of constructive debates on sex for pleasure and male sexual desire.[41] Nonetheless, the close association of HIV/AIDS with gay and bisexual men in the public mind has in many parts of the world intensified the stigma and social marginalization associated with both AIDS and homosexuality.

HIV/AIDS has been a catalyst for both vilification of gay and bisexual men and support for sodomy laws and other means of criminalizing them. In Honduras, for example, gays and lesbians were generally well tolerated in society, even during the repressive regime of the early 1980s. But after HIV/AIDS appeared in the mid-1980s, the government organized violent attacks on gay bars and organized round-ups of gay men for involuntary HIV testing.[42] Public officials condemned gays as "promiscuous" and "abnormal," and the Honduran Medical Association called gay men a health risk to the country. Honduras has the worst AIDS epidemic in Central America,[43] and people with AIDS have few legal protections.

In India, a country transformed by its role in the global economy, HIV/AIDS has similarly brought men who have sex with men into the spotlight. Men who sometimes have sex with men but would identify themselves as heterosexual are numerous in all classes of Indian society.[44] Both strict social separation of women from men and relative freedom from masculine stereotypes beyond the imperative to marry and reproduce have contributed to the seeking out of same-sex partners by men and boys. "Gay identity" and a gay rights culture does not exist as in the North American context. Asthana and Oostvogels argue that HIV/AIDS service programs or awareness campaigns in India that, influenced by Western attitudes or donors, assume a community identity on the part of men who may have sex with men are ill fated.[45] They suggest, moreover, that the phrase "men who have sex with men" or MSM widely used by international agencies and in the epidemiological literature was an attempt to break the equation of same-sex behavior with a gay identity but that, in practice, MSM and "gay" are often used as synonyms.[46]

A kind of backlash against the globalization of a human rights movement based on a gay identity and mobilized to fight AIDS may be coming home to roost in the United States. In the United States, MSM who identify themselves as heterosexual have emerged as an especially high-risk group for HIV. Numerous studies suggest that African American MSM in particular eschew being identified as gay, an identity they perceive as white, effeminate, and associated with AIDS. They may choose to live double lives as men in long-term unions with women but also having sex with men secretively or on the "down low."[47] HIV risk, of course, is high not only for these men but for their wives or girlfriends as men having sex with men on the "down low" shun condom use with their female partners.[48]

In Africa, AIDS, politics, and traditional values combine to pose particular challenges to MSM. Gay rights movements have emerged in southern African countries that both have more contact with the global economy than other African states and have significant white minority populations. None of this context has been lost on African leaders who have cast gays and lesbians as "perverts" who personify corrupt European values.[49] In South Africa, characterizing homosexuality as a part of apartheid's deformation of African values has added another dimension to the politics of discrimination against sexual minorities.[50] Largely unable to combat HIV/AIDS, some leaders have resorted to using HIV/AIDS to further stigmatize and persecute homosexuals, while people with AIDS may face additional stigma by being presumed to have engaged in "prohibited" sex.[51]

Religious Fundamentalism, U.S. Power, and HIV/AIDS

Women and MSM facing abuse and discrimination in a globalized society, in some cases exacerbated by HIV/AIDS as noted earlier, are further caught up in waves of religious fundamentalism that some observers see as an inevitable result of the new global economy's challenge to traditional values. From the Taliban to the Christian right in the United States, in the view of Altman, the political power of religious fundamentalists represents a fanatical reaction to global ideas of gender equity.[52] As Altman notes, in a rapidly changing society, fundamentalist political leaders are often able to drum up support for even the most draconian social controls.

The ruling Bharatiya Janata Party (BJP) of India and the Hindu fundamentalist groups under its wing are a case in point. The BJP, which turned up the volume on its Hindu fundamentalist (and anti-Muslim) message in the aftermath of September 11, 2001, has persecuted MSM in the name of upholding "national values" or Hindu values in the way that it has also attacked Muslims. The government has looked the other way as MSM and sex workers and those who work with them to prevent HIV have been beaten and otherwise abused by the police.[53] Even before September 2001, the Hindu political party Shiv Sena organized violent attacks on cinemas showing the film "Fire" by Deepa Mehta, which included the depiction of a love affair between two women.[54] BJP's women's organization has frequently decried sex workers as women with no rights because of their "immorality."[55]

With respect to HIV/AIDS, perhaps the most harmful wave of religious fundamentalism in the corridors of power has been in the United States. The global AIDS initiative of President Bush announced in January 2003 became a vehicle for the institutionalization of the values of the Bush's fundamentalist Christian supporters. The Republican-controlled Congress, reflecting the wishes of the White House, passed a bill in June 2003 that requires one-third of U.S. assistance to HIV prevention programs to support "abstinence only until marriage" approaches.[56] Teaching sexual abstinence as part of a range of choices in HIV prevention is an accepted strategy, but the Bush administration's version of "abstinence only" entails sending messages that condoms are ineffective for HIV prevention, pandering to Christian conservatives who believe that talking about condoms and sex leads to sexual promiscuity.[57] Since the United States previously was a principal global supplier of condoms for HIV prevention programs,[58] this shift has potentially dire consequences for the fight against AIDS.

The Bush administration has made it clear that there is no longer U.S. support for delivery of services to MSM or sex workers or research on their health problems.[59] For example, a colleague at an NGO that receives large amounts of U.S. funding for work on HIV/AIDS recently told me that the government was discouraging its grantees from using the term "sex worker" because it implicitly denigrated "real" workers. As HIV/AIDS programs around the world remain heavily dependent on external donor support and the United States is the biggest donor to many countries, these developments may have dire consequences for many women and MSM at risk of or living with AIDS.

Conclusion and Recommendations

Factors related to the global restructuring of the economy and society have on a massive scale rendered women highly vulnerable to poverty, leading them often to engage in work that puts them at risk of sexual abuse and HIV/AIDS. Violence and discrimination faced by women and girls in many societies are exacerbated by HIV/AIDS as men seek younger, "purer" girls for sex and women known to be HIV-positive face violence from society and their husbands. Men who have sex with men are vilified because of the identification of HIV/AIDS as a "gay disease," even in places where gay identity has little cultural currency. Religious fundamentalists in political power, including in the United States, further demonize the expression of sexual identity and desire, greatly undermining the possibility for approaches to HIV/AIDS that promote and respect gender equity and the human rights of people affected by or at risk of AIDS.

The transformation of HIV/AIDS policies and programs that is needed to begin to combat these developments may be easiest to articulate in the language of human rights. Jonathan Mann, the first director of the Global Programme on AIDS of the United Nations, the precursor to UNAIDS, was visionary in his early realization that respecting the human rights of MSM, sex workers, women, prisoners, migrants, and others who are vulnerable to HIV was the only way to move forward in combating the epidemic.[60] There is enormous rhetorical consensus around Mann's ideas in international circles, but there remains little support for the kinds of measures that would allow human rights–based approaches to HIV/AIDS to become "globalized."

With respect to women and girls, these conclusions lend support to an agenda for fighting AIDS with the following as central elements:

- Measures that allow girls to realize their right to education. As Heise and Elias note, the most effective anti-AIDS program may be paying or subsidizing the school fees of girls so they do not have to resort to trading sex for income or to stay in school.[61] Girls' right to education in highly AIDS-affected countries also means more support for the care of people living with AIDS so that girls do not have to be pulled out of school to provide that care.
- Measures that protect women and girls, including migrant workers, from sexual abuse, harassment, and coercion in the workplace.
- Legislative and policy changes to rid all countries of property, inheritance, and divorce laws that discriminate against women and render them economically dependent on their husbands.
- Measures to facilitate the reporting of sexual and domestic violence and to ensure prosecution of offenders. This includes laws that render marital rape a crime.
- Measures to ensure that women and girls have equal access to health services and information on and care for HIV/AIDS and other sexually transmitted diseases.

More broadly, women's empowerment should be an objective and a strategy of AIDS programs. The collectivization and empowerment of sex workers to fight HIV/AIDS in several states of India have been enormously successful in increasing condom use and access to information on HIV transmission.[62] One would expect that such achievements by the most marginalized women in India could be replicated in many other settings with the right kind of support. Similarly, there is a need for more support to programs that work with young men to explore the pressures they feel to engage in behavior that reinforces subordination of women and girls.[63]

With respect to MSM, there is an urgent need for governments and donors to understand the formal criminalization of same-sex behavior and extrajudicial harassment of MSM to be directly counterproductive to fighting HIV/AIDS. The recent decision of the U.S. Supreme Court to strike down the sodomy law of the state of Texas[64] should set an example for countries such as India that are hearing challenges to such laws.[65]

This analysis raises a number of research questions for public health and the social sciences, including:

- How are MSM who identify themselves as heterosexual best approached for the purposes of delivery of services and information on HIV/AIDS? What elements of their gender identity are most programmatically important?
- How can the use of the public health tools of fighting HIV/AIDS, such as widespread voluntary or "opt-out" testing for pregnant women, be optimized without discriminating against or endangering women in places where HIV/AIDS is highly stigmatized?
- There is an urgent need to accelerate existing research on women-controlled HIV prevention methods such as vaginal microbicides, which while they do not alter power relations, would provide millions of women with protection from HIV that they do not now have.

Finally, the struggle for access to antiretroviral treatment for people living with HIV/AIDS has galvanized a strong global movement in recent years. There have been some recent successes in opening the way toward greater access to generic antiretrovirals, all the more remarkable since activists have pitted themselves against such quintessential stewards of the globalized economy as the World Trade Organization, multinational pharmaceutical companies, and the U.S. Trade Representative. If the early promise of these victories holds and millions more people with AIDS gain access to treatment, vigilance will be required to ensure that women and girls, who have borne the burden worldwide of caring for people with AIDS, as well as men who have sex with men, who have borne a burden of stigma and abuse, will not face new discrimination in treatment access.

Notes

1. D. Wolfe and K. Malinowska-Sempruch (2004), Illicit drug policy and the global HIV epidemic, *Working Paper for the HIV/AIDS Task Force of the UN Millennium Project*, New York: Earth Institute, Columbia University.

2. UNAIDS and WHO (2002), *Report on the Global AIDS Epidemic Update 2002*, Geneva: United Nations.

3. C. Beyrer (2003), Global sex: Book review, *Social Science and Medicine* 56(6): 1369–1370.

4. R. Parker (2002), The global HIV/AIDS pandemic, structural inequalities, and the politics of international health, *American Journal of Public Health* 92(3): 343–347.

5. Human Rights Watch (2003), Women's work: Discrimination against women in the Ukrainian labor force, *Human Rights Watch Reports* 15(5): D.

6. In its annual reports on the HIV/AIDS pandemic, the United Nations used to include an estimate of cumulated deaths from AIDS but no longer does so. The last such estimate from the United Nations, about 22 million deaths, was at the end of 2001, since which time the United Nations has estimated that at least 6 million more people have died of AIDS. See UNAIDS and WHO, 2002 and 2003.

7. UNAIDS and WHO (2003), *AIDS Epidemic Update 2003*, Geneva: United Nations (pp. 3–17).

8. Global Campaign for Microbicides (2003), *About Microbicides: Women and HIV Risk* (available: http://www.global-campaign.org/womenHIV.htm).

9. L. L. Heise and C. Elias (1995), Transforming AIDS prevention to meet women's need: A focus on developing countries, *Social Science and Medicine* 40(7): 931–943.

10. UNAIDS and WHO (2002), *Report on the Global AIDS Epidemic Update 2002*, pp. 25–26.

11. Human Rights Watch (2002), Ignorance Only: HIV/AIDS, human rights and federally funded abstinence-only programs in the United States, *Human Rights Watch Reports* 14(4):G (September 2002): 13–15.

12. See, e.g., <http://www.sodomylaws.org>.

13. G R. Gupta (2000), Gender, sexuality, and HIV/AIDS: The what, the why and the how, *XIIIth International AIDS Conference*, Durban, South Africa: UNAIDS.

14. D. Altman (2001), *Global Sex*, Chicago and London: University of Chicago Press, p. 38.

15. B. Ehrenreich and A. R. Hochschild (2002), Introduction, in B. Ehrenreich and A. R. Hochschild, eds., *Global Woman: Nannies, Maids and Sex Workers in the New Economy*, New York: Henry Holt & Co.

16. B. Ehrenreich (2001), Veiled threat, *Los Angeles Times* (op-ed), November 4; M. A. Espino (2000), Women and Mercosur: The gendered dimension of economic integration, In DePauli, L., ed., *Women's Empowerment and Economic Justice: Reflecting on Experience in Latin America and the Caribbean* (pp. 20–21), New York: UNIFEM.

17. I. Fernandez (1998), *Migration and HIV/AIDS Vulnerability in South East Asia*, paper presented at the 12th World AIDS Conference, Geneva.
18. S. Sassen (2002), Global cities and survival circuits, in B. Ehrenreich and A. R. Hochschild, eds., *Global Woman* (pp. 264–265), New York: Henry Holt & Co.
19. UNAIDS and WHO (2003), *AIDS Epidemic Update 2003*, pp. 14–17.
20. Human Rights Watch (2003), *Women's work: Discrimination against women in the Ukraiman Labor Force.*
21. A. Whiteside (1999), *Reform in Eastern Europe: Assessing Its Impact of Parallel HIV, TB and STD Epidemics*, prepared for the Third International Conference on Healthcare Resources Allocation for HIV/AIDS and Other Life-Threatening Illnesses, Vienna, October 11–13.
22. C. Beyrer, Global sex: Book review, 1369–1370.
23. S. Sassen (2002), Global cities and survival circuits, in B. Ehrenreich and A. R. Hochschild, eds., *Global Woman* (pp. 264–265).
24. I. Wolffers, I. Fernandez, S. Verghis, and T. Painter (2000), *A Model for Evaluating HIV/AIDS Interventions for Mobile Populations*, report of Coordination of Action Research on AIDS and Mobility (CARAM), available at http://caramasia.gn.apc.org/Ivan_UNDP_migrant.htm.
25. I. Fernandez, *Migration and HIV/AIDS Vulnerability in South East Asia.*
26. G. Hugo (2001), *Population Mobility and HIV/AIDS in Indonesia*, Bangkok: United Nations Development Programme, Southeast Asia HIV and Development Programme.
27. Human Rights Watch (2001), Hidden in the home: Abuse of domestic workers with special visa status in the United States, *Human Rights Watch Reports* 13(2): G, June 2001.
28. See e.g., Human Rights Watch (2003), Policy paralysis: A call for action on HIV/AIDS-related human rights abuses against women and girls in Africa, *Human Rights Watch Special Report*, New York, pp. 23–26; Human Rights Watch (1995), *The Human Rights Watch Global Report on Women's Human Rights*, New York: Human Rights Watch, pp. 1–24.
29. S. Sengupta (2003), Congo war toll soars as U.N. pleads for aid, *New York Times*, May 27.
30. M. Tesfa (2002), Congo-The Profits, and Costs, of War, *World Press Review*, October 24 (available: http://www.worldpress.org/Africa/772.cfm).
31. G. Simpson and G. Kraak (1998), The illusions of sanctuary and the weight of the past: Notes on violence and gender in South Africa, *Development Update* (Braamfontein) 2(2): 8.
32. Human Rights Watch, Policy Paralysis, pp. 23–26.
33. D. Altman, *Global Sex*, p. 73.
34. L. Vetten and K. Bhana (2001), *Violence, Vengeance and Gender: A Preliminary Investigation into the Links between Violence against Women and HIV/AIDS in South Africa*, research report written for the Centre for the Study of Violence and Reconciliation, Johannesburg, p. 9.
35. D. Altman, *Global Sex*, p. 71.
36. Associated Press (1998), HIV-positive South African woman murdered. December (available: http://www.aegis.com/news/ap/1998/AP981219.html).

37. Human Rights Watch (2003), Just die quietly: Domestic violence and women's vulnerability to HIV in Uganda, *Human Rights Watch Reports* 15(15): A.

38. Centers for Disease Control and Prevention (2003), *New CDC Initiative would Increase HIV Testing and Enhance Prevention for Persons Living with HIV* (press release), Atlanta, April 17 (available: http://www.cdc.gov/od/oc/media/pressrel/r030417.htm).

39. K. M. DeCock, D. Mbori-Ngacha, and E. Marum (2002), Shadow on the continent: Public health and HIV/AIDS in Africa in the 21st century, *The Lancet* 360: 67–72; (2003), A serostatus-based approach to HIV/AIDS prevention and care in Africa, *The Lancet* 362: 1847–49.

40. See, e.g., U.N. Office of the High Commissioner for Human Rights and UNAIDS (1998), *HIV/AIDS and Human Rights: International Guidelines*, New York and Geneva: United Nations (HR/PUB/98.1).

41. E. Connell (2001), Women and HIV/AIDS, *Canadian Women Studies/Les Cahiers de la Femme* 21(2): 68–71.

42. ILGA (International Gay and Lesbian Association) (1996), *Cleaning up the Streets: Human Rights Violations in Colombia and Honduras*, Brussels: International Gay and Lesbian Association (available at http://www.ilga.org/Information/americas/cleaning_up_the_streets_.htm).

43. UNAIDS and WHO (2002), *Report on the Global AIDS Epidemic Update 2002*, p. 200.

44. S. Dube (2000), *Sex, Lies and AIDS*, New Delhi: HarperCollins Publishers India, pp. 53–56.

45. S. Asthana and R. Oostvogels (2001), The social construction of male "homosexuality" in India: Implications for HIV transmission and prevention, *Social Science and Medicine* 52(5): 707–721.

46. D. Altman, *Global Sex*, p. 74.

47. B. Denizet-Lewis (2003), Double lives on the down low, *New York Times Magazine*, August 3.

48. L. Villarosa (2001), AIDS Education is Aimed "Down Low." *New York Times*, April 3, p. A1.

49. Human Rights Watch and International Gay and Lesbian Human Rights Commission (2003), *More Than a Name: State-Sponsored Homophobia and its Consequences in Southern Africa*, New York: Human Rights Watch.

50. N. Hoad (1998), Tradition, modernity and human rights: An interrogation of contemporary gay and lesbian rights' claims in Southern African nationalist discourses, *Development Update* 2(2): 23–24.

51. Human Rights Watch and IGLHRC, pp. 4, 7.

52. D. Altman, *Global Sex*, p. 139.

53. Human Rights Watch (2002), Ignorance only: HIV/AIDS, human rights and federally funded abstinence-only programs in the United States, 13–15.

54. D. Altman, *Global Sex*, p. 139.

55. M. S. Seshu (2003), Personal communication. (Meena Saraswathi Seshu is general secretary of SANGRAM, an organization that supports empowerment of women sex workers in Sangli, India. She is a 2002 winner of the Human Rights Watch "Human Rights Defender" Award.)

56. United States Congress (108th Congress) (2003), H.R. 1298, United States Leadership Against HIV/AIDS, Tuberculosis and Malaria Act of 2003 (available: http://frwebgate.access.gpo.gov/cgibin/useftp.cgi? IPaddress= 162.140.64.88& filename=h1298enr.pdf&directory=/diskb/wais/data/108_cong_bills).

57. Human Rights Watch (2002), Epidemic of abuse: Police harassment of HIV/AIDS outreach workers in India, *Human Rights Watch Reports* 14(5):C; SIECUS (Sexuality Information and Education Council of the United States) (2003). *On World AIDS Day, SIECUS Calls for Renewed Efforts to Expand Comprehensive Prevention Efforts Based in Sound Science* (press release), New York, December 1.

58. United States Agency for International Development (USAID) (2002), Overview of contraceptive and condom shipments, FY 2001, Washington, DC: PHNI Project for USAID, p. 18.

59. E. Goode (2003), Certain words can trip up AIDS grants, scientists say, *New York Times*, April 18; N. S. Padian (2003), Censoring research on AIDS, *San Francisco Chronicle* (op-ed), November 6.

60. J. M. Mann (1999), Human rights and AIDS: The future of the pandemic, in J. M. Mann, S. Gruskin, M. A. Grodin, and G. J. Annas, eds., *Health and Human Rights: A Reader* (pp. 216–226), New York and London: Routledge.

61. L. L. Heise and C. Elias (1995), Transforming AIDS prevention to meet women's need: A focus on developing countries, *Social Science and Medicine* 40(7): 931–943.

62. See, e.g., C. Dugger (1997), Going Brothel to Brothel, Prostitutes Preach About Using Condoms, *New York Times*, January 4, p. A1; M. Menon (1997), An NGO gets sex workers to enforce condom use, *InterPress News Service*, August 20; Heise and Elias, Transforming AIDS prevention to meet women's need, 931–943.

63. G. Barker (2000), Gender equitable boys in a gender inequitable world: Reflections from qualitative research and programme development in Rio de Janeiro, *Sexual and Relationship Therapy* 15(3): 263–82.

64. *Lawrence et al. v. Texas* (2003), 539 U.S. 1 ff., decided June 26.

65. Human Rights Watch (2003), *World Report 2003: India*, New York: Human Rights Watch, pp. 243–245 (available: http://www.hrw.org/wr2k3/asia6.html).

In Perspective

Tanzania Living with HIV/AIDS

Theresa Kaijage

In the context of globalization and health, Tanzania's experience, like its neighbors, is rooted in its history and place in the world. Africa's role in the global economy dates back to the time when African people and their goods were commodities in the global market.[1] During colonization the health of Africans was maintained just enough to ensure the production of commodities needed for the global market.[2] In other words, people were kept healthy enough to remain functional and productive.[3]

There was also a time in global history when Africa's development was seen as a burden to its colonizers, the "white man's burden." Today, HIV/AIDS is bringing back those memories because, due to the HIV/AIDS epidemic, Africa is again viewed as a burden to the developed world.[4] In essence, Africa has not been able to develop its own economic base to fund its own health infrastructure, so the African HIV/AIDS epidemic is not the same as the HIV/AIDS epidemic in the rest of the world.[5] With insufficient internal resources for the funding of HIV/AIDS programs,[6] Africa is dependent on the goodwill of the international donor community to fund HIV/AIDS treatment and prevention strategies.[7]

This reliance on external assistance has only resulted in the following conditions: after three decades of the epidemic, no HIV infected pregnant woman in Africa is guaranteed treatment. Even in 2005, with the WHO's "3 by 5" initiative (3 million people on ARV treatment by 2005) there remains a 72 percent unmet need for treatment in sub-Saharan Africa and in Tanzania, only 1 percent of people requiring antiretrovirals (ARVs) are currently on treatment.[8] Africa has lost generations due to HIV/AIDS.

The effect of all the 15–40-year-olds who have died, of the unborn children who could not be carried to term, or who died in the womb when their HIV-infected mothers died of AIDS, and of those HIV-infected infants who have died of AIDS, will not be truly felt for another decade, when those people would have been at their peak in productivity. Some of the children left behind are also dying because of poor nutrition and inadequate care.[9] While the infected die due to AIDS, some young children die due to lack of parental care because their parents are too ill, or, are dying too early due to lack of antiretroviral treatment.[10] Grandparents are now taking over the burden of child care and patient care as well as funeral expenses without the means to sustain large households because it is the breadwinner generation that is dying.[11] This AIDS-related social and physical disintegration of the family is often represented today in the media reports like it is a new phenomenon; however, this social crisis has been documented by researchers for 15 years.[12]

Tanzania, which was drawn into the global economic network partly through the eighteenth- and nineteenth-century Arab slave and ivory trades—and from the late nineteenth century was colonized by Germany and Britain—has all the hallmarks of the African predicament in the era of HIV/AIDS. The 35–36 million inhabitants of this East African country survive on an average per capita Gross Domestic Product (GDP) of less than $500 a year.[13] More than three-quarters of the population live in rural areas where they derive a precarious existence from small-scale agriculture. The bulk of the country's exports consist of unprocessed agricultural commodities, whose common characteristic is a progressive decline in their world market prices. Globalization in the economic sphere continues to subject Tanzania's tiny industrial sector to intense competition. The country's fragile economy, as is the case in the rest of sub-Saharan Africa, is hopelessly ill-equipped to shoulder the social burdens wrought by the HIV/AIDS pandemic.

At the moment, it is estimated that at least 2 million Tanzanians may be living with HIV/AIDS. From a mere three cases of AIDS in 1983, the number of cumulative AIDS cases reported to the National AIDS Control Program (NACP) in Tanzania rose to 783,865 in 2002, but in 2001 alone, the number of reported AIDS cases was 14,112.[14] The prevalence rate in the sexually active population aged 15–49 years is estimated at 12 percent. All this may explain why AIDS is the nation's number one killer and HIV/AIDS–related illnesses have been responsible for than half of all hospitalized patients for more than a decade.[15]

Women and children have borne the brunt of the epidemic. As far back as the late 1980s, data showed that 3.6 percent of pregnant women and 29 percent of barmaids in Dar es Salaam were HIV positive; in Bukoba region where the epidemic was more severe, 16 percent of pregnant women tested positive.[16] In the same year, 20 percent of all infant-and-child deaths were attributed to HIV/AIDS–related complications.[17] In 2002, surveillance data on women attending ante-natal clinics for the first time indicated that HIV-prevalence rates among them ranged from 42 to 32 percent. In Dar es Salaam, Tanzania's capital city, HIV prevalence among women is as high as 31.2 percent, compared to 18.2 percent among men.[18] Mother-to-child transmission of HIV accounts for about 5 percent of the total infections.[19] Hence, the protection of women and children against HIV and the development of strategies that address the socioeconomic, psychosocial, and public health consequences of HIV/AIDS in Tanzania are of utmost importance. Controlling AIDS in this population contributes significantly to the control of AIDS nationally, as well as internationally. Neither Tanzania nor Africa can do it without international collaboration.

However, today's global health arena will only meet the gender challenge posed by HIV/AIDS if the same strategies that are applied to HIV/AIDS treatment and prevention in the developed world are the same as those for the developing world. Too often double standards in the prevention messages promoted in Africa compared to those in the North not only fail to prevent the spread of HIV but they only serve to enhance the existing inequities in health as well as other socioeconomic inequalities that make AIDS care so difficult in Africa. If we are to win the battle against HIV in Africa, such inequities and inequalities cannot be ignored.[20]

One striking example of these double standards was the differing sets of guidelines for breastfeeding in the developed world versus the developing world. Until 1996, WHO, UNICEF, and UNAIDS recommended that all women in developing countries breastfeed, even if HIV positive; while HIV positive women in the richer countries were told to use replacement feeding.[21] Breastfeeding was recommended for these resource-poor nations in an effort to prevent infant mortality due to malnutrition and diarrheal diseases. These were the conclusions from a 1990 meeting in Geneva that I attended to present a case of a mother who I encouraged to find alternative feeding for her infant. The breastfeeding lobby did not like what I presented.

In essence, it was pronounced that the women in the developed world should be counseled not to breastfeed and to find alternative sources of breastfeeding, but the women in Africa and the rest of the world where sources of alternative feeding are difficult to come by should be encouraged to breastfeed, because the benefits of breast milk outweigh the risks of contracting HIV. That was the statement: one message to the North and another message to the South. This is an example of selective globalization. Only after 1997, and a move toward a human rights framework did the guidelines begin to change.[22] UN agencies including UNICEF and the WHO now recommend that HIV-infected mothers avoid all breastfeeding, but only when "replacement feeding is *acceptable, feasible, affordable, sustainable and safe*. When replacement feeding does not meet all of these criteria, exclusive breastfeeding is recommended during the first months of life."[23]

To personalize the repercussions of this statement in the developing world, I will relate to you the story of an HIV-positive woman and her baby who came to live with me in 1989. I quickly noticed the pattern that after every breastfeeding she was out of breath and she was passing out. Often I had to rush her to the emergency room. I began to wonder whether alternatives to breast milk existed. The woman said they did, and we went out of our way to find them.

Fortunately, I knew that this baby was born by caesarean section, so I knew that one risk for the baby in contracting HIV was not there. After the baby went on an alternative-milk diet, the woman suddenly began to blossom. Before, she thought she was dying, she was not eating much, and when she gave her breast to her child there was little milk to be drunk. The woman felt depressed, like giving up. However once she had an alternative, she was able to actually gain her energy and thrive, and the baby also started to thrive. Today, the baby is 16 years old and the mother is still alive. Mother and child are both doing well.

With stories like these all around me, at the same time as this woman came to live with me, I threw my own energy into mobilizing a group of like-minded Tanzanians to form an organization called WAMATA (*Walio Katika Mapambano na AIDS Tanzania*). This was the first grassroots AIDS Service Organization (ASO) in Tanzania. WAMATA is a Kiswahili acronym for the "people in the battle against AIDS in Tanzania." WAMATA's main mission has been to mobilize the families affected by HIV/AIDS as a front-line force for the prevention of the spread of HIV/AIDS as well as the care of people living with and affected by HIV/AIDS, including the widows, orphans, and surrogate parents (mostly grandparents). We have paved the way for more involvement by HIV/AIDS–affected individuals and families in the local and national endeavors to fight HIV/AIDS, and it has inspired many people and organizations to be partners in promoting this vision. Today, WAMATA is no longer the only ASO in this struggle in Tanzania; it is one of many.

Part of what we do at WAMATA is to work to break down the barriers in health care by bringing AIDS care to the homes of those unable to leave their beds (or sleeping mats if they have no beds). However, our wish is to move beyond the regional and national efforts and work together *globally* to delay that end stage by providing the necessary care to people living with HIV/AIDS (PLWHAs) so they live in good health for as long as possible, both in Tanzania and throughout the world. Even earlier than this, we must work for the unborn children of the world to engage in a dialogue with world governments together with their corporate partners to develop, promote, and fund policies that will ensure a future in which no child is born HIV-positive anywhere in the world. And, for the children that are born to HIV-infected mothers today, we must encourage the exploration of affordable alternatives to breastfeeding and advocate for policies that enable mothers to access both the formula, clean water, and the education to not only survive but thrive. The rationale that developing countries cannot afford either the formula or the clean environment to make the formula safe for babies simply cannot continue being used as an excuse to allow HIV-infected mothers in Africa and other less developed parts of the world to continue exposing their infants to the possible risks of HIV-infected breast milk.

Indeed, I do not know of any other epidemic that has different sets of messages for a global epidemic, but that has been the reality of HIV/AIDS. Right now in America, with all of the antiretroviral drugs and alternatives to breastfeeding, there is really no reason for any child to be born HIV-positive at all. But in Tanzania, with few to none of those resources, children are born HIV-positive all the time, and where does the blame go? It goes on the mother who, for example, has been with us at WAMATA for one year and is now pregnant. She has to be made to feel guilty, because there is nothing I, nor the counselors, can do for her. ARV drugs only became available in WAMATA in 2003 and their access to the broad population of people infected is very limited nationwide. In addition to the burden of guilt mothers and caretakers may feel when an infant is born infected, we have the loss; the funerals we go to every day.

As a Catholic, I have given talks to priests and to seminarians. Some listeners in these groups think what they have taught people regarding abstinence has helped people develop a conscience where they can always make rational and moral choices in their own lives. Since no religion uses police to go and sanction the lives of people to see if they are actually using what is preached to them be it on Sundays—or Fridays for Muslims, how can we assume that everybody will abstain? On top of these complexities, today the developed world seems to say, "Really too many people are infected in the developing world. There isn't enough money for that." And then they say, "They should abstain; we taught them to abstain. If they don't abstain, it's their own fault. There are too many of them anyway." In the end, we, Africans, are blamed for our failure to stop the spread of HIV/AIDS.

The fact that some people have been educated all along with little resulting change in behavior means that additional strategies must be considered alongside the messages being preached. If it were that easy, we would have no worries. It does not matter whether it is 1 percent or 50 percent of the people taught who are not going to follow the lessons preached to them. It is on that 1 percent or 50 percent who do not follow what is being taught that we must focus. And it is that 1 percent or 50 percent who make up my clients. They are the people I want to create alternatives for so that we together prevent the spread of infection.

With these clients in mind, it is simply not acceptable to continue promoting one set of values for HIV-infected mothers and their infants in the developed world while adopting an entirely different attitude toward the HIV-infected mothers and infants of the developing world. My main objective in founding WAMATA was to provide an opportunity for Tanzania to give people living with HIV/AIDS the chance to get involved in the national efforts and struggles against HIV/AIDS. Now that this objective has been achieved, our next objective in WAMATA is to have the world listen to the voices of Africans living with HIV/AIDS. These voices include the voices of children living with HIV/AIDS and children losing parents due to AIDS. They all want to see justice served in access to information, treatment, and services pertinent to HIV/AIDS prevention, treatment, and care.

Notes

1. BBC World Service (2003), *The Story of Africa: The East African Slave Trade*, (available: http://www.bbc.co.uk/worldservice/africa/features/storyofafrica/9chapter3.shtml); R. W. Beachey (1976), *The Slave Trade of Eastern Africa*, London: Collings.
2. M. I. Dougherty (1966), Tanganyika during the "Twenties": A study of the social and economic development of Tanganyika under British mandate, *African Studies* 25.
3. C. Cohen (1993), The natives must first become good workmen: Formal education provision in German South West and East Africa compared, *Journal of Southern African Studies* 19: 115–134; T. O. Ranger (1979), European attitudes and African realities: The rise and fall of the Matola Chiefs of South-East Tanzania, *Journal of African History* 20: 63–82.
4. F. J. Kaijage (1993), AIDS control and the burdens of History in northwestern Tanzania, *Population and Environment* 14: 279–300.
5. I. Bazira (1994), The spread of HIV/AIDS and its consequences in Africa: The Tanzania experience, *International Conference on AIDS* 10(1): 441, abstract no. PD0373. Medical Aid Foundation, Dar es Salaam, Tanzania; J. Donnelly (2003), African AIDS epidemic is at its worst, *Boston Globe*; L. W. Karanja (2002), Vertical transmission of HIV/AIDS in Sub-Saharan Africa: An epidemiological review, dissertation Abstract International, MAI 41/01, p. 210. (UMI No.1409521); R. Sabatier (1989), *Blaming Others: Prejudice, Race and Worldwide AIDS*, Philadelphia: New Society Publishers.

6. Y. Museveni (1991), *AIDS and Its Impact on the Health and Social Service Infrastructure in Developing Countries*, paper presented at the International Conference on HIV/AIDS in Florence, Italy, June 16.

7. R. Laing and K. Pallangyo (1990), *Background Study on Alternative Approaches to Managing the Opportunistic Illnesses of HIV-Infected Persons: Costs and Burden on the Tanzanian Health Care System (on the Basis of Field Work in August, 1990)*, Boston: Management Sciences for Health; J. Mann, D. J. M. Tarantola, and T. W. Netter, eds. (1992), *AIDS in the World: A Global Report*, Boston: Harvard University Press; K. A. Hartwig, E. Eng, M. Daniel, T. Ricketts, and S. C. Quinn (2005), AIDS and "shared sovereignty" in Tanzania from 1987 to 2000: A case study, *Social Science and Medicine* 60(7): 1613–1624.

8. WHO/UNAIDS (2005), "3 by 5" Progress—December 2004, Geneva: Joint Fact Sheet WHO/UNAIDS/283 (available at: http://www.who.int/3by5/en/factsheet.pdf).

9. UNICEF, UNAIDS, and USAID (2004), *Children on the Brink 2004: A joint report of new orphan estimates and a framework for action*, New York: United Nations Children's Fund.

10. WHO (2005), Lack of AIDS drugs for children. *The "3 by 5" Target newsletter*, November 2004–January 2005, Geneva: World Health Organization; G. Bicego, S. Rutsteien, and K. Johnson (2003), Dimensions of the emerging orphan crisis in sub-Saharan Africa, *Social Science and Medicine* 56(6): 1235–1247.

11. P. Mujinja and M. Over (1995), *Expenditures on Medical Care and Funerals in Households Experiencing Adult Deaths in Northwestern Tanzania*, paper presented at the Ninth International Conference on AIDS and STDs in Africa, Kampala (abstract WeD268).

12. S. Hunter (1990), Orphans as a window on the AIDS epidemic in Sub-Saharan Africa: Initial results and implications of a study in Uganda, *Social Science and Medicine* 31(6): 681–690; World Bank (1992), *Tanzania AIDS Assessment and Planning Study*, A World Bank Country Study, Washington, DC.

13. UNDP (2002), *Human Development Report 2002*, New York: United Nations Development Program.

14. National AIDS Control Program (NACP)-Tanzania (2003), *HIV/AIDS Surveillance Report*, Dar es Salaam.

15. National AIDS Control Program (NACP)-Tanzania (2002), *HIV/AIDS Surveillance Report*, Dar es Salaam; Adult Morbidity and Mortality Project (1997), *Policy Implications of Adult Morbidity and Mortality: End of Phase I Report*, Dar es Salaam: The United Republic of Tanzania and the United Kingdom Department for International Development.

16. Fred Mhalu et al. (1987), Prevalence of HIV infection in healthy subjects and groups of patients in Tanzania, *AIDS* 1: 217–221.

17. UNICEF (1990), The situation of women and children in Tanzania, Dar es Salaam, Tanzania.

18. Tanzania Commission for AIDS (TACAIDS) (2002), *National Multi-sectoral Strategic Framework on HIV/AIDS (2003–2007)*, Dar es Salaam, Tanzania.

19. National AIDS Control Program (NACP)-Tanzania, *HIV/AIDS Surveillance Report, January–December 2001*.

20. J. Killewo, S. Gregorich, G. Sangiwa, and T. J. Coates (1998), Sexual risk behaviors, knowledge and attitudes in a population-based probability sample of Dar es Salaam, Tanzania: Results from the Voluntary Counseling and Testing Efficacy Study, paper presented at the 12th World AIDS Conference, Geneva, June 28–July 3; Laing and Pallangyo, *Background Study on Alternative Approaches to Managing the Opportunistic Illnesses of HIV-Infected Persons: Costs and Burden on the Tanzanian Health Care System (on the Basis of Field Work in August, 1990)*.

21. J. Levy and K. Storeng (2004), Contingent choice: HIV and infant feeding, *AIDS & Anthropology Bulletin. The Newsletter of the AIDS and Anthropology Research Group* 16(2): 5–7.

22. Ibid.

23. UNICEF (2002), HIV and Infant Feeding—A UNICEF Fact Sheet (available at: http://www.unicef.org/publications/files/pub_hiv_infantfeeding_en.pdf); UNICEF, UNAIDS, WHO, UNFPA (2004), *HIV Transmission through Breastfeeding: A Review of Available Evidence*, Geneva: World Health Organization (available at: http://whqlibdoc.who.int/hq/2004/9241562714.pdf).

In Perspective

Two Sides to Home: Cross-Border Sexualities

Michael L. Tan

Csete's choice of the title, "A Comfortable Home," for her chapter on globalization, reminded me of how important it is to look into the issue of HIV/AIDS risks for migrant workers. Such risks have to be understood in the context of cross-border sexualities, the plural used here to emphasize how risks are transformed as one moves from a comfortable home to the often radically different environment of a host country.

The need to look into cross-border risks is particularly salient for Southeast Asia with large numbers of migrant workers. The concern over HIV risks for migrant workers has often concentrated on those migrants involved in the sex industry. In mainland Southeast Asia, for example, border areas have often been identified by epidemiologists as HIV/AIDS "hot spots" because of the sex industry servicing tourists as well as itinerant populations such as truck drivers. The vulnerabilities are not limited to contiguous land areas; even in insular Southeast Asia (i.e., Indonesia and the Philippines), ports around common fishing areas have also been identified as possible HIV/AIDS hot spots, again because of the sex industry.

Csete's chapter discusses the problem of sex work and HIV/AIDS, pointing out how poverty and gender inequalities amplify the risks for workers in the sex trade. In addition, Csete cites other analysts such as Ehrenreich and Hoschild[1] and Fernandez[2] on the global feminization of poverty and how this increases risks for HIV/AIDS in other sectors besides the sex industry, for example, among women migrant workers in household jobs.

I wanted to elaborate further on the way gender relations interact with other social variables to amplify risks for HIV/AIDS, and to look into the implications of these situations for advocacy as well as policies and programs. My framework for analysis links gender to sexuality, which I feel is essential if we are to develop more responsive policies and programs for HIV/AIDS prevention. This gendered sexuality is then linked back to the social and political aspects of globalization.

While I believe gender—as socially defined statuses and roles—is extremely important in shaping risks and vulnerabilities, I feel that a gendered analysis needs to link back into sexualities, both of "self" as well as of "others." Understanding how these perceptions and images are formed helps us to understand that globalization is not just a movement of bodies and of the virus, but of a whole gamut of feelings, emotions, aspirations, desires, and expectations that increase or decrease one's risks.

I focus on overseas Filipino workers (OFWs) as a case study. The data from the Philippines comes mainly from a research project I directed with a nongovernment organization, Health Action Information Network (HAIN) in 2000, a project commissioned by the National Economic Development Authority (NEDA) that looked into the adverse impact of HIV/AIDS on the Philippines, involving several case studies of populations at risk, one of which was OFWs.

While the emphasis will be on Filipino workers, I hope this chapter highlights the importance of looking at the situation of migrant workers in general, especially in Asia, where populations have become highly mobile in this age of globalization.

Background Information on Overseas Filipino Workers

There are between 6 and 7 million Filipinos working overseas, out of a total population of about 84 million. These OFWs are found, literally, in all countries of the world, from Afghanistan to Zimbabwe, although the largest numbers are in Hong Kong, Singapore, Taiwan, and Saudi Arabia, as well as a mobile population of seafarers.

The large numbers of OFWs is part of a government policy of exporting labor, one that was institutionalized in the 1970s by Ferdinand Marcos. Prior to that, the export of Filipino labor consisted mainly of physicians and nurses, with the United States as the largest recipient. Seeing the opportunities for foreign exchange, the Marcos government set up several government agencies to look for other "markets" and to rationalize processing of workers. Today, remittances from these overseas workers constitute a major source of foreign exchange, helping to keep the economy afloat and providing a channel for social mobility for Filipino families. In the first half of 2004 alone, remittances from overseas workers ran to US$4 billion.[3]

The largest numbers of overseas workers are deployed as seafarers, domestic helpers, construction workers, and nurses. Many of the workers have working visas from their host countries but there are also considerable numbers of undocumented workers, such as Muslim Filipinos in Malaysia, many of whom first left the Philippines in the 1970s to flee armed conflict between government and Muslim rebels. In the United States, there are also large numbers of undocumented Filipinos who first entered as tourists but stayed on and are called TNT (tago ng tago, meaning hiding and hiding).

It is significant that the first HIV case reported in the Philippines, in 1983, was actually an overseas Filipino who had returned home from the United States. The vulnerability of OFWs continues to be borne out today by statistics on infections. In its May 2004 monthly report, the government's HIV/AIDS Registry notes that of 2,073 HIV sero-positive cases reported to the government, 639 or 32 percent were OFWs, "of which two hundred forty-eight (37%) were seafarers, one hundred nineteen (18%) were domestic helpers, sixty-six (10%) were local employees, forty (6%) were entertainers and thirty-four (5%) were nurses."[4]

I do not attempt an epidemiological analysis of the figures since we do not have the numbers of serological tests that were conducted for each of the occupational categories. Note that mandatory HIV/AIDS testing is banned under a Philippine law but several countries that import Filipino labor do require the tests, which is why large numbers of OFWs have taken the HIV antibody tests several times, almost always as a precondition for overseas deployment and yielding the statistics that I just cited. These figures do raise some questions that relate to the topics of gender and globalization.

First, the numbers show clearly that seafarers are among those at risk for HIV. In the research I directed in 2000, our interviews with seafarers, including several who had been positive, clearly showed how gender increased their risks. A powerful machismo ideology operates among seafarers, including the "need" to prove one's masculinity by visiting bars and brothels at each port. Not to go to the brothels and to pay for sex is to invite suspicions of being homosexual. The seafarers I have interviewed say that in some ports, there may not even be a need to go to shore leave, since brothel owners will bring the women sex workers to the ships.

All the HIV-positive seafarers interviewed in our research project said they were infected by sex workers, some of them even claiming to remember the foreign port where they had the fateful encounter.

I will return to the seafarers shortly, but wanted to move on to a second observation about the reported HIV infections. While OFWs figure prominently among those infected, we do find other vulnerable groups. What is striking though is that one group of overseas workers does not quite have the large numbers of infections as one would have expected.

I refer to the category of "entertainers." The term is rather loose, including, for example, many singers and band players who are hired by hotels and resorts. In addition, there are other "entertainers" who are actually sex workers. The demand is particularly strong from Japan, with literally hundreds of recruitment agencies in the Philippines specializing in the hiring of women, men (referred to as "hosto," a coined word meant to be the equivalent for "hostess") as well as male transvestites. There is a long recruitment process for these *jappayuki* (Japanese words meaning "destined for Japan" but now used by Filipinos to refer to those who leave for Japan to work as entertainers), including training in "cultural activities" and the issuance of an Artist's Record Book (ARB) before they are sent off to Japan.

Yet the figures from the Health Department show a fairly small number of infected entertainers. This cannot be attributed to low levels of testing because the *jappayuki* do in fact take HIV antibody tests.

Contrast the low numbers of reported infections among entertainers with those for domestic helpers. These figures support some of the research findings from our interviews with OFWs in 2000 around HIV vulnerability, especially our suspicion that this vulnerability may actually be higher in OFWs who do not leave as sex workers.

Part of the explanation lies in the nature of sex work, especially when it takes on legal (as in Japan) or semi-legal status (as in the Philippines). The sex workers themselves, as well as their recruiters and employers, know that a sick sex worker means reduced profits. It is therefore to the stakeholders' advantage to keep the sex worker "clean," that is, safe from sexually transmitted infections (STIs). The *jappayuki* I interviewed, for example, are aware of the risks of HIV/AIDS, including the proper use of condoms. In contrast, seafarers tended to shrug off the risks, dismissing condoms as cumbersome.

Gender inequity further complicates the risks for HIV infection, and this is best illustrated by the case of Glenda, whom I interviewed in 2000. Four years before the interview, when she was 16, Glenda was recruited to work in a factory in Malaysia. Because she was under age, her travel papers had to be forged. When she got to Malaysia, she realized she had actually been recruited for sex work. Young, isolated without social support, and without any awareness of HIV/AIDS, Glenda was trapped in a situation that can only be described as chattel slavery. Her recruiters kept her travel papers to make sure she paid back the money she owed for travel. Eventually, she was infected by a client in Malaysia. Glenda's case is that of a migrant worker disempowered in circumstances of illegal recruitment. Remember she was recruited as a factory worker.

There could be other cases of OFWs holding legal jobs overseas, but who remain vulnerable when it comes to HIV/AIDS. The numbers of domestic helpers listed in the statistics for HIV cases bear more investigation. Certainly, there have been reports of sexual abuse by employers, which should not be surprising given the skewed power relations of the domestic helpers, one shaped in part by gender.

In addition, there have been reports of domestic helpers, as well as other OFWs in other occupational categories, who may engage in occasional sex work or transactional sex while overseas. I have in fact interviewed Filipinas who had gone to work in Singapore as domestic helpers and Taiwan as factory workers, but who do occasional transactional sex, not just for additional income, but as a way of possibly getting a local boyfriend who might marry them and allow them to stay on. We see in this transactional sex the links between gender and sexuality, and between sexuality and economics.

Finally, much too little attention has been given to noncommercial, non-transactional sex. Away from home, many migrant workers will inevitably go into intimate relationships as a way of countering isolation and loneliness, what we might call "comfort sex." In such situations, condoms may even be anathema since the relationship is seen as one built on trust, even love.

My point is that in sexual relationships outside of a brothel or commercial environment, many migrant workers will not recognize HIV risk. Inadvertently, the messages in mass media, both from back home in the Philippines and in the host country, may further reinforce this denial of one's risks because the HIV campaigns tend to emphasize sex workers as "core transmitters." Rare are the instances where campaigns refer to how loneliness and love may also put one at risk for HIV.

Two Sides to Each Border

I have, so far, described the risks for HIV infections among subpopulations of OFWs to show how these risks are closely related to gender. I have also linked the discussions of gender to sexuality, with a focus on individual perceptions of their own risks.

My analysis of gender, sexuality, and risk can further be expanded beyond the individual, if we recognize how gender and sexuality become even more complicated for mobile populations. This is where we can return to the title of Csete's chapter, "A Comfortable Home," which reminds us that migrant workers shuttle two worlds, a "comfortable home" left behind, and a host country which, no matter how affluent, will never become home. It is the shuttling of these two worlds that carries the tense contradictions of opportunities as well as inhospitable, even hostile, circumstances.

Put another way, we might want to consider the two "S's" that describe the circumstances around cross-border sexualities and sexual health, of being separated from their home environment, even as they are segregated away from mainstream services in a new country.

Globalization has certainly expanded the possibilities in this shuttling, in terms of geographical distances as well as the bewildering variety of images that shape and reshape one's views of self as well as of partners.

This is a good time to return to the Filipino seafarer. Here, we have someone who leaves home already with a machismo ideology, which is further reinforced while overseas, not just by peers but by being away from home, away from the social controls that come with the wife, relatives, and neighbors.

There are many other similar situations involving other nationalities of migrants and host countries. Lyttleton and Amarapibal's article on the behavior of males and females in a border area between Thailand and Laos provide an illustration. Males from Thailand, economically more affluent than Laos, now find themselves with a "sing song fang" identity, literally translated as "a lion on two sides (of the border)."[5] In these border areas, commercial sex has actually been on the decline, replaced by "negotiated sex" with the Thai men and Lao women seeking "degrees of intimacy." Moreover, Lyttleton and Amarapibal note how in Laos, ". . . the Thai men are able to suspend everyday social constraints within this field of desire and with this a prohibitive fear of AIDS that has lessened commercial sex interactions so markedly in Thailand."[6]

In the case of the Filipino seafarer, note that even as he plies the seas, the social dynamics on two sides of the "border" (of home and the seas) continue to determine vulnerabilities and risks. Machismo becomes more complicated here, gendered expectations mixed with exoticism, the idea that one must "taste" different dishes while overseas. The interviews I conducted with seafarers are consistent in the way they describe women as different "food dishes" (putahe) in different ports. It is not surprising that the HIV-positive seafarers I interviewed tended to blame their infection on Latin American sex workers, who they describe as being particularly desirable because they were *mestizas* (mixed-blood).

It does not matter whether they were actually infected in a Latin American port; what is more important for our analysis is the conflation of images and desires: the Latin American sex worker is seen as "exotic" because the encounter occurred in a distant port, but at the same time there is a preference for the *mestiza*, part of the machismo ideology from back home, which sees sex with the *mestiza* as a conquest of a "white" woman. This idea of conquering "white" women is a legacy from an earlier "globalization," the colonial period—the Philippines was under Spain for 300 years and the United States for 50 years—directly impacting on sexualities.

Lyttleton and Amarapibal's description of the Thai "lion on both sides" reminds me of notions of entitlement among Filipino seafarers as well, the men speaking of how they have to bear with hardship and loneliness while overseas, all for the family. Ironically, because they endure all this for their families back home, they also feel they are entitled to have a "good time," to spend on wine, women, and song when on shore leave.

The statistics on HIV infection reflect the vulnerability in terms of seafarers who are eventually infected, but those numbers fail to capture the full tragedy of each of these infections. I am referring here to the wives of the seafarers—who are classified under "others" in the statistics—infected by their husbands when they return home with the virus. (Lost, too, in the statistics, are the other sexual partners the seafarers may have infected in other ports before they returned home.)

The tragedy here is that these wives do know that they are vulnerable as well. The wives of seafarers do internalize the gender-stereotyped view of a testosterone-driven promiscuity on the part of seafarers. Wives I have interviewed are consistent in describing how they try to detect STIs in their returning husbands. For example, in a rather roundabout way they become suspicious if their husbands come home and avoid alcohol. This is because many Filipinos believe that they should not mix antibiotics with alcohol. A seafarer, being "male," is expected to go into drinking bouts when he returns so if he seems to be abstaining, then he's probably taking antibiotics, and those antibiotics are probably for an STI.

The irony is that despite these elaborate urban myths around disease detection, the seafarers' wives will not be in the position to demand that he use a condom since it is her conjugal "duty" to agree to sex, without the encumbrances of a condom. The condom suddenly represents mistrust, besides carrying all the connotations of unpleasurable sex, anathema for conjugal sex especially when a husband has returned after a long absence. On one hand then, both the seafarer and his wife know seafarers "play around" while overseas, yet the idea of "protected sex" is a major conceptual leap that can be difficult to make given existing ideologies around both gender and sexuality.

Implications for Research and Policy

There is increasing awareness of the problems of HIV risks in cross-border areas but much more work needs to be done in terms of research, policies, and program planning to help mobile populations to face up to the risks for HIV.

I argue here for going beyond the stereotyped and simplistic view of HIV risk as being associated only with sex work, with the gender dimension reduced to helpless women sex workers and predator male customers. I have tried to show how much more complicated HIV risk is, gender interacting with sexualities, and this gendered sexuality taking on many permutations in a broader social and economic context, from the need to work away overseas to the need for companionship and intimacy while away from home.

The gendered nature of these needs and feelings, and the way they are transformed as workers move from one setting to another, needs to be documented and analyzed, especially for its implications for HIV risk, of being separated from home and of being segregated in a new country. I reiterate my earlier observation that risks do not come with commercial sex alone but also with transactional sex and maybe even "comfort sex."

In such circumstances, it is clear that HIV prevention campaigns cannot be reduced to information activities around viral transmission. Policies and programs need to be reviewed to evaluate how appropriate they are, perhaps even how they may inadvertently be contributing to HIV risks. Information campaigns that keep reinforcing stereotyped notions of HIV risk as being confined to the sex industry builds up denial among populations of migrant workers who do not self-identify as sex workers.

Efforts to enhance HIV prevention will have to consider programs both at home and in a host country. For example, in the Philippines the government has integrated HIV/AIDS education into predeparture orientation seminars for workers about to leave. But I have always felt these HIV/AIDS seminars, currently limited to biomedical information about viral transmission routes, need to tackle issues of gender and sexuality as well, helping workers to understand how their vulnerabilities are affected by their notions of masculinity and femininity and how these relate to sexuality, including notions of "pleasure" and "risk." Workers need to be given tools for reflecting on what all these sexual risks means in relation to their own hopes and aspirations for their families.

Such seminars in the home country will, however, be meaningless if the migrant workers move into a new environment where there are no support systems available. Migrant workers need to know where they can turn to for the reproductive and sexual health services when they arrive in a new country, and I do not mean only HIV/AIDS programs. In Hong Kong, I have talked with Filipino women working as domestic helpers and their needs span the whole range of gynecological services, including access to contraception and abortion.

Whether it's domestic workers or seafarers, HIV/AIDS is in fact a marginal concern for many of these migrant workers, which again highlights the need to integrate prevention efforts into a broader program of services. A few years back I helped the Philippine Seafarers Association Program (PSAP) in Rotterdam to put HIV/AIDS into their newsletter, which is given to Filipino seafarers who come through their port. The newsletter carries many other news and feature items that relate to the seafarers' many concerns, including salaries, working conditions, and being away from home. In this context, HIV/AIDS becomes more personal, more concrete.

I realize that the situation of illegal workers will be even more difficult, but this only highlights the need to conduct research to map out the many different situations of migrant workers, within the framework of "separation" and "segregation." The potentials for risk reduction start even before workers leave home, and need to be sustained as they begin their new lives in their new environments. Ultimately, the goal of risk reduction for HIV prevention ties into the need to help migrant workers to tap into, or, where needed, to create new networks of social support so that eventually, there is a sense of a home away from home.

Notes

1. B. Ehrenreich and A. R. Hochschild (2002), *Global Woman: Nannies, Maids and Sex Workers in the New Economy*, New York: Henry Holt and Co.
2. I. Fernandez (1998), Migration and HIV/AIDS vulnerability in South East Asia, paper presented at the 12th World AIDS Conference, Geneva.
3. Cecilia C. Gonzales (2004), Overseas Workers Send $4B in 1st-half, *BusinessWorld*, 13 (August 2004): 1.
4. Department of Health (2004), HIV/AIDS Registry, May 2004.
5. C. Lyttleton and A. Amarapibal (2002), Sister cities and early passage: HIV, mobility and economies of desire in a Thai/Lao border zone, *Social Science and Medicine* 54(4): 505–518.
6. Ibid., p. 515.

7

Opening a Global Gold Mine: Globalization, Gender, and Transnational Tobacco Companies

Jeff Collin

Introduction

A key factor driving the shifting regional priorities of transnational tobacco companies (TTCs) toward developing countries has been the often huge disparity in smoking prevalence rates between men and women. The prospect of narrowing this gap is hugely enticing, and selling tobacco products to women has been plausibly described as "the single largest product marketing opportunity in the world."[1] This echoes the situation in the United States in the first half of the twentieth century, when cigarette manufacturers first began to target women in a sustained effort to expand the smoking population. In the 1920s George Washington Hill, then president of American Tobacco, famously likened successfully boosting smoking among women to "opening a new gold mine right in our front yard."[2] This resonance is of more than merely historical interest, since methods originally developed to target American women are now being applied by TTCs in emerging markets.

The pandemic of death and disease from tobacco highlights key features of the complex interrelationships between globalization, gender, and health. Both the trajectory of this pandemic and the structure of the tobacco industry are undergoing substantial transformations, and are doing so as a result of global change across multiple dimensions. Global tobacco consumption is increasingly inequitable in its distribution and impacts. A broad decline in smoking prevalence across most high-income countries over recent decades has coincided with substantial increases among low- and middle-income countries (LMICs), with the latter already accounting for 82 percent of the world's smokers. Around 4.9 million deaths were attributable to tobacco use in 2000, an increase of 45 percent since 1990, and it is predicted that by 2030 the global total will reach 10 million, or around one in six adult deaths, when 70 percent of such deaths will occur in developing countries.[3]

This transition is being driven by the globalization of the tobacco industry, and just four companies now control 75 percent of the world cigarette market: Philip Morris, British American Tobacco (BAT), Japan Tobacco/ RJ Reynolds, and the China National Tobacco Corporation.[4] The latter's share reflects its dominance of the huge Chinese market, but the remainder have been assiduous in their pursuit of growth through restructuring and major investments in developing countries. Such growth has been facilitated, in particular, by changes in the global economy, highlighting the impact of trade liberalization in increasing tobacco consumption across LMICs.[5] The significance of TTCs as agents of social change[6] (Collin 2003a) highlights the importance of adopting a broad interpretation of globalization, and here the term is used in accordance with Lee's definition as "a set of processes that are changing the nature of how humans interact across three types of boundaries—spatial, temporal and cognitive."[7]

It is equally evident that patterns of tobacco consumption, usage, and disease are highly gendered. At its most basic, this has been evident in the variation in smoking prevalence rates between men and women, a variation that primarily reflects much lower prevalence among women in developing countries. Whereas the World Bank estimated smoking prevalence among men and women in high-income countries at 38 percent and 21 percent respectively, in LMICs these figures were 49 percent and 9 percent.[8] There has been a broad convergence between male and female smoking rates across much of Europe and North America, and indeed uptake among girls is now higher than for boys in several European countries.[9] A stark contrast to such convergence is provided by China, where adult male smoking prevalence of 53.4 percent contrasts with only 4 percent among women. The magnitude of this divide in developing countries should, however, be treated with some caution. In countries where powerful cultural pressures have traditionally inhibited smoking by women, underreporting is liable to result in underestimating actual tobacco use. Perhaps more significantly, the principal emphasis of research on cigarette smoking ignores traditional widely practiced noncommercial forms of tobacco use among women. In India, for example, female cigarette use in urban centers is estimated to be as low as between 2 percent and 5 percent whereas up to 67 percent of rural women use smokeless tobacco.[10]

The relevance of gender is both more pervasive and more complex than can be deduced from simple variation in prevalence rates. As has been argued by Ernster et al.: "gender relations—defined as roles and responsibilities that are socially determined between men and women—affect the prevalence, determinants, treatment and eventual outcome of tobacco-related diseases among women".[11] There are, for example, substantial differences in motivations underlying tobacco usage. Women are generally more likely than men to use cigarettes as a mechanism for coping with negative feelings and typically have less confidence in their ability to give up smoking.[12] There is also a strong relationship with the perceived importance of being thin, with increasing value on thinness being associated with a greater risk of smoking initiation among female adolescents.[13] Tobacco use raises additional health risks among women including complications during and after pregnancy and exacerbation of osteoporosis, the higher prevalence of depression among women suggests increased vulnerability to nicotine dependence,[14] while exposure to passive smoke is greater among women and children.[15] Significant differences have also been identified with respect to responsiveness to specific tobacco control policies, with young men being much more responsive to changes in the price of cigarettes than young women.[16]

The importance of examining tobacco and gender is emphasised by indications that the globalization of the tobacco industry could have a significant impact in narrowing the gender gap in cigarette consumption. Young women appear to be particularly likely to begin smoking when TTCs become significant actors in national tobacco markets, a vulnerability that reflects the efficacy of targeted marketing and promotional activities. In Lithuania, for example, smoking among women doubled over a five-year period in the 1990s and increased by fivefold amongst the youngest groups.[17] Smoking surveys elsewhere in the former Soviet Union also indicate that smoking prevalence has increased particularly amongst young women in cities.[18] In South Korea the smoking rate among female teenagers was reported to have quintupled (jumping from 1.6 to 8.7 percent) during the year following the opening of the market to U.S. tobacco companies (U.S. General Accounting Office 1990), while in Japan market liberalization was similarly found to have contributed to increased smoking prevalence among young women and adolescents.[19]

Torches of Freedom: Cigarettes, Marketing, and Women

Early attempts to target women as potential smokers established core themes that have proved to be remarkably persistent, remaining central to contemporary marketing strategies. Edward Bernays, a key figure in the emergent practice of public relations, was recruited by Hill with the specific remit of reviving American Tobacco's Lucky Strike brand via a concerted appeal to women. A 1925 campaign built around the slogan "Reach for a Lucky instead of a sweet" more than doubled the brand's market share,[20] a first manifestation of long-standing efforts to associate smoking with slimness. Bernays led a similarly innovative foray into the world of fashion in a 1934 strategy designed to make the distinctive green of the Lucky Strike pack the fashionable color of the season, while 1930s advertisements featuring endorsements by movie stars Jean Harlow and Claudette Colbert were part of the industry's broader (and continuing) effort to link cigarettes with the glamor of Hollywood.[21]

Underlying such tactics was the core challenge of overcoming entrenched cultural (and occasionally legal) prohibitions against women smoking. In undertaking such efforts cigarette manufacturers clearly positioned themselves as self-conscious catalysts of social change. The manipulation of opinions and values was central to what Bernays referred to as "the engineering of consent": Age-old customs, I learned, could be broken down by a dramatic appeal, disseminated by the network of media.[22]

Critical to the ability of the tobacco companies to recruit women smokers was their success in associating the cigarette with broader social change. Subverting the long-standing disreputability of tobacco use by women, the cigarette had come to be presented by some as "the symbol of emancipation, the temporary substitute for the ballot"[23] or as "a provocative badge of honour."[24] In an early example of the powerful iconography of the cigarette, Bernays arranged for a "torches of liberty contingent" of debutantes to smoke Lucky Strike cigarettes during the 1929 Easter parade in New York City,[25] an event that generated enormous media coverage. The theme was developed during the course of an advertising campaign that sought to directly associate Lucky Strike cigarettes with advances for women in U.S. society. Under the heading of "An Ancient Prejudice Has Been Removed" the advertisements claimed:

> *Today, legally, politically and socially, womanhood stands in her true light. AMERICAN INTELLIGENCE has cast aside the ancient prejudice that held her to be inferior. "TOASTING DID IT"—Gone is that ancient prejudice against cigarettes—Progress has been made. We removed the prejudice against cigarettes when we removed from the tobaccos harmful corrosive ACRIDS (pungent irritants) which are present in cigarettes manufactured in the old-fashioned way. Thus "TOASTING" has destroyed that ancient prejudice against cigarette smoking by men and by women. "It's toasted" No Throat Irritation-No Cough.[26]*

The use of cigarettes as signifiers of independence has remained central to the strategies of tobacco companies, and has increasingly been used in conjunction with imagery and language connoting economic progress and prosperity.

This approach reached its apogee with Philip Morris's extensive promotion from 1968 of its overtly female-oriented Virginia Slims brand under the tag line "You've come a long way, baby."[27] The imagery used in this long-standing campaign typically contrasted a contemporary picture of an ostensibly successful and carefree career woman smoker with a historic depiction of domestic (nonsmoking) drudgery. The glamor of the product was reinforced by contrasting its sleek lines with the traditional "fat" cigarettes smoked by men, while the campaign provided reassurance to the prospective Virginia Slims smoker that, notwithstanding such gains, she remained someone's "baby."[28] An attempt to reconcile imagery of freedom and progress with traditional femininity is equally evident as the primary motivation behind BAT's Kim brand.

A 1977 document entitled "Channelling the tide of fashion: the development of Kim" asserts: "The KIM smoker is a woman in search of emancipation and equality with men. But she does not want to adapt to the male world. She wants a status of her own and to show it . . . The slim format and greater length were designed to compliment the slim feminine hand, and from this came the copy line: 'Smart and slim—far too chic for the hands of men.' "[29] Following the 1964 U.S. surgeon general's report highlighting the health impacts of smoking, the desire to allay health concerns also became established as a distinctive and key additional element in marketing cigarettes to women. A 1966 report for Philip Morris on the commercial prospects for a "health cigarette" concluded that "(w)omen, and particularly young women, would constitute the greatest potential market for a health cigarette," hence advertising for such a product "should be directed to both sexes but in such a way as to have the greater appeal to women."[30]

Subsequently, the marketing of cigarettes that incorporate implicit if fraudulent health claims has overwhelmingly centred on women. Most prominent among such cigarettes have been those marketed using what are now recognised as misleading descriptors, deploying terms such as "mild" or "light" that denote products with purportedly reduced yields of low tar and nicotine. For smokers concerned about the health consequences of smoking, switching to such products seemingly offers an alternative to cessation and has disproportionately appealed to women. In the United Kingdom three times as many women smokers as men smoked lights in 1983,[31] while for the European Union around half (48 percent) of women smokers use lights by comparison with about a third (32 percent) of men.[32]

The commercial importance of ensuring that cigarettes are attractive to women is demonstrated by its consistently critical role in the product development and marketing strategies of leading manufacturers. Successive innovations in cigarette technology, including the introduction of filters, the addition of menthol, and (most significantly) the development of low tar and nicotine products have been primarily oriented toward sustaining and enhancing the appeal of smoking among women. A 1992 review by Philip Morris of key stages in the development of the U.S. cigarette market explained the contrast between the successful introduction of longer, slimmer cigarettes and the failure of subsequent gimmicks in such terms:

> It is perhaps more reasonable, however, to interpret the success of small-circumference cigarettes as one more step in a long process through which smoking became more and more acceptable among women. The first cigarettes, themselves, made tobacco use more attractive to women than the use of chewing tobacco, snuff, pipes, and cigars had been. In succession, longer cigarettes, filters, menthol and lower delivery were steps which further removed cigarettes from what tobacco use had originally been and made them more acceptable among women. In that context, then, slim cigarettes can be seen not as just some quirky unique selling point that happened to do well in the market, but as another step in the long process through which cigarettes became more acceptable to a demographic segment which, by 1970, represented nearly half of the market. Slim cigarettes' chance for success were further enhanced by the fact that their introduction coincided with a feminist movement and by the way their advertising and promotion by Philip Morris capitalized on that timing.[33]

This analysis neatly encapsulates the success with which leading cigarette manufacturers positioned themselves to take advantage of opportunities presented by broader social changes during the twentieth century to dramatically increase smoking among women in North America and in Western Europe. As Brandt has noted,[34] the fact that smoking had already assuming specific meanings and a restricted appeal among women before the onset of targeted advertising does not detract from the significance of their marketing efforts in recruiting women as smokers. Similarly, the contemporary significance of TTCs as agents of emergent social change in developing countries rests upon their recognition and exploitation of broader socioeconomic and cultural transformations, transformations that are strongly associated with globalization.

Segmenting the Female Market

None of the abovementioned is intended to portray tobacco manufacturers as omniscient with reference to the social dimensions of tobacco use, and their pursuit of women smokers has not been conducted without embarrassing miscalculation. In 1971, for example, Joseph Cullman then head of Philip Morris responded to questioning about the impact of smoking during pregnancy on birth weight with the claim that some women would prefer having smaller babies.[35] Yet the enormity of the economic opportunity presented by maximizing the number of women smokers has required the industry to pay persistent and rigorous attention to gender roles, and in particular to how changes in them may impact upon tobacco use. If far from flawless, research undertaken on their behalf has frequently been innovative and impressive, and has often contrasted starkly with the persistence of gender-blind approaches to health promotion.[36]

It is not too fanciful to suggest that a basic appreciation of the strategic utility of a rudimentary understanding of gender dynamics dates back to the start of the twentieth century, when women were depicted in early promotional materials to entice male smokers.[37] While the use of such imagery remains hugely important in marketing cigarettes to young men, the 1970s witnessed the adoption of a more systematic, albeit initially very crude interest in gender as the scale of future reliance upon women smokers became increasingly evident.

The corporate documents of the tobacco companies reveal an ongoing interest in the divergent attitudes to cigarette consumption between male and female smokers. Initial interest, unsurprisingly, proceeded from a clear presumption that the former constituted the norm with attention focusing on the extent and manner of deviation from it by women. An internal report on "The Smoking Behaviour of Women" conducted by BAT in 1976 highlighted a number of distinctive findings, including evidence that while women found it harder to quit this varied significantly by class with "higher social classes being much more successful at quitting than those of lower social classes." The report concluded:

> In some respects it appears that female smokers are, or consider themselves to be, more highly motivated to smoke than male smokers and there is evidence that they find it harder to stop smoking. Although it is not completely clear why this should be the case, it may be related to the observations that women are more neurotic than men and more likely to need to smoke in stressful situations, presumably because they are less well able to deal with stress.[38]

The significant role of stress alleviation in smoking by women was also highlighted in a similar review by Lorillard of "The Female Smoker Market."

The perceived ability of the cigarette to assist in reducing tension was viewed as a particularly important attribute to "working women" by comparison with "homemakers." The review recommended considering the development of a product that could more effectively appeal to this key group as "a socially acceptable tranquilizer" than existing female brands like Eve and Virginia Slims:

> The most loyal female smokers are the working women, and these women will soon outnumber full time homemakers. A cigarette positioned for the working woman, to relax and steady her nerves when the tension is mounting by serving as a socially acceptable tranquilizer deserves investigation. Unlike Eve, her cigarette will not symbolize passive femininity; unlike Virginia Slims, her cigarette will not be an overt demand for equality. She *is* liberated in her lifestyle and her cigarette is part of that lifestyle.[39]

Arguably of greater significance than the analysis of differences in tobacco use between men and women has been the increasing interest of the cigarette manufacturers in understanding the often dramatic variation within them.

The basic distinction between women in paid employment and domestic workers represented the starting point for increasingly sophisticated and complex categorizations. Importantly, subsequent marketing and product development strategies have been consistently characterized by the recognition that "women smokers" do not constitute a single undifferentiated category. As summarized by a report for American Tobacco: "There is significant opportunity to segment the female market on the basis of current values, age, lifestyles, and preferred length and circumference of products. This assignment should consider a more contemporary and relevant lifestyle approach targeted toward young adult female smokers."[40]

Market segmentation refers to the practice of subdividing populations according to how they respond to a given set of marketing messages, and the tobacco industry has used diverse criteria for their definition including demographics, geography, attitudes, and preferred product benefits.[41] Such varying approaches are of far more than mere semantic interest, since they are driven by the desire to formulate products or marketing campaigns that most effectively target strategically significant subgroups. In 1981, for example, social trends among female smokers were analyzed for Brown and Williamson with reference to "Project Delta," exploring the development of new products targeted at women.[42] The study rested on the identification of four social value groups labeled Personal Experience, Self-Achievement, Aimless, and Retreaters. The first two of these groups collectively accounted for 70 percent of all women smokers, and subsequently received more detailed analysis. In demographic terms, Self-Achievers were identified as "relatively middle aged, married, college educated, white collar, upscale" while the Personal Experience group was "relatively young, married, high school educated, blue collar, downscale."

The clusters were then assessed with reference to responses to smoking restrictions and individual attitudes to smoking. The Personal Experience group showed the greatest concern that they smoked too much while Self-Achievers group were more likely to agree that low tar and nicotine cigarettes represented a major step in harm reduction.[43] The analysis culminated in the identification of the following marketing proposition for Project Delta: "Develop and market separate new low tar brands for female Self-Achievers and Personal Experiencers who are socially concerned, and feel that they smoke too much; yet are still looking for a new brand, and believe that there should be a cigarette especially for women."[44]

Notwithstanding the success of female-specific brands such as Virginia Slims, they remain a comparatively small part of the overall market of women smokers. This indicates something of the complexity of the relationship between gender and tobacco use, and obviously raises questions about what the larger part of this market find appealing in other brands. Of particular interest is the substantial number of women smokers who select products that have long been promoted via overtly masculine imagery, including leading brands such as Winston, Camel, and (pre-eminently) Marlboro. This seemingly curious phenomenon was noted in a report for BAT examining the appeal of Marlboro across several European markets:

> Given the apparent dynamism, aggression and machismo of Marlboro it is perhaps surprising to note the substantial representation of female franchise. The study reveals two bases of explanation a) females are passive in early brand choice, typically sharing the brand of their partners/social peers b) the ubiquity and normality of Marlboro is appealing because it does not provoke strong differentiation from the group and females in general favour social conformity.[45]

Expanding the Epidemic: Targeting Women in Emerging Markets

The prospect of narrowing the gender gap in tobacco consumption among developing countries is paramount among the commercial opportunities presented to TTCs by globalization. Unsurprisingly, the techniques that have proved so successful in increasing smoking prevalence among women in North America and Western Europe are now being deployed in emerging markets. Marketing campaigns that are similarly designed to associate cigarettes with female independence and prosperity are being implemented, often assisted by the greater latitude afforded by less restrictive advertising regulations. While such efforts are designed to appeal to the same core themes long established in traditional markets, it is important to note that typically they are not simply transplanted in their existing format. The value of adaptation to local context has long been recognized by TTCs and is particularly significant in attempting to navigate the complexities of the conflicting images often evoked by women smoking in different parts of the world.

Though there remains a need for more sustained analyses of tobacco industry documents that are informed by gender, work that has already been undertaken is sufficient to clearly demonstrate the potential value of this resource. The corporate documents demonstrate the central importance of expanding smoking prevalence among women in developing countries to the future of the global tobacco industry. This is inextricably linked with the broader opportunities associated with global change, and comparative success in appealing to women smokers is likely to be a key determinant of competition between TTCs. It is clear that BAT is particularly concerned about the lead enjoyed by Philip Morris International (PMI) in this respect. Research into female smoking presented to BAT's marketing team in December 2000 highlighted the current differential, but suggests that there is a significant opportunity for BAT to develop a female-oriented global brand:

1. There is a correlation between the Gender Development Index and the incidence of female smoking. Approximately a quarter of BAT's consumers are female, compared with over 40% for Philip Morris. There are many reasons for this, but it is partly due to geographic mix and brand mix.
2. The research shows that the role of smoking for males concerns satisfaction, while for females it concerns sensory pleasure. The majority of women want "real" cigarettes rather than superslims which are niche products. They would prefer a brand that includes femininity but is multi-dimensional. Female smokers often default to the market leader because the category is not of high interest to them.
3. The project team concluded that there is an opportunity for a global female brand for contemporary, open-minded pleasure seekers, the "free-feeling woman". They proposed a premium-priced Lights brand targeted at FASU30,[46] with brand muscles: multi-dimensional me; contemporary femininity; and sensory pleasure.[47]

BAT is a particularly significant company from a perspective of global health since 70 percent of its sales are in Africa, Asia, Latin America, and Eastern Europe.[48]

Notwithstanding the global strength of Marlboro, PMI is more weighted toward declining traditional markets while BAT enjoys greater market share in emergent markets.[49] This suggests that any erosion by BAT of PMI's currently substantial lead among women smokers is likely to occur among developing countries. BAT's documents indicate that targeting women smokers is a key element in its strategy to displace PMI as the leading tobacco transnational via global expansion.

A road map prepared to clarify the future role of BAT's Central Marketing team in June 2000 asserted that "Lights growth optimisation plus gaining a higher share of females is a key challenge in all markets."[50] The grammatical error of identifying these two objectives as a single challenge captures a greater truth, since (as discussed earlier) the rise of light cigarettes is inextricably linked with their appeal to women. The ongoing significance of this linkage is clear from its strategic importance in shaping BAT's investment decisions. In Uzbekistan, for example, the expectation of success in recruiting more women smokers was a core element of the company's marketing strategy, and lights were identified along with menthol cigarettes as the means of attaining this objective: "Historically, local products have been too strong to attract large numbers of female smokers. Female smoking is now more socially acceptable and females can be drawn into the market via menthol offers or lighter brands."[51] In similar vein, BAT planned investment in Moldova on the basis of substantial predicted market growth, reflecting an anticipated combination of increased incomes, improved distribution, and "higher incidence" (and thus new smokers), particularly amongst women.[52]

An indication of the potential profitability of such a development to the future of the TTCs is provided by the case of Indonesia.[53] Identified by BAT as "the fourth most populous country in the world, the second largest cigarette market in Asia Pacific (including kreteks) and experiencing high growth,"[54] an overall adult smoking prevalence rate of around 34 percent disguises a huge gender-based disparity, 69 percent among men in contrast with only 3 percent among women. While it is clear that the efforts of TTCs to narrow this gap are based on techniques and strategies developed in their traditional markets, the precise nature of their appeal may differ according to local context. Consequently, the assessment of prevailing social, economic, and cultural factors affects the manner in which such strategies are implemented. In many developing countries the very transnationality of the transnational tobacco companies is deployed as an important element in marketing their products.

A global brand cigarette constitutes a comparatively accessible and affordable signifier of Western-, and often specifically American-style prosperity and modernity.[55] Among Indonesians who smoked both the locally dominant kretek, a clove cigarette, and conventional white stick cigarettes, research conducted for Philip Morris demonstrated the preference of such dual users for smoking white cigarettes "when 'prestige' requires (particularly for women)."[56] Such research was based on an assessment that reported incidence of smoking among urban women was depressed by underclaiming and that there was indeed scope for significant gains. Effective marketing to women would, however, have to be predicated on a recognition of the divergent images evoked by women smoking in Indonesia:

> As women are an important possible target, we feel we should point out that female smoking in Indonesia evokes two contrary perceptions. One is of modernity and sophistication, the other of disreputability (the bar-girl image). The latter is stronger the lower the socio-economic status . . . That is not to say that they are not a valid target. A correctly positioned brand may be able to increase smoking incidence as well as win share.[57]

This complexity is illustrated by the place among the views about female smokers subsequently expressed in interviews of existing female smokers that the activity was "cheap" and gave a bad impression in public. While it was also held to be modern and impressive, the subsequent report noted that their perception of women smoking as emancipated, intellectual, and independent were "not totally positive assessments, even amongst these women."[58]

Any substantial narrowing of the gender divide in tobacco consumption in countries such as Indonesia is, of course, liable to occur only over a long time frame. The corporate documents do, however, provide indications that recent investments by TTCs in key emergent tobacco markets among LMICs are already leading to increased smoking of their products among women. BAT's relaunch of its Kent brand in Chile, Russia, Romania, and Hong Kong resulted in a 65 percent increase in total volumes, an assessment of which reported "clear evidence that the rounded corner pack has proved vital in growing market share amongst ASU30[59] consumers and females in particular."[60] Kent's relaunch in Hong Kong also seems to have been successful in both rejuvenating the brand's profile and increasing its appeal to women, a business review reporting that "(i)n terms of user profile, improvement was seen in the 18–24, 25–29 and female franchise."[61]

Conclusion and Recommendations

Globalization is widely cited as being characterized by the increasing economic, social, and political power of transnational corporations, but compelling analyses of the mechanisms by which such alleged influence is exerted have proved elusive. J. K. Galbraith has observed the paradox that in a context of the declining capacity of the nation-state and the primacy of the modern corporation "(t)he institution that most changes our lives we least understand."[62] The release of over 40 million pages of internal tobacco industry documents following litigation in the United States provides an opportunity to partially redress this dearth of understanding.

From the perspective of global health, this is an opportunity of enormous significance. The documents cover a period in which the leading tobacco companies transformed themselves, becoming genuinely transnational actors. They offer an insight into the strategies adopted during a critical period that witnessed the revitalization of the tobacco industry, switching from primary reliance on profitable but gradually declining traditional markets in high-income countries and Western Europe to exploit opportunities for growth in LMICs. Countering the consequent shift in the burden of tobacco-related death and disease requires a major shift in global health governance, a process instigated by negotiations for the Framework Convention on Tobacco Control, WHO's first international health treaty.[63] This process was itself partially reliant upon the insights from and political momentum facilitated by revelations of misconduct in the industry documents. There remains, however, a need for far more research into the conduct of the TTCs in developing countries if their political influence is to be countered and effective tobacco control policies broadly adopted.

Determining how the marketing strategies of TTCs shape temporal, cognitive, and spatial notions of prosperity and success in LMICs may help health analysts better understand poverty as it relates to gender, health, and globalization. A study looking at the economic impact of tobacco consumption in Bangladesh concluded that associated expenditures greatly exacerbated the effects of poverty, creating the greatest impact on the most poor by decreasing income available for combating malnutrition and accessing health care.[64] More research examining the diverse gendered implications arising from family spending patterns in poor countries is needed, since increased spending on tobacco can critically decrease already limited funds for the purchase of food.

There has been comparatively little research into the documents that is informed by a gender perspective, and that which has been undertaken has primarily focused on North America. That which has been attempted has, however, been sufficient to demonstrate their potential value as a resource in advancing understanding of the complex role of gender relations in the development of the tobacco pandemic and to subsequently inform appropriate policy responses. In particular, the documents demonstrate the importance of recognizing the enormous diversity within the overarching categories of male and female. TTCs have long since acknowledged that women do not constitute an undifferentiated unitary group, developing increasingly sophisticated approaches to segmenting the female market. Health promotion research and policy has much to learn from this recognition of the inadequacy of a one-size-fits-all approach.

Future research into the relationships between globalization, gender, and health also needs to be more serious in the frequently avowed intention not to restrict the consideration of gender, to the study of women. This is a persistent failure that this chapter has arguably perpetuated. The global variation in smoking prevalence rates between men and women reiterates the importance of encouraging cessation among men while attempting to restrict uptake among women. Gender-informed analyses have much to offer in this. For example, it has been argued that tobacco companies were first interested in women as a way of selling cigarettes to men, and the persistent reliance on the promise of attraction in selling their appeal to adolescent males requires greater study, particularly from a global perspective. TTCs have increasingly recognized the complexity of identity politics and there is a need for additional analyses of efforts to promote cigarettes to minority ethnic groups as well as to lesbian, gay, bisexual, and transgender communities.

While the status of TTCs as the primary vectors of the tobacco pandemic makes it entirely appropriate that they should be the subject of further research, global health research also needs to look beyond them. The ongoing relevance of diverse traditional tobacco products requires the avoidance of a narrow fixation on the white stick cigarette. Recognition of the distinctive threats posed by the entry of TTCs into developing countries should not lead to an assumption that domestic tobacco industries are somehow benign.

Notes

1. N. Kaufman and M. Nichter (2001), The marketing of tobacco to women: Global perspectives, in J. Samet and Soon-Young Yoon, eds., *Women and the Tobacco Epidemic: Challenges for the 21st Century*, WHO/NMH/TFI/01.1, Geneva: WHO, p. 69.
2. A. M. Brandt (1996), Recruiting women smokers: The engineering of consent, *JAMWA* 51(1&2): 63–66, p. 64.
3. C. K. Gajalakshmi et al. (2000), Global patterns of smoking and smoking-attributable mortality, in P. Jha and F. Chaloupka, eds., *Tobacco Control in Developing Countries*, Oxford: Oxford University Press, p. 11; World Health Organization (2003). *The World Health Report 2003: Shaping the Future*, Geneva: WHO, p. 91.
4. M. Crescenti (1999), The new tobacco world, *Tobacco Journal International* (March): 51–53.
5. F. Chaloupka and A. Laixuthai (1996), *US Trade Policy and Cigarette Smoking in Asia* (Working Paper No. 5543), Cambridge, MA: National Bureau of Economic

Research; A. Taylor, F. Chaloupka, E. Gundon, and M. Corbett (2000), The impact of trade liberalization on tobacco consumption, in P. Jha, and F. Chaloupka, eds., *Tobacco Control in Developing Countries* (pp. 343–364), Oxford: Oxford University Press.

6. J. Collin (2003), Think global, smoke local: Transnational tobacco companies and cognitive globalization, in K. Lee, ed., *Health Impacts of Globalization: Towards Global Governance* (pp. 61–85), Basingstoke: Palgrave.

7. K. Lee (2003), Introduction, in K. Lee, ed., *Health Impacts of Globalization: Towards Global Governance* (pp. 1–12), p. 5.

8. C. K. Gajalakshmi, et al. (2000), Global patterns of smoking and smoking—attributable mortality, in P. Jha, and F. Chaloupka, eds., *Tobacco Control in Developing Countries*, Oxford: Oxford University Press, p. 11.

9. M. Thun, and V. L. da Costa e Silva (2003), Introduction and overview of global tobacco surveillance, in O. Shafey, S. Dolwick, and G. E. Guindon, eds., *Tobacco Control Country Profiles*, second edition, Atlanta, GA: American Cancer Society.

10. J. M. Samet and S-Y. Yoon, eds. (2001), Women and the tobacco epidemic, *Challenges for the 21st century*, Geneva: World Health Association; M. Morrow and S. Barraclough (2003), Tobacco control and gender in South East Asia, Part 1: Malaysia and the Philippines, *Health Promotion International*. 18(3): 255–264.

11. V. Ernster, N. Kaufman, M. Nichter, J. Samet, and S-Y. Yoon (2000), Women and tobacco: moving from policy to action, *Bulletin of the WHO*, 78(7): 891–901, p. 891.

12. L. Doyal (1995), *What Makes Women Sick: Gender and the Political Economy of Health*, Basingstoke: Macmillan.

13. K. Honjo and M. Siegel (2003), Perceived importance of being thin and smoking initiation among young girls, *Tobacco Control*, 12(3): 289–295.

14. R. Fant, D. Everson, G. Dayton, W. Pickworth, and J. Henningfield (1996), Nicotine dependence in women, *Journal of American Medical Women's Association*, 51(1&2): 19–25.

15. J. M. Samet and S. Yoon, eds., Women and the tobacco epidemic, Gajalakshmi, et al., Global patterns of smoking and smoking-attributable mortality, p. 11.

16. F. J. Chaloupka and R. L. Pacula, Sex and race differences in young people's responsiveness to price and tobacco control policies, *Tobacco Control* 8(4): 373–377.

17. A. Amos and M. Haglund (2000), From social taboo to "torch of freedom": the marketing of cigarettes to women, *Tobacco Control* 9(1): 3–8.

18. A. B. Gilmore, C. Radu-Loghin, I. Zatushevski, and M. McKee (April 19, 2005), Pushing up smoking incidence: A review Of transnational tobacco company plans for a privatised tobacco industry in Moldova, *The Lancet* 365(9467): 1354–1359.

19. K. Honjo and I. Kawachi (2000), Effects of market liberalisation on smoking in Japan, *Tobacco Control* 9(2):193–200.

20. A. Amos, and M. Haglund (2000), From social taboo to "torch of freedom," 3–8.

21. C. Mekemson and S. Glantz (2002), How the tobacco industry built its relationship with Hollywood, *Tobacco Control* 11(Supplement 1): i81–i92.

22. E. L. Bernays (1965), *Biography of an Idea: Memoirs of Public Relations Counsel Edward L. Bernays*, New York: Simon and Schuster, cited: A. M. Brandt (1996), Recruiting women smokers: The engineering of consent, *JAMWA* 51 (1&2): 63–66, p. 65.

23. *Atlantic Monthly* 1916, cited: Brandt, Recruiting women smokers, 63–66, p. 63.

24. J. Walton, ed. (2000), *The Faber Book of Smoking*, London: Faber and Faber, p. 142.

25. M. Dowie (1995), Introduction; torches of liberty, In J. Stauber, and S. Rampton, *Toxic Sludge is Good For You! Lies, Damn Lies and the Public Relations Industry*, Monroe, ME: Common Courage Press, p. 1.

26. American Tobacco Company (1929), "An ancient prejudice has been removed," advertisement—Lucky Strike http://roswell.tobaccodocuments. org/pollay/images/Luck02.01_display.jpg (accessed January 2005).

27. B. Jacobson (1988), *Beating the Ladykillers: Women and Smoking*, London: Victor Gollancz, p. 55.

28. Ibid., p. 56.

29. BAT (1977), *Channelling the Tide of Fashion: The Development of Kim*, Guildford Depository, Bates No. 686031825/1858.

30. M. Johnston (1966, June), *Special Report No. 248 Market Potential of a Health Cigarette*, Philip Morris, http://legacy.library.ucsf.edu/tid/bdw67e00.

31. ASH (1998), *Big Tobacco and Women*, www.ash.org.uk/html/conduct/html/ tobexpld8.html (accessed August 30, 2004).

32. Joossens and Sasco (1999), *Some Like It "Light": Women and Smoking in the European Union*, European Network for Smoking Prevention, http://www. ensp.org/files/ACF39C3.doc.

33. J. Tindall (February 13, 1992), *Cigarette Market History and Interpretation and Consumer Research, MMTP Presentation*, Philip Morris, Bates No: 2057041153–1196.

34. A. Brandt, Recruiting women smokers, p. 65.

35. Walton, *The Faber Book of Smoking*, p. 113.

36. J. N. Kabeer (1994), Gender-aware policy and planning: A social relations perspective, *Gender Planning in Development Agencies*, Oxford: Oxfam; N. Christofides (2001), How to make policies more gender-sensitive, in J. Samet and S. Yoon, eds., *Women and the Tobacco Epidemic: Challenges for the 21st Century*, WHO/NMH/TFI/01.1. Geneva: WHO.

37. V. Ernster et al., Women and tobacco, p. 891.

38. R. Thornton (November 12, 1976). *The Smoking Behaviour of Women, Report No. RD.1410 Restricted*, BAT Group Research and Development Centre, Brown & Williamson, Bates No: 650008159–8191.

39. V. Frideman (June 28, 1973). *The Female Smoking Market*, Lorillard, Bates No. 03375503–5510.

40. V. Ernster et al., Women and tobacco, p. 894.

41. P. Ling and S. Glantz (June 12, 2002). Using tobacco-industry marketing research to design more effective tobacco-control campaigns, *JAMA*, 287 (22): 2983–2989.

42. McCann-Erickson Inc. (1981), Social trends among female smokers—application to project delta, Brown & Williamson, Bates No. 677046079/6106.

43. This exercise provided further evidence of the greater appeal of low tar and nicotine products to women than men: "As a cross reference, female responses were compared to combined male/female responses, i.e., a more representative sample size. We believe that the variation in the total agreement of Self-Achievers, is due to an actual difference in the beliefs held by male vs. female respondents. Female Self-Achievers are then interpreted as being possibly more responsive to low T&N appeal" (McCann-Erickson 1981).

44. McCann-Erickson Inc., Social trends among female smokers—application to project delta.

45. [Schweitzer] (1992), TSG Report: Marlboro pan-European study. British American Tobacco, Guildford Depository, Bates No. 202215366–5378.

46. Female adult smokers under the age of 30.

47. H. C. Barton (December 19, 2000). *Marketing Committee [Notes from the meeting held on 6th December 2000.]* [BAT DoJ Minnesota] 325051442–1444.

48. Y. Saloojee, and E. Dagli (2000), Tobacco industry tactics for resisting public policy on health, *Bulletin of the World Health Organization*; 78 (7): 902–910.

49. B. Fisher (June, 2001), The power of regionalism, *Tobacco Reporter*.

50. BAT (2000), Marketing Road Map (Draft handed out at Drive Team meeting June 8) BAT. Minnesota Tobacco Document Depository, Bates No. 325421407–1408.

51. D. Sims (1993), Marketing Report Uzbekistan, Field Visit October 6, 1993 to October 15,1993, Guildford Depository, BAT, Bates No. 203465873–93.

52. A. Gilmore et al. (in press), Pushing up smoking incidence.

53. S. Lawrence and J. Collin (2004), Competing with Kreteks: British American Tobacco, Globalisation and Indonesia, *Tobacco Control* 13(Suppl 2): ii96–ii103.

54. BAT (1996), Asia Pacific Regional Conference: Strategy Exercise Data Pack, 5 January, Bates No. 503909616.

55. J. Collin (2003), Globalization, the tobacco industry and policy influence, in A. K. Varma, ed., (2002), *Tobacco Counters Health. Vol 2: Proceedings of the 2nd World Assembly on Tobacco Counters Health* (pp. 39–50), Macmillan India Ltd.: New Delhi.

56. BAT Indonesia (n.d.), [A study on the smokers of International Brands], British American Tobacco, Guildford Depository, Bates No. 400458940.

57. N. Fincher (1988) [Re: Philip Morris Research], Survey Research Indonesia. 5/02/88, Philip Morris, Bates No.2504054603/4615 [accessed November 2002]

58. BAT (1996), Asia Pacific Regional Conference: Strategy Exercise Data Pack, 5 January, BAT. Guildford Depository. Bates No. 503909616.

59. Adult smokers under the age of 30.

60. BAT (2000), *Kent Key Conclusions* BAT, Minnesota Tobacco Document Depository, Bates No. 325422554–2556.

61. BAT (n.d.), *KENT Business Review, China* BAT, Minnesota Tobacco Document Depository, Bates No. 325422559–2569.

62. J. K. Galbraith (1977), *The Age of Uncertainty*, London: Penguin, p. 275.

63. World Health Organization (2003), Framework Convention on Tobacco Control, final text, May 21, http://www.who.int/tobacco/areas/framework/final_text/en/ (accessed August 30, 2004); J. Collin, K. Lee, and K. Bissell (2004), Negotiating the framework convention on tobacco control: The politics of global health governance, in Wilkinson R. and Murphy C., eds., *Global Governance: A Reader*, London: Routledge.

64. D. Efroymson, S. Ahmed, J. Townsend, S. M. Alam, A. R. Dey, R. Saha, B. Dhar, A. I. Sujon, K. U. Ahmed, O. Rahman, Hungry for tobacco: An analysis of the economic impact of tobacco consumption on the poor in Bangladesh, *Tobacco Control* 2001(10): 212–217.

In Perspective

Women's Health under Fire: Does It Need to Go Up in Smoke?

Stella A. Bialous

Jeff Collin's comprehensive overview of the implications for women's health of increased tobacco use by women due to globalization is at once brilliant and maddening. While such exceptional discussion of the multiple, complex layers of the epidemic of tobacco-related diseases among women is a "must read" for the researcher in me, as a women's health's advocate I want to scream, "yes, yes, and what are we going to do about it?" Although Collin's discussion does not go into great detail about the issues that are specific to Latin America, to Brazil, or to the Latina population in the United States, the tobacco industry strategies he describes, and the health impact of women being perceived as a major growth market are, unfortunately, too easily translated.

I am always amazed and frustrated to observe that tobacco use among women struggles to find its rightful place on the agenda of organizations that advocate for women's health and women's rights. Certainly, there are an increasing number of laudable exceptions, and I am honored to be part of the International Network of Women Against Tobacco (INWAT) and a tobacco control network in Brazil that was developed by the Human Development Network (REDEH), a "feminist organization that holds as its mission to promote human rights."[1] However, in the vast majority of countries, in both the developed and developing worlds, focus is placed on other women's health issues, and tobacco, the big elephant in the room, remains an afterthought at best. Tobacco companies are ready, willing, and eager to take advantage of this situation.

In their efforts to portray themselves as socially responsible corporate citizens, an effort that seems more a public relations campaign than truly an ethical epiphany,[2] tobacco companies heavily invest in women-related issues, funding, for example, domestic violence prevention programs and women's shelters throughout the world, gaining the tacit approval, if not the active support, of many women's organizations. Could we not equate decades of aggressive marketing to women throughout the world with just another form of abuse? I would never minimize the seriousness of domestic violence, HIV infection, and other crucial issues in women's health. But the epidemic proportions and the future projections for the impact of tobacco use on women's health leaves no room for partnership with tobacco companies. The companies' goal is to be profitable—and to grow profits they need to sell more and, as discussed by Collins, women in middle-and low-income countries make the most desirable target from the industry's perspective for expansion. Women's groups that compromise now will pay later.

As a Brazilian, a nurse, and a Latina immigrant there are just too many overlapping ways in which I have closely witnessed the issues described by Collins and have seen the impact that growing tobacco prevalence among women has had on the health of the population. Recent data from the Global Youth Tobacco Survey in Brazil show that tobacco experimentation and smoking prevalence remain higher overall for boys than for girls in the 13–15 age group, but in many of the 12 state capitals included in the study this difference was minimal, and in two of the cities experimentation and prevalence were higher among girls.[3] This trend was seen throughout the region and, in fact, the world, as Collins described. Also of note from the findings is that despite Brazil's comprehensive legislation restricting tobacco marketing, the majority of children included in the study stated they could recall seeing positive tobacco messages in the media. These data indicate that the tobacco industry's message continues to get across, often through innovative marketing strategies, and is reaching young girls at escalating rates in Brazil as much as in many other parts of the world.

Growing up in the 1980s, it was almost impossible to escape the lure of tobacco and its insidious presence. I did, mainly because I failed miserably at repeated inhaling attempts and could not maintain a "glamorous" image between fits of coughing and tearing eyes. I did have a clique of girlfriends who were "un-cool" like me, but I always envied the girls who, at school, at parties, and on the beach, could smoke with the boys, almost all of whom smoked at that time. Being a nonsmoker did not keep me from whole-hearted participation in many industry-sponsored cultural events, which were then, as with smoking itself, the social norm. In Brazil, too, cigarette brands were created and marketed directly to women, with ads showing sophisticated, gorgeous women. And a major success story in Brazil is the marketing of "Free," a premium (i.e., more expensive) brand with ads depicting cutting-edge men and women, now garnering approximately 14 percent share of market overall and 50 percent share in the so-called lights segment.[4] Free's earlier tagline stated that it was simply a matter of "common sense." As described by Collins, "light" cigarettes are heavily marketed toward a more health-conscious public, mainly women. Brazilian legislation stopped the sponsorship of events such as the Free Jazz Festival, but Free's new point of sales campaign is based on the premise that one is supposed to create, relax, and have fun "in excess," but to smoke in moderation.[5] This campaign ignores scientific knowledge about addiction and adds insult to injury to women, who may have a more difficult time quitting than men.[6]

Entering nursing school in Brazil did not bring about a change in the smoking that surrounded me. Several of my nursing student colleagues, the nurses on the floor, and the physicians were smokers, and much as it was the case a decade or so earlier in developed countries, smoking was part of shift report meetings and of the bonding process for the health care team. I have no recollection, as a student in the early 1980s, of tobacco-related content being part of either the theoretical or the clinical teaching, but looking back, I see that countless times, both as a student and as a young staff nurse, I was directly confronted with the end-result of tobacco use and saw suffering and death that could have been entirely prevented. This experience is not unique to Brazil, or even to the region, although it might be more extreme there. A recent survey of U.S. nursing schools shows that even in that country, tobacco-related content is not sufficiently or satisfactorily addressed in the curricula.[7]

But there is a deeper issue at stake here: nursing, in many parts of the world, remains a predominantly female occupation, thus issues associated with women's health are intrinsically associated with nurses' health. Not coincidentally, much of what is known about the harmful health effects of tobacco on the female body was learnt through the Nurses' Health Study.[8] This ongoing longitudinal study has told the world much of what is known about women's health and tobacco, but we often overlook that nurses are the subjects, and this study could be interpreted as one of the larger studies of the impact of smoking on a single, largely female occupation. In many developed countries, and increasingly in developing ones, nurses' smoking rates remain higher than those of other health care professionals and or at a similar prevalence to the general female population, reflecting many of the gender and class issues seen across the board in the tobacco epidemic. Nonetheless, unlike many of the women who use tobacco, nurses are confronted by high societal expectations of exemplary behavior. Too often, we forget that these nurses were once young and impressionable, seduced by the images of success and slimness of tobacco marketing.

Knowledge about the harmful effects of tobacco use is not enough to overcome addiction.

Also while in nursing school, I saw how women were, and continue to be, used as "bait." On one hand the tobacco companies' advertising tell women that smoking will lead to independence; women, on the other hand, are used as walking advertising in events sponsored by the tobacco companies. Unfortunately, this is neither part of the past nor unique to Brazil. A Peruvian advertisement where a cigarette pack is safely tucked in a woman's bosom is often used as an example of such exploitation.[9] In college, I had friends who wore miniscule shorts as they either distributed free samples of cigarettes, or just circulated among the public attending music or sports events (the Formula 1 and motocross races being most desirable). My lack of participation was not due to some higher standards, or even in protest of the required "uniforms"—it was simply that going to college full time, I had no time left to take on additional work, and I felt once again on the fringe of coolness. But never once did it cross my mind that we were being used to sell a product that causes suffering and death. I can never forget when, years later, I was sitting at an open café with American friends who were visiting Brazil and a van parked in front of the café disgorged what seemed like an endless wave of gorgeous, scantily dressed young women distributing free samples of a new brand of cigarettes. At the time I was already working on tobacco control and tried to engage the young woman who came to our table, asking a few questions about her current job but she could not see anything wrong with what the tobacco companies were doing. This confirmed to me that the industry's "adult choice" argument was still going strong, and much remained to be done in order to educate the female population on tobacco issues. Knowing now what I didn't know then solidifies my commitment to work on tobacco control and to focus on tobacco companies' behavior. One of the Americans with us could not believe such blatant promotion (which is more common now in North America), and through his shock I realized that, yes, when it comes to the tobacco companies marketing to women, there are a variety of standards. Victories achieved by health advocates in one country are not easily incorporated and translated to another. When it comes to tobacco, globalization applies to marketing and trade, but not yet health. So we, women of developing countries, continue to be oxymoronic independent objects, manipulated by the desire for profits of a handful of tobacco companies.

As I enter my mid-years, I am part of a very large community of Latino immigrants (according to the census data, one of the fastest growing segments of the U.S. population), and have the unfortunate privilege of continuing to witness the same targeted marketing strategies that I saw in my home country. Latino women smoke less than their white counterparts in the United States and women from lower socioeconomic class and from ethnic minorities are as much of a target in the United States as are women in developing countries.[10] Whereas in developing countries smoking is still often associated with social status and success, and in many parts of the world somewhat limited to women of higher socioeconomic and educational level status, in developed countries, smoking has become an entrenched social and gender justice issue. As in extensive marketing analysis conducted by tobacco companies all over the world, U.S. companies also took the same in-depth approach to market segmentation. This is why, for example, one such analysis, from 1989, found among the now public internal industry documents, described how Latino women in New York differ from Latino women in Los Angeles: "the Hispanic woman in Los Angeles has not reached a comparable level of attitudinal or social liberation as her counterpart in either Miami or New York." The document further states that:

> The message of reassurance appears to be the most relevant one for the [Hispanic] women. Although they talked about the liberated, modern women, and said they identified with her, several obviously *wished* they could identify more. A few even admitted that they are still struggling to be liberated and independent. This was not surprising given that they are still part of the "downtrodden" minority, being both women and Hispanic. Therefore, reassurance for smoking is much closer to their actual reality, and is a message worth retaining.[11] [emphasis in original]

Therefore, unlike the often nationality- and gender-neutral approaches of tobacco control counter-marketing, the tobacco industry recognizes the many differences among women of the same broad category and plans its strategies accordingly.

It is evident that the lower prevalence rate of smoking among women in most of the world is a tragedy waiting to happen unless global action is taken. As discussed by Collins, there is still much we can learn from in-depth analysis of the now publicly available internal industry documents. We also need more research on tobacco initiation and cessation among women, and whether or not there are cultural and gender-specific issues that can guide tobacco control measures.

We need more research about tobacco use and cessation of women in developing countries and women in subgroups of the population: class and ethnic issues, image, self-esteem, and body weight—what role these factors play in women's tobacco use in the developing countries? Of additional concern is the current debate about whether a particular form of smokeless tobacco, called snus, should be advocated as a form of reduced harm nicotine for those smokers who are unable to quit. It is largely based on the experience of Swedish men and the reduction of lung cancer rates in Sweden.[12] Until now, utterly lacking from the debate is the impact the recommendation of snus as a reduced harm tobacco would have on women, particularly those in developing countries. Some have argued that women who would not otherwise smoke, because of societal norms against it, may uptake the use of snus, which while allegedly less harmful than smoking, is not without any health risks. Before any decision on recommending snus as a harm reduction public health strategy, more research is needed on the impact of this proposed policy change on the health of women.

From a policy perspective, the World Health Organization Framework Convention on Tobacco Control (WHO FCTC), a major attempt at globalization of the solution for the tobacco epidemic, may start to offer some solutions. The WHO FCTC calls for a stop of gender-blind tobacco control measures, while also advocating broader policies to the benefit of all. Research and policy can provide a wealth of information that will only be of practical use when the current and future devastation of tobacco on women's health make it to the top of women organizations' agendas. Tobacco use is the worst form of gender equality. So, as stated earlier, what are we going to do about this? The debate continues and hopefully sustained action will follow.

Notes

1. Rede de Desenvolvimento Humano, available: http://www.redeh.org.br/.
2. B. Burton, and A. Rowell (2002), British American tobacco's socially responsible smoke screen, *PR Watch* (Fourth Quarter): 6–12.
3. Global Youth Tobacco Survey Collaborating Group, report presented at the 12th World Conference on Tobacco or Health, August 3–8, 2003, Helsinki, Finland, http://www.cdc.gov/tobacco/global/gyts/globaluse01.htm. Ministerio da Saude, Instituto Nacional de Cancer (2004), Vigescola. *Vigilancia de Tabagismo em Escolares*, Vol. 1. Rio de Janeiro: p. 15.
4. Souza Cruz Website, Marcas, available: http://www.souzacruz.com.br/oneweb/sites/SOU_5RRP92.nsf/vwPagesWebLive/DO5QKJC6?opendocument&SID=6B05F86E2651DD81556991B78537BED3&DTC=20040717&TMP=1 (accessed July 15, 2004).
5. Ibid.
6. K. A. Perkins (2001), Smoking cessation in women: Special considerations, *CNS Drugs* 15(5): 391–411.
7. M. Wewers, K. Kidd, D. Armbruster, and L. Sarna (2004), Tobacco dependence curricula in U.S. baccalaureate and graduate nursing education, *Nurse Outlook* 52(2): 95–101.

8. The Nurses' Health Study, available: http://www.channing.harvard.edu/nhs/.

9. For this and other examples, see: http://www.tobaccofreekids.org/adgallery/.

10. United States Department of Health and Human Services, Centers for Disease Control and Prevention (May 28, 2004), Cigarette Smoking Among Adults—United States, 2002, *MMWR*, 53(20): 427–431.

11. Leo, Burnett (November 8, 1989), *Research Among Hispanic Women Smokers*, prepared for Philip Morris, Leo Burnett Research Department, Bates No. 2047934426/2047934438. www.pmdocs.com, access date: November 19, 2002.

12. J. Foulds, L. Ramstrom, M. Burke, and K. Fagerström (2003), Effect of smokeless tobacco (snus) on smoking and public health in Sweden, *Tobacco Control* 12: 349–359; C., Bates, K., Fagerström, M. J. Jarvis, M. Kunze, A. McNeill, and L. Ramström (2003), European Union policy on smokeless tobacco: A statement in favour of evidence based regulation for public health, *Tobacco Control* 12: 360–367.

In Perspective

Globalization, Gender, and the Pandemic of Disease in Women Caused by Tobacco

Norbert Hirschhorn

The World Health Organization (WHO) has described the prevalence of the use of tobacco and subsequent mortality as an evolving four-stage multi-decade pandemic. As shown in figure 7.1, historic tracing in northern countries reveal the stages[1]: In the first stage, the prevalence of smoking is low, and mostly by men, as is mortality from cancer, lung, and heart disease related to tobacco, which take several decades to be manifest. In the second stage, over half the men smoke, more women begin taking up the addiction, and smoking-related diseases in men is on the rise. The third stage sees a slowly falling rate of smoking among men, converging on a still-rising rate in women, and now a rise in the death rate in women. The fourth stage sees a downturn in smoking rates among both men and women, a beginning downturn in tobacco-related mortality in men, but a continued rise in death rates among women.

If one imposes on this trace the patterns of smoking and disease in the world's regions today we may find sub-Saharan Africa in the first stage; Asia and North Africa in the second stage; Latin America, Southern and Eastern Europe in the third stage; Western Europe and the English-speaking nations in the fourth. The paradigm, while not a perfect match, nevertheless indicates to which populations the tobacco industry is and will be most active in promoting tobacco; and also, coincidentally, where tobacco control is still at its weakest. By stage four, one-third of all men die from tobacco-use, and quarter of all women.[2]

Epidemiologic data, both retrospective and prospective, show that tobacco kills half of its users, half of those between the productive ages of

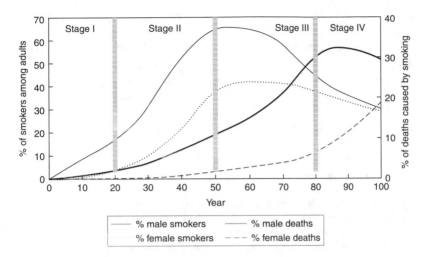

Figure 7.1   A model of the cigarette epidemic.

Source: A. D. Lopez, N. E. Collishaw, and T. A. Piha, Tobacco Control, 1994, p. 246. Copyright: BMJ Publishing Group Ltd.

35 and 69.[3] Today, over 1.3 billion humans smoke; the majority beginning in their teenage years. Globally 47 percent of men and 12 percent of women smoke (the latter statistic reflecting the numerical influence of China with 350 million smokers, mostly men). WHO estimates that tobacco will be responsible for 5 million deaths annually, 10 million within two decades, and that 70 percent of those deaths will occur in the southern countries that are still at stages 1–3.[4]

By the stages of the pandemic it is apparent that the consequences of tobacco-use are gender-neutral. What is not neutral is the incessant promotion of cigarettes by the tobacco industry and in particular to populations with lower prevalence of smoking; which today means to developing countries, youth, and women. In industrialized countries where there is an increasing disparity in smoking prevalence between the educated and less educated, the well-to-do and the less-well off, there the tobacco industry strives to maintain if not increase the rate of smoking among working-class and disadvantaged women.[5]

"Gender analysis examines the power relationship between men and women and its consequences on their lives. . . . It enables us to examine how women's socially defined roles and relative powerlessness determine their exposure to risk."[6] This definition from a book on health equity applies to smoking because of the way, as Jeff Collin has presented, the tobacco industry assiduously pursues women to become smokers. Collin cites an internal British American Tobacco (BAT) memo's crass observation that *"gaining a higher share of females is a key challenge in all markets."*[7] From my reading of previously secret tobacco industry documents it is clear that the majority of tobacco industry executives, lawyers, public relations and marketing personnel are men.[8] It has been that industry's strategy to pitch smoking to middle-class women with gendered images of slimness, emancipation, and concern over health, leading more of those women to take up so-called light and mild cigarettes; and to lower-class women who mostly smoke Marlboros with "virile" imagery.[9] That the marketing wizards of the tobacco industry do a kind of twisted "gender analysis" is shown in the famous BAT internal memo that stated,

> Smoking behaviour of women differs from that of men. . . . [they are] more highly motivated to smoke. . . . [T]hey find it harder to stop smoking. . . . [W]omen are more neurotic than men and more likely to need to smoke in stressful situations, presumably because they are less well able to deal with stress. . . . Given that women are more neurotic than men it seems reasonable to assume that they will react more strongly to smoking and health pressures. . . . There may be a case for launching a female oriented cigarette with relatively high deliveries of nicotine. . . .[10]

We should be concerned whenever any person is initiated into smoking. What makes us even more concerned when women become the special target?

Three major reports on women and smoking document disquieting statistics of what happens when the prevalence rises as it has in northern countries: two U.S. Surgeon General Reports, and one from WHO/Johns Hopkins.[11]

> Since 1980, approximately 3 million U.S. women have died prematurely from smoking-related neoplastic, cardiovascular, respiratory, and pediatric diseases, as well as cigarette-caused burns. Each year during the 1990s, U.S. women lost an estimated 2.1 million years of life due to these smoking attributable premature deaths.[12]

According to the latest information from the U.S. Surgeon General, the message essentially is: "If you smoke like a man, you die like a man."[13] Adjusted for duration and intensity of smoking, lung and other cancer rates are comparable between genders; chronic obstructive pulmonary disease (COPD, or emphysema), cardiovascular disease, and stroke are equal threats to men and women smokers. (Postmenopausal women smokers are more likely to develop osteoporosis than comparably aged men smokers.) Therefore to target populations of women who are not now smokers is to add fuel to the existing pandemic.

The 2001 Surgeon General's report also documents that deaths in the United States from lung cancer in women have since 1987 surpassed deaths from breast cancer; while this statistic in part reflects the better survival rate of breast cancer under treatment, only lung cancer is almost entirely preventable. Smoking is also a consistent risk factor in cervical and vulval cancers.[14]

When standardized for nicotine concentration in the blood, women are as susceptible to addiction as men.[15] With respect to adolescents, the Surgeon General's Report on Women and Smoking noted that "most risk factors for initiation of smoking appear to be similar among girls and boys."[16] Smoking initiation to control weight seems generally to be gender-neutral,[17] although a recent review of 55 studies on the subject suggests that the positive relationship "was more consistent among female adolescents than among male adolescents."[18] Symptoms of "dependence" from the onset of monthly smoking, however, appear to occur much sooner in adolescent girls than boys: an average (median) of 21 days compared to 183 days.[19]

Cigarettes are a killer no matter who smokes, a consumer product that harms when used as intended. However, since fewer women smoke, they are disproportionately affected by the passive smoke of husbands, partners, and co-workers.[20] In Vietnam, where only 4 percent of women smoke, compared to over 70 percent of men, a woman wishing to marry has little choice but to be passively exposed. As one woman interviewed put it,

> If you hate cigarette smoke, you will still have to marry a man who's heavily addicted to tobacco. Out of 100 men, 99 smoke. If you're afraid of tobacco then you'll have to live alone; it will be very depressing.[21]

Generalized harm also falls on poorer and working-class persons so that within a family where even only the men smoke, family income suffers with disproportionate effect on women and children, their nutrition in particular.[22] The WHO reports that in Bangladesh the poorest families spend ten times as much on tobacco as on education.[23] Education plays a major role in the uptake of smoking: in the United States of America, the prevalence of smoking in women with nine to eleven years of schooling was 33 percent, but only 11 percent in those with sixteen or more years.[24]

The major consequence of smoking for women that differentiates them from men is in their reproductive health, and with latent effects on their children.[25] Thus, smoking by women causes *generational* harm. Active and passive smoking in women are linked to sub-fecundity and sub-fertility (the same pattern holds for heavy smoking by men trying to have their partners conceive). Pregnancy is more hazardous for female smokers: increased incidence of ectopic pregnancy, abruptio placenta, placenta praevia, spontaneous abortion, premature rupture of the membranes, shortened gestation leading to lower birth weight, higher perinatal death rates; but a reduced risk of eclampsia. Children born to smokers (either parent) are more likely to suffer sudden infant death syndrome, and impaired lung function at birth. Later effects include respiratory illness, asthma and ear infections, especially if the mother continues to smoke. Other reports also suggest effects on behavior and intelligence.[26]

In the United States of America, in 2000, nearly 30 percent of high school senior girls said they had smoked cigarettes in the past month.[27] Young women seem not to understand the consequences: For instance, in a cross-sectional survey of American women over the age 25, over-sampling for Blacks and Hispanics, fewer than half identified heart disease as the leading cause of death in women, and only 36 percent identified smoking as a risk factor.[28] Eighty percent of American women still believe breast cancer is their leading risk of cancer death.[29] Yet, as Collin has adroitly summarized, it is painful to recognize how superbly the tobacco companies "educate" women into smoking, while our clinical and public health programs consistently fail them. In a study of prenatal care programs funded by the U.S. government, only a quarter provided cessation to pregnant smokers, and only 28 percent even made smoking cessation a high priority during home visits.[30]

What are the Research and Policy Implications of These Data?

The data strongly suggest that we need to go outside the usual health agencies to help terminate the epidemic of smoking among women. Education, for instance, may be as important to stopping the use of tobacco among women as immunizations are to their children against infectious disease. Barbeau et al. question the current U.S. emphasis on reaching college women with anti-smoking messages and suggest that programs should be designed to reach less-advantaged women.[31] The Women Infants and Children (WIC) nutritional programs would be an ideal venue for such programs, but because so little time is spent counseling each woman on nutrition, little is done on smoking (personal communication, WIC coordinator Minnesota Department of Health). Research is needed to determine the best counter-marketing strategies via mass media.

Second, more progress is critical to help women who smoke quit. In particular, cessation programs for women who relapse into smoking after stopping during pregnancy should be incorporated into routine post-partum health care for themselves and their infants. Support from social networks, partners, and families is crucial.[32]

Tobacco control as defined by the World Health Organization's Framework Convention, is oriented toward a "globalization" perspective: increased taxation, generalized bans on advertising and public smoking, labeling and packaging, public education.[33] But based on experience from the reproductive health movement as a framework for social change, however,[34] it may be that women themselves should take the lead, a "gendered" orientation to public policy. The International Network of Women Against Tobacco (INWAT) has over 1,200 representatives in 70 countries:[35] but more importantly it is tied to many of the powerful women's NGO movements that have arisen in the past two decades for human and social justice, reproductive rights, children's rights, and the environment.[36] While in the United States of America, corporate sponsors can be found to enable tobacco control organizations that directed to women,[37] most of the southern countries' NGOs work on shoe-string or no budgets, and perhaps this is to their advantage: they can thus provide the moral and persuasive force to stop the tobacco industries' cynical predation of women. As Margaret Mead famously wrote, "Never doubt that a small group of thoughtful citizens can change the world. Indeed, it's the only thing that ever has."

Notes

1. A. D. Lopez, N. E. Collishaw, and T. Piha (1994), A descriptive model of the cigarette epidemic in developed countries, *Tobacco Control* 3: 242–247.
2. O. Shafey, S. Dolwick, and E. G. Guindon, eds. (2003), *Tobacco Control Country Profiles, Second Edition*, Atlanta, Georgia: American Cancer Society, World Health Organization, International Union Against Cancer, pp. 7–10.
3. R. Doll, R. Peto, J. Boreham, and I. Sutherland (2004), Mortality in relation to smoking: 50 years' observations on British male doctors, *BMJ* 328: 1519–1528.
4. A. Lopez et al., A descriptive model of the cigarette epidemic in developed countries.
5. E. M. Barbeau, A. Leavy-Sperounis, and E. D. Balbach (2004), Smoking, social class, and gender: What can public health learn from the tobacco industry about disparities in smoking? *Tobacco Control* 13: 115–120.
6. J. Cottingham and C. Myntti (2002), Reproductive health: Conceptual mapping and evidence, in G. Sen, A. George, and P. Ostlin, eds., *Engendering International Health. The Challenge of Equity* (ch. 4). Cambridge, MA and London: Oxford University Press, p. 83.
7. Ray E. Thornton (November 12, 1976), *The Smoking Behavior of Women*, research report (RD 1410), Minnesota Tobacco Document Depository, British American Tobacco (File B3183), Bates No. 776193337/3365 (also accessible at: http://legacy.library.ucsf.edu/tid/dnd10f00).
8. Tobacco industry internal documents were made publicly available through litigation in American courts and by agreement with U.S. States' Attorney

Generals, in 1998. The great majority may be found on industry web sites, at www.tobaccodocuments.org, and at http://legacy.library.ucsf.edu.

9. E. Barbeau, A. Leavy-Sperounis, and E. Balbach, Smoking, social class, and gender.
10. Thornton, *The Smoking Behavior of Women*.
11. *Women and Smoking*, A Report of the Surgeon General—2001 (available: http://www.cdc.gov/tobacco/sgr/sgr_forwomen/index.htm); *The Health* Consequences of Smoking, A Report of the Surgeon General—2004 (available: http://www.cdc.gov/tobacco/sgr/sgr_2004/index.htm); *Women and the tobacco epidemic, Challenges for the 21st Century* (2001), World Health Organization and Johns Hopkins School of Public Health.
12. *Women and Smoking*, A Report of the Surgeon General—2001.
13. *The Health Consequences of Smoking*, A Report of the Surgeon General—2004.
14. Ibid.; *Women and the tobacco epidemic. Challenges for the 21st Century*, World Health Organization and Johns Hopkins School of Public Health.
15. *Women and Smoking*, A Report of the Surgeon General—2001.
16. Ibid.
17. S. Shiffman, and S. M. Paton (1999), Individual differences in smoking: Gender and nicotine addiction, *Nicotine & Tobacco Research* 1(S2): S153–157; C. A. Tomeo, A. E. Field, C. S. Berkey, G. A. Colditz, and A. L. Frazier (1999), Weight concerns, weight control behaviors, and smoking initiation, *Pediatrics* 104: 918–924; J. A. Fulkerson, and S. A. French (2003), Cigarette smoking for weight loss or control among adolescents: Gender and racial/ethnic differences, *Journal of Adolescent Health* 32: 306–313.
18. B. K. Potter, L. L. Pederson, S. S. H. Chan, J-A. L. Aubut, and J. J. Koval (2004), Does a relationship exist between body weight, concerns about weight, and smoking among adolescents? An integration of the literature with an emphasis on gender, *Nicotine & Tobacco Research* 6: 397–425.
19. J. R. DiFranza, J. A. Savageau, N. A. Rigotti, K. Fletcher, J. K. Ockene, A. D. McNeill, M. Coleman, and C. Wood (2002), Development of symptoms of tobacco dependence in youths: 30 month follow up data from the DANDY study, *Tobacco Control* 11: 228–235.
20. J. M. Samet and G. Yang (2001), Passive smoking, women and children, in *Women and the tobacco epidemic. Challenges for the 21st Century* (pp. 17–45), World Health Organization and Johns Hopkins School of Public Health.
21. N. J. Kaufman and M. Nichter (2001), The marketing of tobacco to women: Global perspectives, in *Women and the Tobacco Epidemic. Challenges for the 21st Century* (pp. 69–98), World Health Organization and Johns Hopkins School of Public Health, p. 139.
22. *Tobacco and Poverty: A Vicious Circle.* (2004), Geneva: World Health Organization. (WHO/NMH/TFI/04.01).
23. Ibid.
24. *Women and Smoking*, A Report of the Surgeon General—2001.
25. Ibid., ch. 5.
26. J. Samet and G. Yang, Passive smoking, women and children; J. R. DiFranza, C. A. Aligne, and M. Weitzman (2004), Prenatal and postnatal environmental tobacco smoke and children's health, *Pediatrics* 113(4S) 1007–1015.

27. *Women and Smoking*, A Report of the Surgeon General—2001.
28. L. Mosca, A. Ferris, R. Fabunmi, R. M. Robertson (2004), Tracking women's awareness of heart disease. An American Heart Association National Study, *Circulation* 109: 573–579.
29. Women and lung cancer survey (available: www.americanlegacy.org , click on "Research & Publications . . . Fact Sheets").
30. L. V. Klerman and C. Spivey (2003), Smoking-related activities in prenatal care programs. *American Journal of Preventive Medicine* 25: 129–135.
31. E. Barbeau et al. (2004), Smoking, social class, and gender.
32. F. W. Li, A. O. Goldstein, A. Y. Butzen, A. Hartsock, K. E. Hartmann, M. Helton, and J. A. Lohr (2004), Smoking cessation in pregnancy: A review of postpartum relapse prevention strategies, *Journal of the American Board of Family Practice* 17: 264–275; P. D. Mullen (2004), How can more smoking suspension during pregnancy become lifelong abstinence? Lessons learned about predictors, interventions, and gaps in our accumulated knowledge, *Nicotine & Tobacco Research* S2: S217–238.
33. Available: http://www.who.int/tobacco/en.
34. J. Cottingham and C. Myntti, Reproductive health: Conceptual mapping and evidence.
35. Available: http://www.inwat.org/.
36. M. Bianco, M. Haglund, Y. Matsui, and N. Nakano (2001), The International women's movement and anti-tobacco campaigns, *in Women and the Tobacco Epidemic. Challenges for the 21st Century* (pp. 209–217), World Health Organization and Johns Hopkins School of Public Health.
37. Available: www.americanlegacy.org, click on "partners." Also see, American Legacy Foundation's Circle of Friends, available: http://www.join-the-circle. org.

8

The Case for Women's Health Research in the United States: Grassroots Efforts, Legislative Change, and Scientific Development

Carolyn M. Mazure

A critical factor in improving the health and health care of all individuals is the development of new scientific knowledge that can be incorporated into clinical and personal practice. Yet, such knowledge referable specifically to women has been in short supply because, historically, women have not been included as full participants in clinical research trials.[1] Furthermore, when women have been included in clinical research trials, studies have not traditionally examined whether there were differences between women and men in study outcomes.[2] This situation has generated tremendous limits in our understanding of the health of women, and of gender-specific aspects of health and disease.

The following case study focuses on the emerging history within the United States regarding the efforts made to include women as study participants in clinical trials in order to generate fundamental health data on women and on gender differences in health and disease. It illustrates how advancing the health of women came about through collaboration between grassroots efforts and legislative action. A brief history as to why women traditionally have not been studied and what initiated a change in this long-standing convention is first explored. Next, I discuss the sequelae to policy changes in health research that now provide for the inclusion of women as participants in clinical investigations. Finally, I highlight what current investigations are needed in women's health research in order to get a more accurate assessment of women's health today. With both the positive and negative attributes of global superpower, the actions of the United States often influence countries and policies outside its own borders. Through this case study, we can see the opportunity of the globalizing influence of the United States. to create a women's health research model with crucial health ramifications worldwide.

Why were Women Excluded?

Women were excluded as subjects in research studies for at least three major reasons. First, women were excluded, in part, due to concerns about exposing women to experimental risk during childbearing years.[3] It is of course true that there is a very serious obligation to insure safety in this regard. However, excluding all women from studies that are required to prove the efficacy of new treatments and from studies to develop preventive interventions has left us with major areas of women's health unexplored. It has also left us without gender-specific data on treatment and prevention that can only be drawn from comparing women and men.

Second, women have been excluded as study participants due to the complexities that women subjects can bring to research as a function of hormonal changes related to the reproductive cycle. Cyclic changes related to reproductive life that occur either over the course of a month or a life span, by definition, do not allow the constancy often sought by traditional scientific methods. However, despite the underrepresentation of women in clinical research studies due to the biological factors that set women apart from men, the assumption frequently has been made that the treatments and prevention initiatives that were developed with men also would work for women.

Third, women have not been the target of research efforts based on the misperception that certain conditions do not affect women to the same extent that they affect the health and lives of men. Further, when women are affected by these conditions, it has been assumed that they will be affected in the same way as men. One of the classic illustrations of this type of misperception is found with regard to cardiovascular disease. Long thought to be primarily "a man's disease," critical studies on cardiovascular illness, including response to medical and surgical therapies and prevention therapies, have focused largely on men. Yet, despite the focus on studying men, ischemic heart disease and cerebrovascular disease are the two greatest causes of mortality in women as well as men worldwide, causing more deaths than any other disease or injury.[4]

Furthermore, it is also now clear that when cardiovascular disease occurs, how it appears, and its clinical course can be different for women and men. For example, investigators from our research program at Yale have now shown that middle-aged women are more likely to die during hospitalization for a heart attack than men the same age (independent of medical history, severity of condition, and treatment given in hospital) and this difference persists when women and men are followed two years after hospitalization.[5] Importantly, these types of studies showing difference lay the foundation for the next step; namely, studying why there *is* difference. It is important to emphasize that in no way should our colleagues in cardiology be singled out. The tradition of including largely or exclusively male subjects is certainly not specific to one discipline.

As an illustration of how, until very recently, convention did not dictate analysis by sex, I turn to my own field of research—depression, for which well-designed epidemiological studies conducted in many countries in the United States, Europe, Asia, and Africa show consistently higher rates of depression in women than men.[6] This area of work has included women in those being studied due to the fact that so many more women than men suffer from depression in its many forms. Yet, even though women have been included in studies of depression, which is the leading cause of disability for women throughout the world, it is only in very contemporary work that we are looking for and finding sex differences in predictors of depression and response to antidepressant treatments.[7]

Grassroots Efforts and Legislative Change

So what has initiated a change in studying the health of women in the United States? A major catalyst came in the late 1980s when concerned scientists, clinicians, and other advocates joined together, and appealed to the U.S. Congress for assistance in evaluating the scope of this apparent crisis. The appeal was made, in particular, to the Women's Caucus for Congressional Issues. The Caucus enlisted the aid of the House of Representatives' Energy and Commerce Subcommittee on Health and the Environment in determining whether research funded by the National Institutes of Health (NIH), which represents the largest single source of public funding for health research in the United States,[8] was considering the health of women in funded protocols. The assistance of this subcommittee was sought because it had responsibility for overseeing the budget recommendations for the NIH.

The chair of this Congressional subcommittee, Representative Henry Waxman, asked the investigative arm of Congress, the General Accounting Office (GAO), for a report on this issue in time for his subcommittee's hearings on NIH reauthorization legislation, which is the legislation required for continued funding of the National Institutes of Health.

Representative Waxman's subcommittee's request noted that in 1986, NIH had adopted a policy to encourage the inclusion of women in their funded clinical research trials, and the question for the GAO study was whether NIH had implemented its policy.

The GAO, in a report issued in June 1990, concluded that the NIH had made little progress in implementing its policy on the inclusion of women and, in fact, no system had been instituted to track the inclusion of women in NIH-funded studies.[9] As a consequence of this report, a clinical research equity provision, entitled "Women and Minorities as Subjects in Clinical Research"[10] was written which required that, going forward, women and minority groups must be considered as subjects in NIH-supported research. This provision was placed in the re-authorization bill for NIH and signed into law on June 10, 1993. In 1993, concerned citizens, working in collaboration with the U.S legislative system, became the agents of change in enacting law that insured the systematic and widespread inclusion of women into clinical research.

The Sequelae of Policy Change in the United States

The efforts toward policy change designed to include women in NIH-funded clinical research trials has had several important results. First, since 1990, the NIH has begun to fund new large studies on circumscribed areas of women's health. Perhaps the best known example, and, by far, one of the very largest studies ever conducted, is the Women's Health Initiative (WHI)—which is, in fact, a set of separate research trials studying several different questions in over 160,000 postmenopausal women between the ages of 50 and 79. There are a number of other large-scale NIH-funded studies, although none the size of the WHI, focusing on hormone use, heart disease, breast cancer, as well as other important targets. Yet, these topics and many, many other areas need large-scale studies to answer crucial questions.

Second, there are continuing, active attempts to incorporate women's health interests into our governmental institutions through appropriately placed offices on women's health and health research at the national, regional, and state levels. At a national level, for example, a bill has been introduced in the last several congressional sessions in the House of Representatives and the Senate that would provide a statutory basis for Offices on Women's Health within every agency in the Department of Health and Human Services (DHHS)—the primary national governmental structure administering health programs and health research within the United States.

DHHS contains agencies such as the NIH, the Administration for Children and Families, the Administration on Aging, the Health Care Financing Administration, the Agency for Healthcare Research and Quality, the Health Resources Administration (HRSA), the Centers for Disease Control and Prevention (CDC), the Food and Drug Administration (FDA), the Indian Health Services, and the Substance Abuse and Mental Health Services Administration (SAMSHA). At this point, only the NIH has an office dedicated to women's health and SAMSHA has a designated position for women's health that is in existence by law.[11] The NIH Office for Research on Women's Health was established in 1993 as part of the NIH Revitalization Act as was the SAMSHA position; all other offices and positions on women's health exist by administrative fiat—which means that, presently, in the event of a change in agency administration, these offices could be subject to dissolution. Such offices are essential because they provide an identifiable base of operations for considering the health status of women and ensuring that women and girls benefit equitably from advances made in medical research and health care services.[12] If this bill eventually passes, there would be programmatic and potentially budgetary stability where none exists today.

A third major development in women's health since the 1993 NIH Revitalization Act, and one that is fundamentally important, involves a change in the questions being asked in scientific investigations as a function of requiring investigators to include women in their research proposals. There has been a steadily growing realization in science that if we want to generate useful new knowledge on human health, we need to study those who were once ruled out of the algorithm for understanding health and disease.[13] In particular, we are learning that the issues presented by studying women are not impediments; rather, they are clues to new knowledge. Consequently, researchers are generating their own "grassroots" efforts by investigating aspects of health and disease referable to women that have never before been the focus of investigation.

What Needs to Be Studied in Women's Health Research?

When we ask what needs to be studied in women's health research, the answer is many content areas need to be studied, across many different disciplines because there is not a single system or set of topics that define women's health. In the past, women's health was conceptualized largely as reproductive health, which is of course critically important. However, reproductive health does not define women's health. We must broaden the definition, and we must insure that one, two or three specific diseases or conditions afflicting women do not become the sole focus of women's health. All communicable and noncommunicable syndromes and conditions that afflict women and for which scientific information is needed must be included in our inquiries. Furthermore, crucial to the success of translating new research data into practical benefit, we cannot see women as one unitary group but as a diverse group from different cohorts and backgrounds, countries and cultures.

In terms of general areas of study, we need to understand more about the causes, mechanisms, and treatments for disorders that are unique to women, including cervical and ovarian cancers, endometriosis, cardiovascular risk during pregnancy, and postpartum disorders. We need a better grasp of the many conditions that are more prevalent in women, including depression and anxiety disorders, breast cancer, migraine, osteoporosis, and the variety of autoimmune disorders.

We need to know more about the conditions that can present differently in women than men and may require different interventions, such as acute coronary syndromes, pain syndromes, and addictive disorders. In the United States, for example, because rates of illicit drug abuse indicate approximately a 2:1 male to female ratio, women have been seriously understudied in this area.[14] Yet, women comprise a large and growing subgroup of individuals abusing drugs in the United States. Estimates from the 1994 National Household Survey on drug abuse indicate that now a full 37 percent of the illicit-drug abusing population in the United States is women and that more women than men are at risk for becoming dependent on prescribed substances.[15] Although men are more likely to use and become dependent on drugs, when women cross the threshold into drug abuse and addiction, they are likely to show a greater number of biological, social, and psychological problems than men.[16] Additionally, because of the primary childcare role of women, drug abuse and addiction in women have a more significant impact on children and families.[17]

We also need to address diseases and conditions that are increasing for women, such as HIV/AIDS and domestic violence, as well as disease-producing behaviors that are becoming more common for women, such as smoking. With regard to smoking, the same lifetime exposure to cigarettes results in a greater risk of developing cancer in women than men; lung cancer has surpassed breast cancer as the leading cause of cancer death in American women; and death rates from other smoking-related diseases are rising for women. Yet, 1 in 4 girls under the age of 18 in the United States now smoke.[18] For women in other parts of the world, particularly women in developing countries where smoking prevalence has been traditionally low, the same trend is occurring as the tobacco industry targets women in these countries as a new market.[19]

It is essential to address injury and disease-producing environmental and occupational conditions and, of course, we must address the inseparable connection between poverty and health—as poverty is clearly a major pathway to disease. Finally, we cannot lose a focus on health-promoting behaviors and predictors of *health*, such as nutrition and exercise, which may differ for women and men, or the need to clarify confusing or incomplete data on health-related options for women, such as hormone replacement therapy.

Conclusion

As a follow up to the 1990 GAO Report on inclusion of women in clinical trials, the GAO conducted a second examination of NIH with regard to this issue. The 2000 GAO Report found that NIH had now made significant progress in increasing the number of women being studied, in part due to the large-scale trials under way;[20] and that the review process for research "treated the inclusion of women and minorities as a matter of scientific merit."[21] However, the report also found that there was still insufficient analysis of data by sex designed to reveal whether interventions affect women and men differently. As some have pointed out, the reason for including women is not to fulfill quotas, but to acquire scientific data that can be applied to the entire population.[22]

Issues of gender underrepresentation in clinical trials may significantly affect men as well in certain cases. For example, when looking at the relationship between life stress and depression, there are approximately a dozen well-done clinical studies clearly supporting the role of stress as a precipitant to major clinical depression. There also are a similar number of community-based studies (non-treatment–seeking samples) showing that in about 85 percent of cases, significant clinical depression was preceded by a serious adverse life event.[23] This information was increasingly being integrated into clinical practice and prevention strategies as generally applicable to both women and men. However, the subject composition of these studies indicated that two to four times as many women as men participated in the clinical studies, and only women were included in the community studies. Consequently, the available studies really showed a consistent and important relationship between life stress and depression only in women. Without a focus on examining sex difference, it remained unknown if stress was really a potent precipitant of depression for men. We subsequently studied sex differences in stress-related risk for depression and found that stress can precipitate depression for men as well as women. However, stress is not as strongly associated with subsequent depression in men as it is in women, and the stressors associated with depression are different for women and men, which has significant implications for treatment and prevention strategies.[24]

The changes of the past decade have made this an exciting time in women's health research and in research uncovering gender differences in health and disease, but we are only at the beginning of a long journey that requires vigilance and further expansion.[25] Dramatic changes are occurring in the health needs of the world's populations, particularly in the developing regions of the world. As indicated in the World Health Organization's report of The Burden of Disease, "noncommunicable diseases, such as depression and heart disease, are fast replacing the traditional enemies, such as infection and malnutrition, as the leading causes of disability and premature death."[26] We must be prepared to confront all disorders and, in that process, advance the health and health care of all populations of women in need of care.

The promise of research is discovery and innovation, finding out what we did not know and using new information to change. Based on research discoveries, we can improve our health, our illness outcomes, and the health and lives of those that come after us. A committee charged by the Institute of Medicine to respond to the question of whether sex matters in our explorations of human health recently reported: "Sex does matter. It matters in ways that we did not expect. Undoubtedly, it matters in ways that we have not begun to imagine."[27]

Notes

1. T. L. Johnson and E. Fee (1997), Women's health research: An historical perspective, in F. P. Haseltine, ed., *Women's Health Research: A Medical and Policy Primer*, Washington, DC: Health Press International.
2. J. LaRosa (1995), Including women and minorities in clinical research, *Applied Clinical Trials* 4(5): 31–38.
3. For a detailed history, see Johnson and Fee, Women's Health Research: An historical perspective.
4. C. J. L. Murray and A. D. Lopez, eds. (1996), *The Global Burden of Disease*, World Health Organization.
5. V. Vaccarino, L. Parsons, N. R. Every, H. V. Barron, H. M. Krumholz (1999), Sex-based differences in early mortality after myocardial infarction, *New England Journal of Medicine* 341(4): 217–225; V. Vaccarino, H. M. Krumholtz, J. Yarzebski, J. M. Gore, and R.J. Goldberg (2001), Sex differences in 2-year mortality after hospital discharge for myocardial infarction, *Annals of Internal Medicine* 134(3): 173–181.
6. M. M. Weissman and M. Olfson (1995), Depression in women: Implications for health care research, *Science* 269: 799–801; S. I. Wolk and M. M. Weismann

(1995), Women and depression: An update, in J. M. Oldham and M. B. Riba, eds., *Review of Psychiatry* 14 (pp. 227–259), Washington, DC: American Psychiatric Press.

7. C. M. Mazure, G. P. Keita, and Blehar, eds. (2002), *Summit on Women and Depression: Proceedings and Recommendations*, American Psychological Association Press.

8. C. M. Mazure, A. Arons, and A. Vitali (2001), Examining structured representation and designated fiscal support for women's health in the U.S. Department of Health and Human Resources, *Journal of Women's Health* 10(9): 849–860.

9. U.S. General Accounting Office (June 18, 1990), Testimony of Mark V. Nadel, Associate Director of National and Public Health Issues, Human Resources Division before the Subcommittee on Health and the Environment, U.S. House of Representatives, *National Institutes of Health: Problems in implementing policy on women in study populations.*

10. United States Public Law 103–43, NIH Revitalization Act of 1993. May 10, 1993, Washington, DC Government Documents.

11. Mazure, Arons, Vitali, Examining structured representation and designated fiscal support for women's health in the U.S. Department of Health and Human Resources.

12. Ibid.

13. C. D. DeAngelis and M. A. Winker (2001), Women's health—Filling the gaps, *Journal of the American Medical Association* 285(11): 1508–1509.

14. J. C. Anthony, A. M. Aria, and E. O. Johnson (1995), Epidemiological and public health issues for tobacco, alcohol and other drugs, in J. M. Oldham and M. B. Riba, eds., *Review of Psychiatry* 14 (pp. 15–50), Washington, DC: American Psychiatric Press.

15. Substance Abuse and Mental Health Administration (SAMSHA) (1995), Preliminary estimates from the 1994 National Household Survey on Drug Abuse, Advance Report No. 10.

16. T. R. Kosten, B. J. Rounsaville, and H. D. Kleber (1989), Sex and ethnic differences in psychopathology of opiate addicts, *International Journal of the Addictions* 20(8): 1143–1162; M. L. Griffin, R. D. Weiss, S. M. Mirin, and U. Lange (1989), A comparison of male and female cocaine abusers, *Archives of General Psychiatry* 46: 122–126; E. F. McCance-Katz, K. M. Carroll, B. J. Rounsaville (1999), Gender differences in treatment-seeking cocaine abusers-implications for treatment and prognosis, *American Journal on Addictions* 8: 300–311; S. F. Greenfield, S. G. Manwani, and J. E. Nargiso, (2003), Epidemiology of substance use disorders in women, *Obstetrics and Gynecology Clinics of North America* 30: 413–446; C. A. Hernandez-Avila, B. J. Rounsaville, and H. R. Kranzler (2004), Opioid-, cannabis- and alcohol-dependent women show more rapid progression to substance abuse treatment, *Drug & Alcohol Dependence* 74: 265–272.

17. S. S. Luthar and K. Walsh (1995), Treatment needs of drug-addicted mothers: Integrated parenting psychotherapy interventions, *Journal of Substance Abuse Treatment* 12: 341–348; T. J. McMahon, and S. S. Luthar (1998), Bridging the gap for children as their parents enter substance abuse treatment, in R. L. Hampton,

V. Senatore, and T.P. Gullota, eds., *Bridging the Fields of Substance Abuse and Child Welfare*, Volume 7: Issues in children's and families' lives (pp. 143–187), Thousand Oaks, CA: Sage Publications.

18. C. G. Husten, J. H. Chrismon, and M. N. Reddy (1996), Trends and effects of cigarette smoking among girls and women in the United States, 1965–1993, *Journal of the American Medical Women's Association* 11–17; U.S. Department of Health and Human Services, *Women and Smoking: A Report from the Surgeon General* (2001).

19. U.S. Department of Health and Human Services, *Women and Smoking: A Report from the Surgeon General*.

20. J. E. Buring (2000), Women in clinical trials—A portfolio for success, *The New England Journal of Medicine* 343(7): 505–506.

21. United States General Accounting Office (2000), *NIH has Increased Its Efforts to Include Women in Research*, GAO/HEHS-00-96.

22. *New York Times* (April 30, 2000), *Studies Find Research on Women Lacking*.

23. C. M. Mazure, Life stressors as risk factors in depression, *Clinical Psychology: Science and Practice* 5(3): 291–313.

24. P. K. Maciejewski, H. G. Prigerson, and C. M. Mazure (2001), Sex differences in event-related risk for major depression, *Psychological Medicine* 31: 593–602.

25. C. M. Mazure, M. Espeland, P. Douglas, V. Champion, and M. Killien (2000), Multidisciplinary women's health research: The national centers of excellence in women's health, *Journal of Women's Health & Gender-Based Medicine* 9(7): 717–724.

26. C. J. L. Murray and A. D Lopez (1996) eds., *The Global Burden of Disease*, pp 1–38.

27. Institute of Medicine (2001), *Exploring the Biological Contributions to Human Health: Does Sex Matter?* Mary-Lou Pardue, Chair, IOM Committee.

In Perspective

Gender in Public Health Research and Policies in Germany and Europe

Ulrike Maschewsky-Schneider

Introduction

Although the United States, Canada, and several other countries began to promote and fund women's health research in the late 1980s, Europe has begun only more recently to take a gender perspective on health and disease and to include women as well as men in clinical research. In 1998–1999, the European Community established a new policy to ensure equal opportunities for women and men—the gender mainstreaming policy.[1] This policy, as applied to research and research funding, requires that gender be a criterion in health studies.

A comprehensive overview of implementation activities and of what has already been achieved in Europe regarding the gender mainstreaming of health research and health care policies does not yet exist due to a lack of data and information. In this chapter, I give a definition of gender mainstreaming, and a brief overview of the main stages of the historical, legal, and administrative implementation processes in Europe, and, more specifically, in Germany.

As a case study, Germany serves as an example of a European nation still at the beginning of the policy implementation process as it continues to work at introducing gender mainstreaming policies at both the federal and state levels,[2] transferring general political guidelines into actual policies, regulations, and practices. In the past, Germany has lagged behind other European countries regarding attention to gender issues in health research, particularly in medicine and health policies. In the last few years however, some good examples of the promotion of women's health and gender sensitive health research have come into being and are reviewed in this chapter. Thus, the German case study will enable us to examine more closely the actual progression of gender mainstreaming policies within health research in several areas, including public health, medicine, and the overarching federal legislation. Germany represents those European countries, which will need some time to transfer the policy from a general political guideline into actual policies, regulations, and practices.

The EU's Gender Mainstreaming Policy

Derived from the Amsterdam Treaty, the EU's gender mainstreaming policy defines gender mainstreaming as "the reorganization, improvement, development and evaluation of policy processes, so that a gender equality perspective is incorporated in all policies at all levels and at all stages, by the actors normally involved in policy-making."[3] An official brochure in Germany gives an additional explanation: "Gender Mainstreaming implies the inclusion of life conditions and needs of women and men, girls and boys, in all social measures and policies, because there is no gender-neutral reality."[4] In essence, the goal across Europe is to ensure equality and equity between men and women in all life sectors and conditions.

A History of Women in Health Research in Germany and Europe

In order to understand the context of the current EU gender mainstreaming policy as it pertains to Germany, it is important to understand some of the history of women's health and women in health research. First, the European roots of women in health lie in the women's health movement of the 1970s comprised most prominently of the struggle for the right to legal abortions, safe and self-determined reproductive health, and general control over their own health. These years witnessed the founding of women's health centers as well as shelters for battered women. The goal of the movement was overall women's empowerment in a world of paternalistic and high-tech medicine. The women's health movement in North America inspired the German women's health movement itself. Indeed, connections can be easily traced between individual colleagues and activists in both the United States and Germany.[5] Further, feminist social sciences influenced women's health research in Germany to extend beyond medicine. Subsequently, concepts for women's health research were developed and initial research projects conducted in the late 1970s.[6]

In the 1980s only a few individual research projects on women's health were conducted, covering such issues as: the social aspects of pregnancy, health and the working conditions of nurses, the epidemiology of psycho-active pharmaceutical drugs, and concepts of health promotion for low-income women. Important women-specific services were established in many regions of Germany that included shelters for battered or abused women, women's health centers, and health counseling for women. However, with the exception of prevention and counseling, these activities were not conducted within the health system itself but instead fell under the rubric of "social services." As a result, the health care system, as well as mainstream health research, failed to recognize the importance of a gender perspective in both health research and health care services. This failure was also the case in the United States but soon after guidelines for clinical trails had been introduced in the early 1980s the establishment of huge studies and research programs on women's health were under way. In the 1990s, although information about women's health research activities in the United States were reported and published in Germany,[7] they impacted neither the German foundations of medicine nor biomedical research. Instead, getting attention for women's health research from the scientific community and in the health care and prevention system depended in large part on the situation of public health sciences in Germany.

After World War II, public health education and research had been shut down at German universities because of the misuse of the discipline to eradicate Jews and other populations in Germany. It was only in the 1990s that public health education and research was reestablished at several German universities. These were promoted by funding programs of the Federal Ministry for Education and Science, and were based on experiences and concepts of the Schools of Public Health in the United States.[8] This development proved to be a boon for the advancement of women's health research. Funding agencies supported the establishment of a network on women's health research within the public health program, and research projects began to be funded.[9] The latter focused on such issues as reproductive health, family planning and sex education, health care needs of female immigrants, and comparative analyses of women's health in the former East and West Germany. Other agencies funded research studies on addiction to illegal drugs, HIV/AIDS, general prevention (drugs, eating disorders, health promotion), fertility, and the life conditions of disabled women. One result of these activities was that female professors with expertise in women's health research were employed in the public health sciences at academic universities and at several universities of applied sciences (Fachhochschulen) in Germany.

In 2001 the first women's health report was published by the Federal Ministry for Family, Seniors, Women and Adolescents.[10] Its 700 pages consisted of 10 chapters that focused on the living conditions of women: socio-demographic indicators; health status of women and men; health behavior and healthy lifestyles of women; violence and gender; reproductive health of women over the course of their lives; women's work at home and at the workplace; health of middle-aged women; the life of women with special health conditions; and gender sensitive health care and health promotion. The report included information on theoretical concepts and the international state of research as well as data from Germany. The report has been not only useful as a resource for data and basic information, but it is also used as a core reference of women's health in Germany. In addition, the report's information illuminated the existence of some gender sensitive and women-friendly approaches in prevention and health promotion as well as the virtual absence of women-friendly health care services.

More concretely, one result of the women's health report was the implementation of a Federal Coordination Center for Women's Health, funded by the same ministry from 2002 to 2004, a center whose tasks included networking and increasing awareness of women's health care needs in the health system. Unfortunately, the center was closed in 2004 due to lack of funding, and no new source of funding has yet been identified.

Parallel to the developments in science, networking and lobbying also became stronger in Germany in the late 1990s. For example, sections on "women/gender and health" were founded in scientific, public health-related associations; the "National Network on Women's Health" and the "Working Group of Women in Medicine, Psychotherapy and Society" were established; and women became more prominent in both federal and state departments of physicians.

Once initiated, these improvements occurred relatively smoothly within public health. However, raising awareness for women's health and women in health research has proven to be more difficult in the field of medicine. On the one hand, despite the reluctance of those in the field of medicine to consider gender issues, associate professorships in women's health have been established at some medical schools, and more female full professors have become involved in medical science; though, only 5–6 percent of all professors at university medical schools are women. And, recently the medical department in Berlin, Charité, established the Center for Gender in Medicine to promote gender issues in education, research, and health care at their medical school.

On the other hand, in 2003 the Joint Federal-State Commission for Education and Science conducted a hearing to update the status of integration of gender issues into medicine. There, it was shown that gender continues to have no visible role in medicine. Medical studies and clinical trials as well as evidence-based guidelines for treatment do not follow gender-sensitive approaches. As mentioned earlier, it was also asserted that women are underrepresented in leadership functions at universities. The long-term impact of this hearing's results on medicine will have to be evaluated in the future.

In terms of federal legislation, the federal government began to implement gender mainstreaming policies by training top ministerial officials, followed by the initiation of individual pilot projects in each of the federal ministries. However, implementation has not proven to be consistent among the ministries. For example, while the Federal Ministry for Families, Seniors, Women and Adolescents has been very active in regarding women's health since the 1970s when the first women's shelter in Berlin was established and evaluated, the Federal Ministry for Health and Social Security has been more reluctant to address this issue. Aside from funding a few women's health research projects in the previous decades, it was not until 2003 that the Ministry started a pilot project on gender mainstreaming and established a position for women's health within the Ministry. At that time, a cooperative working group of three ministries (Health and Social Security; Education and Science; Family, Seniors, Women and Adolescents) began to work on guidelines regarding the inclusion of both sexes into research (in progress). This is especially important because although some calls for research proposals already ask for the inclusion of women in proposed studies, unlike in the United States, this is a recommendation only and not a prerequisite for funding.

Implementation of the European Union's Gender Mainstreaming Policy

With some of the history of women's health and women in health research in mind, let us turn back to Europe's gender mainstreaming policy to examine some important aspects of its implementation into the health sector both in Germany and throughout Europe. The gender mainstreaming directive of the European Community is based on a normative concept that claims for inclusion of the gender perspective into policy, legislation, administration, research, and education. Gender mainstreaming in health requires that gender be considered at all levels of the health system, including the definition of health targets, health reporting systems, laws and regulations, health care services and models of new practice, health-promotion and prevention programs, evidence-based medicine and treatment guidelines, quality standards for good health care services, and the allocation of resources. Further, in order to gauge the consideration being given to gender, and to illuminate areas that need attention, it is important to conduct a gender assessment and evaluation at each of these levels.

Despite the existence of the policy, its full implementation will still need time. A study on the funding policy within the huge biomedical research program of the European Community (life science program) showed what can be achieved by a gender assessment. The study found that gender was not at all considered in research nor in funding policies.[11] Based on this study the EU-funding program relased recommendations on how to include gender into studies.

Another example is the new EU directive for "Good Clinical Practice"[12] that suggests gender differences be included in clinical drug research trials. EU–member states are expected to adjust their national legislation to fit this directive. In Germany, such adjustments can already be seen through the gender guideline that was included in the draft for the new Pharmaceutical Products Law. Norway had been ahead and had already issued guidelines for the inclusion of women in medical research.[13]

No research or documentation regarding the implementation of gender mainstreaming into the health systems of the European member states is available to the author. It can be assumed that this implementation process is still in an early stage. Gender mainstreaming policies will be different in each country because the member states have the authority for the organization and structure of its own health system and in fact the systems are quite different. Each country is free to set its own priorities to gender mainstream health and the health system. WHO-Europe states "Although gender goals appear in health policies and programmes, they are not reflected in actions; they remain at the principles level. Thus, in many cases, mainstreaming suffers policy evaporation and no concrete actions result."[14]

Concepts of Gender Based Analysis: Examples from Research

As seen through the German case study, carrying out these guidelines is not always simple. A study performed within a public health research program in Germany evaluated the inclusion of gender in all program-funded research projects ($N = 317$) as well as a sample of public health-related publications in three German public health journals.[15] Eichler's concept of gender-based analysis was used as the theoretical framework for the analysis.[16] In this analysis, three major sources of gender bias are identified in science: androcentricity/overgeneralization, gender insensitivity, and double standards (see table 8.1). These can be found in all steps of the theoretical and/or empirical research process.

Table 8.1   Sources of gender bias (adapted from Eichler 2002)

Androcentricity/ overgeneralization The adoption of the male perspective	—Exclusion or under-representation of females —Using males as the norm against which females are assessed
Gender insensitivity —Ignoring sex or gender as a socially or medically important variable —Gender neutrality/gender blindness	—Household unit of analysis: household as a measurement unit instead of the individual— or gender-specific unit —De-contextualization: gender blind concepts hide social differences between both genders —Assumed gender homogeneity
Double standards Evaluation, treatment, or measurement of identical behaviors, traits, or situations that are conducted differently on the basis of sex or gender	— Sexual dichotomy: understanding men and women as distinct groups when actually common attributes exist between both genders —Reification of gender stereotypes

Overall, study results showed how little current research endeavors consider gender. In particular, we found that only 40–50 percent of the evaluated publications paid attention to possible gender differences in the following steps of the research process: research questions, main variables, sample description, data analysis. Specific conclusions from the results had been drawn for women and men separately in only 35 percent of the publications. However, we also found that the awareness of and readiness for gender-based analysis is actually quite high among health researchers. How should this readiness be harnessed? One way is to continue to apply Eichler's framework both in assessment and evaluation. For example, Eichler's approach is currently being extended to a pilot project on gender mainstreaming conducted by the German Federal Ministry of Health and Social Security: "Analysis of the Implementation of the Gender Mainstreaming Policy in Health Promotion and Prevention for Children and Adolescents."[17] The goal is to evaluate the gender sensitivity of child- and adolescent-directed health-promotion and prevention programs on nutrition, physical activity, tobacco, alcohol, illegal drugs, and HIV/AIDS. Publications, research projects, measures and campaigns of the Ministry and its institutes will be examined to detect gender bias or to identify models of good practice regarding Eichler's three concepts. Guidelines for a systematic and sustainable implementation of the gender mainstreaming policy in the health promotion and prevention programs for children and adolescents of the Ministry will be proposed.

Conclusions

For Germany, the inclusion of the gender perspective into research, health care, and preventive services, and the ongoing changes of the German health system is a prerequisite for equal opportunities for men and women in the society and for overall high-quality health care and health research. The first women's health report[18] and the first health report in the united Germany,[19] illustrated the need for general prevention and health promotion programs in Germany. It also uncovered immense research gaps regarding the health of women in Germany, prevention needs, women-friendly health services, and gender-sensitive health research. Further, it is clear that researchers in public health have been much more aware and ready to address these gaps than those in medicine and medical research.

It is because of these gaps that the gender mainstreaming policy of the European Community is so important. To move forward, the following recommendations for gender mainstreaming research and science could be implemented:

- Evaluation and monitoring of the impact of gender guidelines into research and funding policies in the European Community and member states;
- Development of gender guidelines and gender-sensitive methods for clinical trials; inclusion of gender guidelines into regulations and procedures of ethic committees; surveillance of the impact of gender guidelines on clinical trials;
- Initiation of interdisciplinary cooperation between medicine and public health to develop concepts and methods for gender-sensitive medical research, health care, and health services research.

The goal of gender mainstreaming is to ensure equality and equity between men and women in the society. Health systems and its services have to be organized in such a way that these goals can be reached—but it will still need much effort to reach these goals. The good health of men and women are the best indicators for the achievement of these goals.

Notes

1. Council of Europe, ed. (1998), Gender Mainstreaming—Konzeptueller Rahmen, Methodologie und Beschreibung bewaehrter Praktiken, *Schlußbericht über die Taetigkeit der Group of Specialists on Mainstreaming (EG-S-MS)* (98)2.
2. Die Bundesregierung (2002), Gender Mainstreaming: Was ist das? Bonn: Bundesministerium fuer Familie, Senioren, Frauen und Jugend. www.gender-mainstreaming.net.
3. Council of Europe, Gender Mainstreaming-Konzeptueller Rahmen, Methodologie und Beschreibung bewaehrter Praktiken, p. 14.
4. Die Bundesregierung, Gender Mainstreaming: Was ist das?

5. I. Kickbusch (1981), Die Frauengesundheitsbewegung—ein Forschungs-gegenstand? in U. Schneider, ed., *Was macht Frauen krank?* *Ansaetze zu einer frauenspezifischen Gesundheitsforschung*, Frankfurt/New York: Campus.
6. U. Schneider ed. (1981), Was macht Frauen krank? Ansaetze zu einer frauen-spezifischen Gesundheitsforschung, Frankfurt/New York: Campus.
7. C. Helfferich and O. J. von Troschke, eds. (1993), *Der Beitrag der Frauengesundheitsforschung zu den Gesundheitswissenschaften/Public Health in Deutschland.* Freiburg: Schriftenreihe der Koordinierungsstelle Gesundheitswissenschaften/Public Health an der Abteilung Medizinische Soziologie der Universität Freiburg, Bd.2; U. Maschewsky-Schneider, ed. (1996), *Frauen—das kranke Geschlecht? Mythos und Wirklichkeit*, Leverkusen, Opladen: Leske und Budrich.
8. DGPH—Deutsche Gesellschaft für Public Health, ed. (1999), Public Health-Forschung in Deutschland, Bern-Göttingen-Toronto-Seattle: Hans Huber.
9. G. Berg, U. Haertel, and U. Maschewsky-Schneider (1995), Frauengesundheitsforschung—eine Aufgabe von Public Health? *Forum Public Health* (10).
10. Verbundprojekt zur gesundheitlichen Situation von Frauen in Deutschland (2001). Untersuchung zur gesundheitlichen Situation von Frauen in Deutschland. Eine Bestandsaufnahme unter Beruecksichtigung der unter-schiedlichen Entwicklung in West- und Ostdeutschland. Bundesministerium für Familie, Senioren, Frauen und Jugend. Cooperative project on the health situation of women in Germany. 2001. A study on the health status of women in Germany. A situation analysis taking into consideration the different devel-opments in west and east Germany. Ministry of family, older persons, women, and youth.
11. I. Klinge and M. Bosch (2001), Gender in Research: Gender Impact Assessment of the specific programs of the Fifth Framework Program, Quality of Life and Living Resources: A study for the European Commission, Maastricht.
12. Good Clinical Practice, accessed October 12, 2004. http://pharmacos.eudra. org/F2/eudralex/vol-3/pdfs-en/3cc1aen.pdf.
13. National Committee for Medical Research Ethics in Norway, ed. (2001), *Guidelines for the Inclusion of Women in Medical Research—Gender as a Variable in All Medical Research*, http://www.etikkom.no/Etikkom/Engelsk/ Publications/women.
14. World Health Organization, Regional Office for Europe, *Gender and Health/Areas of Work*, http://www.euro.who.int/GEM/areas/20030811_3.
15. J. Fuchs, and U. Maschewsky-Schneider (2002), Geschlechtsangemessene Publikationspraxis in den Gesundheitswissenschaften im deutschsprachigen Raum?—Ergebnisse einer Literaturreview, *Das Gesundheitswesen* 64: 278–283; J. Fuchs and U. Maschewsky-Schneider (2003), Beruecksichtigung des Gender-Aspekts in der deutschsprachigen Public-Health-Forschung: Ergebnisse einer Projektbefragung. *International Journal of Public Health* 48: 227–233; U. Maschewsky-Schneider and J. Fuchs (2003), Gender bias—gender research in public health, in W. Kirch, ed., *Public Health in Europe:10 years EUPHA*, Berlin-Heidelberg-New York: Springer Verlag, pp. 119–128.

16. M. Eichler (June 2001), Moving forward: Measuring gender bias and more, in Berlin Center of Public Health, European Women's Health Network, German Society for Social Medicine and Prevention, eds., *Gender Based Analysis (GBA) in Public Health Research, Policy and Practice*, Documentation of the International Workshop, Berlin. http://www.ifg-gs.tuberlin.de/workshop/ workshop.phtml; M. Eichler, et al. (2002), Zu mehr Gleichberechtigung zwischen den Geschlechtern. Erkennen und Vermeiden von Gender Bias in der Gesundheitsforschung, in J. Fuchs, K. Maschewsky, and U. Maschewsky-Schneider, eds., Deutsche Uebersetzung und Bearbeitung. Berlin: Blaue Reihe-Berliner Zentrum Public Health. http://www.ifg-gs.tu-berlin.de/ handbuchGBA.pdf.

17. U. Maschewsky-Schneider, P. Rattay, and B. Sorg (2003), Umsetzung des Gender Mainstreaming-Ansatzes in der Gesundheitsvorsorge für Kinder und Jugendliche, in U. Koch and S. Pawils-Lechner, eds., *Psychosoziale Versorgung in der Medizin, zugleich 2. Kongress für Versorgungsforschung*, Lengerich: Pabst Science Publishers, p. 205.

18. Verbundprojekt zur gesundheitlichen Situation von Frauen in Deutschland, *Untersuchung zur gesundheitlichen Situation von Frauen in Deutschland. Eine Bestandsaufnahme unter Beruecksichtigung der unterschiedlichen Entwicklung in West-und Ostdeutschland.*

19. Gesundheitsbericht für Deutschland: Gesundheitsberichterstattung des Bundes (1998), Statistisches Bundesamt. Stuttgart: Metzler-Poeschel.

Notes on Contributors

Liliana Acero, Ph.D., is a Visiting Professor and Course Director at the Institute of Women's Studies, the University of Ottawa on New Reproductive Technologies, Gender and Women in Development, Professor at the Virtual Master's Programme on Gender, Society and Policies at FLACSO and at the Master on Business and International Relations, the University of Belgrano, Argentina and directs two NGOs on Gender, Education, and Health in Argentina and Chile. In 1983, she obtained an Honour's Ph.D. and was a Research and Visiting Fellow at Science Policy Research Unit and the Institute of Development Studies, The University of Sussex, as well as, an Associate Professor and Postdoctoral Researcher at the Universities of Massachusetts, at Amherst and at Brown University. IPSA awarded her as best Senior Researcher on Developing Countries (1993–1994), due to her work on the social, household, and gender impacts of new technologies.

Cynthia Lee Andruske, Ph.D., is a new scholar, recent graduate from the University of British Columbia (UBC) in the Department of Educational Studies, and adjunct professor at the University of Houston Clear Lake where she teaches distance courses on multiculturalism. Through her doctoral dissertation, *"I'm Not Sitting on the Couch Eating Bonbons!"*: *Women's Transitions from Welfare to Paid Work and Education,* she explored women's resistance, welfare policy, self-directed learning, and citizenship. As a Research Associate for the Liu Institute for Global Issues at UBC, she worked with Dr. Spiegel on gender, health, social organization, and globalization issues. She is associated with the Centre for Research in Women's Studies and Gender Relations at UBC. Her publications have featured marginalized women, resistance, popular theater, and literacy. Dr. Andruske's current research focuses on gender, health, cultural influences, resistance globalization, Latin America, and women's citizenship through hospitality.

Stella Aguinaga Bialous, R.N., MSCN, Dr. PH., is a nurse, tobacco policy consultant, and the president of Tobacco Policy International. She is the co-investigator of the Tobacco Free Nurses initiative and works as a consultant for the World Health Organization. She is also a former board member of the International Society of Nurses in Cancer Care and is Chair of the Society's Tobacco Control Task Force. She has published several articles on issues related to international tobacco control policy, monitoring the activities of the tobacco industry, and on nurses and tobacco control. Dr. Bialous is also a member of California's Tobacco Education and Research Oversight Committee (TEROC) and, in 2003, was the first recipient of the American Legacy Foundation's Sybil G. Jacobs Adult Award for Outstanding Use of Tobacco Industry Documents for public health.

Lisa Sowle Cahill, Ph.D., M.A., an active voice in theology and ethics today is J. Donald Monan, S.J., Professor at Boston College. Dr. Cahill is a past president of the Catholic Theological Society of America (1992–1993), and the Society of Christian Ethics (1997–1998), and is a fellow of the American Academy of Arts and Sciences. Her works include *Theology, Bioethics, and Society* (Georgetown University Press, 2005), *Bioethics and the Common Good* (Marquette University Press, 2004), *Family: A Christian Social Perspective* (Fortress, 2000) and *Sex, Gender, and Christian Ethics* (Cambridge University Press, 1996). She is the editor of *Genetics, Theology, Ethics: An Interdisciplinary Conversation* (Crossroad, 2005). Dr. Cahill received her M.A. and Ph.D. degrees from the University of Chicago Divinity School.

Jeff Collin, Ph.D., M.A., is lecturer in the Centre on Global Change and Health at the London School of Hygiene & Tropical Medicine with additional appointments at Cambridge and Bristol. Dr. Collin's research interests are in globalization, tobacco control, health inequalities, and health policy. Currently, he is involved in research projects based on the analysis of tobacco industry documents, funded by the U.S. National Cancer Institute and the Rockefeller Foundation. His recent publications based on these projects include five articles on the tobacco industry in Asia in the special regional supplement of *Tobacco Control*, 2004; 13 (Suppl 2). He is also the author of "Think Global, Smoke Local: Transnational tobacco companies and cognitive globalisation" in Lee K., ed., *Globalization and Health: Case Studies* (London: Palgrave, 2002) and, with K. Lee, *Globalisation & Transborder Health Risk in the UK* (London: Nuffield Trust, 2003).

Joanne Csete, Ph.D., M.P.H., is the Executive Director of the Canadian HIV/AIDS Legal Network. Dr. Csete was most recently the founding director of the HIV/AIDS and Human Rights Program at Human Rights Watch. In this capacity, she oversaw the development of a body of research and an agenda of advocacy actions related to a range of human rights issues linked to HIV/AIDS, including numerous reports on gender-related human rights abuses. She was previously chief of policy and programs in the regional office of UNICEF in Nairobi, working especially on HIV/AIDS, and before that senior advisor in the Programme Division of UNICEF's New York headquarters. She worked in Africa for about ten years on public health and nutrition programs, mostly in Rwanda, Burundi, Democratic Republic of Congo, and Kenya. Having a doctoral degree in public health nutrition from Cornell University, she was on the faculty of Nutritional Sciences at the University of Wisconsin–Madison from 1988 to 1993.

Manisha Desai, Ph.D., is Associate Professor of Sociology, Acting Director of Women and Gender in Global Perspectives, and Associate Director of the Program in South Asia and Middle Eastern Studies at the University of Illinois at Urbana Champaign. Her research and teaching interests include gender, globalization, feminism, social movements, human rights, and contemporary Indian society. Her most recent book is an edited volume on Women in Asia and Oceania published by Greenwood in 2003. She is currently finishing a book on Gender and Globalization for the Gender Lens Series of Altimira Press.

Lesley Doyal, M.Sc., is Professor of Health and Social Care, School for Policy Studies, University of Bristol and Visiting Fellow, University of Cape Town. Professor Doyal has published widely on international health policy, gender, and health care and gender, health and development. She has a particular interest in the links between gender studies and health studies and in the interface between biological and social sciences. She has acted as a consultant to the WHO, UN, Commonwealth Secretariat, and the Global Forum for Health Research.

Caren A. Grown, Ph.D., M.A., is Director of the Poverty Reduction and Economic Governance team at the International Center for Research on Women, where she leads research on asset accumulation and women's property rights and the impact of multilateral and national economic policies on gender equality. From 1992 to 2001, Grown was a Senior Program Officer at the John D. and Catherine MacArthur Foundation in Chicago, Illinois, where she managed research networks and competitions on a wide range of economic issues. Before joining the MacArthur Foundation, Grown was an economist with the Center for Economic Studies at the U.S. Bureau of the Census. She has guest coedited three special issues of *World Development* on macroeconomics, international trade, and gender inequality, and has written widely on gender and development issues. Grown holds M.A. and Ph.D. degrees in economics from the New School University and a Bachelor's degree in Political Science from UCLA.

Wendy Harcourt, Ph.D., Programme Advisor and Editor of *Development* quarterly journal of the Society for International Development (S.I.D.) (published by Palgrave Macmillan). After receiving her Ph.D. from the Australian National University in 1987, Dr. Harcourt joined S.I.D. in 1988 and since 1995 has been editor of the *Development* journal. She has contributed to S.I.D.'s policy and research work in the fields of gender in development, alternative economics, sustainable development, culture, health, globalization, and reproductive health and rights. She is currently Chairperson of Women in Development Europe.

Norbert Hirschhorn, M.D., is a physician specializing in global public health, and an adjunct lecturer at the School of Public Health, Yale University. His career spans four decades of research and teaching in maternal and child health; more recently he researched the tobacco industry documents released as a result of court cases in the United States. Nominally retired, he provides pro bono services to a global network of tobacco control advocates, and to the National Public Health Institute, Finland.

Gillian Lewando-Hundt, Ph.D., is an applied medical anthropologist. She is the Professor of Social Sciences in Health at the University of Warwick and is Co-director of the Institute of Health (healthatwarwick.ac.uk). She studied at the Universities of Edinburgh and Warwick. She has held posts at Ben Gurion University of the Negev, Israel, at the University of Birmingham and the London School of Hygiene and Tropical Medicine, UK. Her research program "Eliciting Local Voices on Global Health Issues" focuses on working with disadvantaged groups in the area of health inequalities of care and access. She is currently carrying out research in the Middle East, South Africa, and the United Kingdom.

Theresa Kaijage, Ph.D., M.P.H., M.S.W., is with the Institute of Social Work in Dar es Salaam, Tanzania. In 1989, Theresa Kaijage founded WAMATA, a Tanzanian advocacy and counseling group for families affected by HIV/AIDS—the first AIDS service organization in Tanzania. (WAMATA is a Swahili acronym for "People in the Fight Against AIDS in Tanzania.") Kaijage's research focuses on changing behavior and gender roles in a state transitioning from socialism to capitalism under the shadow of HIV/AIDS. Ms. Kaijage is the recipient of a number of distinguished awards in recognition of her unique contributions to Tanzania including the 2000 Teresa Maximus Distinguished Professor of Social Work Award, Marywood University in Pennsylvania; 2002 Shepherd Wellness Community AIDS Candlelight Memorial Award, Pittsburgh, Pennyslvania; 2004 James E. Dixon Humanitarian Award for HIV Education, The Seven Project, Inc.,

Pittsburgh, PA; and the 1997 Distinguished Social Work Alumni Award, George Warren Brown School of Social Work.

Ulrike Maschewsky-Schneider, Ph.D., is Professor at the Institute for Health Sciences, Technical University of Berlin. She is chair of the Berlin Center for Public Health and has been a member in the Executive Committee of the German Society for Social Medicine and Prevention and the German Society of Public Health. Previously, Dr. Maschewsky-Schneider was the Chief of the Department of Epidemiology at Bremen Institute for Prevention Research and Social Medicine. Her research focuses on sociological concepts and methods of the health sciences; evaluation research in health promotion and prevention; and women's health research (including work on women and tobacco). Dr. Maschewsky has published several articles and books and has been involved in numerous research projects, including the first Women's Health Report for Germany and a public health project entitled "Gender Bias-Gender Research?"

Mahesh Maskey, M.B.B.S., M.P.H., D.Sc., is Assistant Professor in Epidemiology in the Department of Community Medicine and Family Health, Institute of Medicine, Tribhuvan University, Nepal. His major research interests are in the field of reproductive health and globalization. He has developed and applied an alternative method of measuring perinatal and neonatal mortality in developing countries. He is actively involved in efforts promoting public health and the health of women and children.

Carolyn M. Mazure, Ph.D., is a Professor of Psychiatry, the Associate Dean for Faculty Affairs at the Yale University School of Medicine, and the Director of Women's Health Research at Yale, an interdisciplinary program focusing on sex differences in health and disease. Her research focuses on factors determining illness onset and treatment response particularly in depression and, more recently, in addictive disorders. Professor Mazure is the Principal Investigator for the NIH-funded Yale Interdisciplinary Women's Health Research Scholar Program on Women and Drug Abuse, the Core PI for the Sex-Specific Factors Core of the NIH-funded Transdisciplinary Tobacco Use Research Center studying sex-related factors in nicotine-dependence and treatment, and the Scientific Program Director for Yale's Specialized Center of Research on Sex, Stress and Cocaine. She has served on review committees for the National Institutes of Health, has been an invited speaker to the U.S. Women's Congressional Caucus, and testified in three consecutive years to the U.S. Congress on the importance of research funding and its practical applications.

Josephine Nhongo-Simbanegavi, Ph.D., is currently a professor of history at the University of Alabama and, until 2003, was at the University of

Zimbabwe. Much of her research focuses on gender and cross-border migration in Southern Africa, looking at sexuality, health, citizenship, and cross-cultural issues. Her most recent book entitled *For Better or Worse? Women and ZANLA in Zimbabwe's Liberation Struggle* is a thought-provoking analysis of women's experiences with ZANLA during the war of independence. Josephine Nhongo-Simbanegavi was recently coordinating a University of Zimbabwe–based research project on the Historical Dimensions of Human Rights and Democracy, of which her own study of gender and international migration was a part. She takes an active interest in research that promotes the integration of the Southern African region into the global network for mutual benefit. As a member of the Overseas Advisory Board and editorial board of the *Journal of Southern African Studies* (JSAS), she contributes to the process by which JSAS identifies its research priorities.

Jerry Spiegel, Ph.D., is Director, Global Health, Liu Institute for Global Issues, Assistant Professor, Health Care and Epidemiology, and Director of the Centre for International Health at University of British Columbia (UBC). Dr. Spiegel currently directs research programs on globalization, social organization, and health and eco-system approaches to human health that place particular emphasis on gender. His focus is on Latin America and he currently heads research projects in Cuba, Mexico, and Ecuador on matters such as the impacts of tourism development on gender and health in coastal communities, sustainable prevention and control of dengue, and effective intersectoral and transdisciplinary methods for managing environmental health risks. Recent publications include: Spiegel JM, Yassi A. "Lessons from the margins of globalization: Appreciating the Cuban health paradox," *Journal of Public Health Policy*, 2004, 25(1): 96–121.

Michael L. Tan, D.V.M., Ph.D., is Associate Professor and chairperson of the Department of Anthropology, University of the Philippines, Diliman, Quezon City, and coordinator for the university's Health, Society and Culture Program. He is a medical anthropologist who has worked on gender and sexuality issues for many years, including, currently, a research capability building project for the Southeast Asian Consortium on Gender, Sexuality and Health. He has worked as an adviser in various government projects and in 1995 he was appointed to the Philippine National AIDS Council, a presidential advisory body. He has acted as a consultant to the World Health Organization, UNICEF, European Commission, DANIDA and other international agencies, and is currently the Philippine Country Program Adviser for The David and Lucile Packard Foundation.

Index